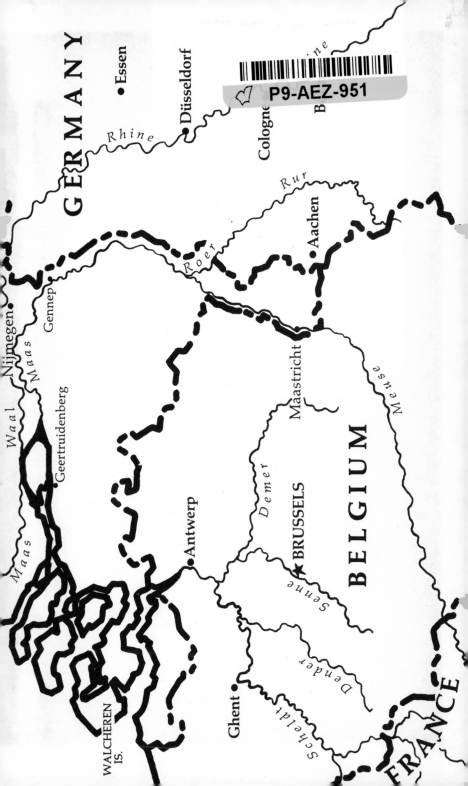

The Netherlands at War: 1940-1945

THE NETHERLANDS
AT WAR: 1940-1945

by WALTER B. MAASS

Abelard-Schuman

London   New York   Toronto

© Copyright 1970 by Walter B. Maass
Library of Congress Catalogue Card Number: 68-14569

First published in the United States of America in 1970
First published in Great Britain in 1970
Standard Book Number 200.71552.6

LONDON	NEW YORK	TORONTO
Abelard-Schuman	Abelard-Schuman	Abelard-Schuman
Limited	Limited	Canada Limited
8 King St. WC2	257 Park Ave. So.	1680 Midland Ave.

An Intext Publisher

Printed in the United States of America

This book is dedicated to the men
and women who lost their lives in the Netherlands'
resistance against Nazi oppression.

CONTENTS

PHOTOGRAPHS

MAPS

PREFACE

This book has been written mainly for the American reader. The events in the Netherlands during World War II are not very well known in the United States. Most Americans have only some vague memories about the air raid on Rotterdam, inundations, air landings, and deportations. Partly this is because comparatively few Americans took part in the liberation of the Netherlands. U.S. troops fought in Limburg and participated in the advance on Nijmegen, but the war in Holland was always considered primarily a British operation. A second reason is the only brief mention of operations in Holland in the great memoirs of World War II by Churchill, Eisenhower, Montgomery, Bradley, and Alanbrooke. Conditions in the occupied country are hardly enumerated at all. The only book on this subject that has achieved international fame is Anne Frank's beautiful *Diary of a Young Girl.* An intensely personal document, however, it views life from a hiding place in an attic in Amsterdam.

Werner Warmbrunn's scholarly account *The Dutch under German Occupation* is extremely valuable, but not known to the average reader. A few personal military reports, like General R.E. Urquhart's *Arnhem* and Bernard Ferguson's *The Watery Maze,* with its fine description of the Walcheren episode, deserve the highest praise, but they tell only fragments of a greater story.

In German writings, the war in the Netherlands has been almost completely ignored except for Hermann Giskes' interesting book, the *Englandspiel,* which is also available in an English translation.[*]

[*] H. Giskes: *London Calling Northpole* (Kimber, 1953).

By far the greatest number of books on the subject are written in the Dutch language; only very few have been translated. In writing this book, I have drawn heavily from Dutch government reports, memoirs, factual literature, novels, and most important, on my personal experiences during the eight years I lived in the Netherlands. Of these, the last three were spent under rather unusual circumstances. I lived by means of forged documents, but unlike many persons in hiding, I continued to work and travel, and witnessed many events that are described on the following pages.

This book has not been written to revive old hatreds or to indulge in horror stories. It does not claim to be a completely impartial document. I saw many of my friends imprisoned, deported, and executed. It is difficult to remember them with complete equanimity even after the passage of more than 20 years.

Regardless of my own experiences, I believe that to write comparatively recent history in a completely impartial manner is hardly possible and, perhaps, not even desirable. Later chroniclers may view things differently, but it is my honest belief that the fight against oppression will generally find most narrators on the side of the oppressed. Holland's war of independence against Spain provides an excellent example. It is still hard to find accounts of that period that favor Philipp II and the Duke of Alba.

I wish to thank the Netherlands Institute for War Documentation for a number of reports, not obtainable in other publications, that have been extremely helpful in writing this book.

CHAPTER ONE

In the autumn of 1939, a long shadow seemed to fall over the Netherlands. For the first time since 1914, statesmen and generals nervously discussed the possibility of an invasion, and ordinary citizens looked anxiously at the sky when they heard the noise of approaching planes. The streets were full of mobilized soldiers, and work on fortifications rose in the eastern border regions. But business still went on as usual. One of the few outward signs of tension was everyone's tendency to follow closely the news on the radio. Whenever men gathered, the discussion soon turned to the political situation and to the question: "Shall we be left alone?"

Holland had been at peace since the days of Napoleon, except for a brief war in 1830 when Belgium gained its independence from the House of Orange. Some minor campaigns were also fought in the Dutch East Indies, but for all practical purposes the country had known an almost uninterrupted period of peace since Napoleon's defeat at Waterloo, where Dutch troops had formed part of the Duke of Wellington's army. During World War I, the Netherlands had maintained an uneasy neutrality, often imperiled by incidents, threats, and blockade, grateful for being spared the terrible ordeal of neighboring Belgium. Swarms of hapless refugees from the latter country had made it quite clear to the Dutch what war and occupation meant. In the last days of the war, the German Kaiser had sought and found asylum at Doorn, much to the annoyance of the Allies and to the relief of some of his countrymen.

Until 1933, there had been a lull in foreign events, except for some minor conflicts with Belgium regarding the Scheldt estuary that had been solved. The country, therefore, was able to maintain its time-honored, strict neutrality. Even the rise of Adolf Hitler and the complete change in German foreign policy seemed not to affect the Netherlands. Holland and Germany had never been enemies. The House of Orange itself had originated in Nassau, Germany, a fact referred to in the Dutch anthem.* Dutch princesses had frequently married German royalty; the late husband of Queen Wilhelmina had been German, and Juliana, the crown princess, had married a German only a few years previously. Germany was traditionally an excellent market for Dutch goods, especially foodstuffs, and a considerable number of German firms were active in Amsterdam, Rotterdam, and other cities. German was the most widely spoken foreign language in Holland, and many Dutchmen had friends and relatives in Germany. True, Germans as a group had never been particularly popular and were often referred to as *moffen,* an unflattering epithet comparable to the French *boches.* It originally means "muff" and seems to have originated from the high hats of the Prussian cavalry. Many Dutchmen considered the Germans arrogant and overbearing. A popular joke had the German ambassador ask the crown princess when Holland would join the Reich. Juliana's supposed reply was: "It would be too much work for mother to govern so large a domain."

The National Socialist government of Hitler dismayed many Dutchmen because extremists of the Right as well as of the Left were generally unpopular in Holland. However, it was considered a strictly German affair and not an immediate danger. Hitler's often-repeated claim that he wanted a Reich inhabited by Germans only seemed to exclude any threat to Holland's independence. Talk of a "Germanic master race" merely amused the sober Dutch, and even among the Fascist-minded elements it never became very popular. Without being especially nationalistic, the Dutch had always fiercely resisted foreign invaders. German classical literature and music were always an influence, but their cloudy ideals and pomposity were often considered

*It starts with the words: Wilhelmus van Nassouwe, ben ik, van Duitsen bloet. ("I'm William of Nassau, of German blood.")

mildly funny. The rational Dutch mind shrank from the verbosity of Schiller and the pagan mysticism of Richard Wagner. Goethe and Beethoven — the latter a man of Flemish origin — were greatly admired. So were several modern authors, none of them very nationalistic. Few Dutchmen approved wholeheartedly of the Treaty of Versailles, but even fewer thought it right or sensible to avenge it by a new blood bath.

Still, when the loud voices from across the border grew more and more strident, a certain uneasiness rose over the land. In 1938, during the Munich crisis, Dutchmen could still listen to Hitler's speeches and his roaring crowd and joke about it. After the brazen annexation of Czechoslovakia, the mood changed. Things were clearly drifting toward a new war in the west, and the Netherlands might present a tempting prey to the motorized Attila.

Holland's defense was traditionally controlled by the flooding of threatened areas. These tactics had already been used during the Netherlands' war of independence against Spain and again with striking success against the French in 1672. During a visit to England in 1937, Mr. Colijn, the Dutch prime minister, declared that he could stop an invader by merely pushing a button — the same mentality that led France to believe that she was safe behind the Maginot Line. The use of massed air attack and parachute troops went unnoticed by strategists in armchairs who still thought and planned in the terms of World War I.

A second fallacy, very popular in those uneasy days, was the conviction that "England won't permit it." As a seapower of high reputation, the Dutch understood well enough that the Royal Navy would be a decisive factor in case of war. But the difficulty in transporting major armies and all their equipment to an embattled shore was never fully realized, and only after the Allied disaster in Norway did it dawn on many people that this might be a sheer impossibility. In fact, no plan for a British invasion of the Netherlands existed in 1940, and ironically, when such an invasion finally materialized in 1944, it came not by sea but by land and by air. Besides, by maintaining a strict neutrality, the Dutch government made any military cooperation with their potential Allies virtually impossible. There remained the forlorn hope that the Allies would strike like lightning at the invader whenever the need would arise. The attitude of the Belgian government was almost identical.

Basically, the inactivity and fatalistic approach of many small countries was dictated by the all-pervading fear that any "unneutral" action might precipitate the attack. By strictly adhering to the rules of neutrality, they hoped to avoid provoking the monster that already clawed at their doors. In fact, the German government had decided long ago to invade the neutrals, whatever their attitude. The moral issue was never even considered by a group of men whose sole purpose was to conquer. Hitler and his generals must have thought the eagerness of those small countries to maintain niceties hilariously funny. They might respect Switzerland's neutrality, because they considered it useful. Holland, however, represented no such restraining considerations.

The armed forces of the Netherlands were considered a deterrent to the invader. In 1914, the Germans, acting upon the Schlieffen Plan, had moved their right wing through Belgium, but bypassed Holland. That plan almost succeeded; its final failure at the Marne was hardly caused by not violating Dutch neutrality. Later on, when the war turned more static, the Germans were not eager to add another enemy to the growing list of their adversaries. It was, of course, conceivable that the same thing might happen again, but history rarely repeats itself in such detail.

The Dutch armed forces suffered from several major disadvantages; they completely lacked field experience and modern materiel. Between the two world wars, they had been neglected. A strong pacifist movement — its symbol a broken rifle — and a general aversion to great expenses for armaments prevented any purposeful preparation. Only the navy, with an eye on protecting the Dutch East Indies, had maintained a degree of strength. The small air force mainly consisted of fighter planes built in Amsterdam. It was far too weak to match the Luftwaffe, even for one single day. Of its 118 planes, only 23 were of top caliber. The army was quite considerable in number: nine first line divisions plus another five of lesser quality — together about 300,000 men. But the greatest difficulty was the lack of modern equipment for opposing a powerful and meticulously prepared invader. Holland had started to arm very late, and its own industry was inadequate to produce enough for defense. By that time, importation of foreign equipment had become almost impossible because all of Europe was arming frantically; few countries had any excess material to export.

The tragedy of the small European countries was that they avoided any real alliance with the West, but lacked the means to defend themselves. When it became clear in 1935 that the League of Nations was incapable of decisive action, small nations like Holland, Belgium, Norway, and Denmark became convinced that they could only save their liberty by maintaining strict neutrality. When England and France permitted the reoccupation of the Rhineland and the annexation of Austria, they reinforced the feeling that their aid couldn't be taken for granted. Belgium — in World War I — the staunch and heroic ally of the West, retreated into complete neutrality in 1936. When England and France let Czechoslovakia fall to German threats of aggression, their prestige sank even lower. The years of passivity and appeasement had undermined any hope for mutual security.

As Holland had no conflict with Germany, one can hardly question the Dutch government's insistence on strict neutrality, at least until the outbreak of World War II. Considering the military weakness of the Allies at that time, it is even questionable if any alliance would have changed the course of events at so late a date. There was the danger that an overt move towards a Western alliance would trigger an immediate German attack. By remaining neutral, there was still hope that invasion could be avoided as in 1914, or at least postponed. As we have learned later from German documents, it was indeed postponed several times, though for entirely different reasons.

The great majority of the people of the Netherlands were sympathetic to the cause of the Allies, but without any great enthusiasm. The shameful Munich agreement had been greeted with a sigh of relief. But soon enough the conviction spread that once again a small nation had been betrayed by England and France. Indeed, it would have been difficult to feel any great confidence in the politics of Neville Chamberlain. The general attitude was that in case of attack the Dutch troops would stem the invasion on the "water line" until the British rushed to Holland's assistance.

There was a small but dangerous minority who thought very differently. In 1931, an engineer by the name of Anton Mussert had founded the National Socialist Bond (N.S.B.), the Dutch National Socialist party. Originally, that party was independent of Germany, but as Hitler's success grew, it came more and more under German influence. The party had received 8 per cent of the vote at the 1935 election, but then its popularity decreased, and at the last prewar voting it gained only 3.8 per cent (1939). There was no probability that the Dutch Nazis would ever become a very important factor in Dutch politics. But even a small party under foreign direction could form a very serious danger, as history has repeatedly taught us. The threat presented by a "fifth column" was greatly underestimated until Holland was actually invaded. Only then did the hideous face of treason appear visible to all, soon to become the most tragic factor in the following years of occupation.

Aside from the N.S.B. and the even smaller Communist party, Holland's political life was free from antidemocratic forces. The country, one of Europe's oldest democracies, had been ruled by coalition governments for a long period of time. The large number of parties — 13 were represented in Parliament — did not hurt the democratic process and never led to that impotence of government so common in France. Between the two world wars, the great man of Dutch politics had been Hendrick Colijn, a staunch Calvinist and conservative of the old school. He had headed various coalition governments since 1933. In 1939 his government fell and was replaced by a new coalition, with D.J. de Geer as prime minister. In such a critical period, this weak and elderly gentleman was a very poor choice for so responsible a task. In August of that year, two Socialist ministers were added to the government, which now encompassed most large parties from the Right to the Left. A few weeks later, Hitler attacked Poland and World War II began.

CHAPTER TWO

When World War II broke out on September 1, 1939, the Netherlands declared their neutrality, and all belligerents announced
they would respect it. Five weeks later, Hilter ordered General
von Brauchitsch to prepare Army Group B for an invasion of
Holland and Belgium, just one day after he had again proclaimed
in a speech before the Reichstag that he considered the Dutch
border inviolable. On November 23, Hitler held a secret conference with his leading military commanders in Berlin. On that occasion, he spoke his true mind: "I will attack France and England
at the most opportune moment, with the greatest possible speed.
The violation of Belgium's and Holland's neutrality is without
importance. Nobody will question that after we have conquered."
   Originally, there had been some discussion among the generals
about attacking the Netherlands. The opinion of the air force that
the Dutch airfields were essential to the whole action in the
west settled the question.
   The German plan of operation had at first more or less followed
the ideas of 1914. Then, too, an attack on Holland had been in
the planning, but was eventually dropped by the German supreme command, which felt that the country's neutrality could
be advantageous to Germany. Therefore, the German army entered Belgium through a narrow corridor south of Maastricht.
In 1939, a very different approach was used.
   The father of that new plan was a brilliant staff officer whose
name was then little known to the public. During the Polish campaign, Erich von Manstein had been chief of the general staff
under Gerd von Rundstedt. When the latter was moved to the
west, von Manstein followed him and took residence in Coblenz.
In October 1939, he received the original plan of attack, which

closely followed the Schlieffen scheme of 1914. His reaction was very characteristic: "How depressing that our generation could think of nothing else than the repetition of an old formula!" Von Manstein saw clearly that a frontal attack on northern France, with Paris as the immediate object, could easily lead to a long and protracted struggle, because the element of surprise was completely lacking. Germany had concluded a nonaggression pact with the Soviet Union only two months before. But what would the attitude of the Russians be if the German army became bogged down in a static front on the Somme or Aisne?

Von Manstein — partly by intuition, partly from intelligence reports — foresaw also the strategic attitude of the Allies. If Holland and Belgium were invaded, they would advance into Belgium to stop the Germans. Well, let them do so. The really decisive blow would fall elsewhere.

Both the French and the German general staffs had always considered the Ardennes, hilly and with only a few good roads, as unsuitable for armored attack. Von Manstein now questioned that preconceived notion. With the aid of Gereral Guderian, who knew the region well, he developed the following idea: The main armored power of the German army should be thrown through the Ardennes toward the "extended" Maginot Line near Sedan. They should traverse the river Maas and then rush for the Channel ports. In this way, the Allied forces in Belgium would be cut off from their main base. They would be encircled and destroyed, and only then further attacks toward Paris and a seriously weakened France would be undertaken.

It was certainly a brilliant and original plan, though not without risks. It rested on the speed of the Ardennes operation and on the knowledge that the French Ninth Army, which guarded the Maas defenses, consisted of mediocre reserve divisions.

Von Manstein submitted his scheme to the Supreme Army Command at Zossen, but found no sympathy for his ideas. A long correspondence followed, and finally von Brauchitsch, aggravated, appointed von Manstein to a command in which he would have no further dealings with planning the offensive. But in his new function, von Manstein had to present himself to Adolf Hitler. On this occasion, he found the opportunity to explain his plan on the highest level. It is possible that the Fuehrer had already been informed of that daring scheme.

Von Manstein's unconventional idea had finally found the right audience. Hitler, always in favor of risky and surprising actions, approved wholeheartedly. He soon adopted the plan as his own and forced it on the High Command. Characteristically, von Manstein got no recognition at all and took no part in the offensive. When Hitler appointed 12 new field marshals after the fall of France, Manstein's name was not even mentioned. The full story of "Plan Yellow" — the code name for the western offensive — became known only after World War II.

The blow against the Netherlands was also to be composed of very unconventional actions. Hitler is supposed to have remarked: "We will occupy them through the back door." Undoubtedly, a merely conventional frontal attack from the east would eventually have defeated the Dutch army, but it would have taken some time. By using completely surprising methods, the resistance was to be broken within a few days.

It was no secret that any defense of the Netherlands rested on "Fortress Holland," the region north of the big rivers Maas and Waal. It was protected by the Grebbe Line, which ran from Baarn via Amersfoort to Rhenen. A system of inundations between the river Lek and the Zuiderzee and on the southern bank of the Maas would defend its flank. A second "water line" was to be made operative from Muiden — east of Amsterdam — to Utrecht, Leerdam, and Gorinchem. Behind this system of inundations and fortifications, even a weak army could resist for some time, especially if it maintained a link to the Allies via Belgium and the Scheldt estuary.

The German plan was to circumvent the water line by an armored thrust into the "Fortress." For such an unexpected push, the possession of the vital bridges at the Moerdijk and over the Maas near Rotterdam was mandatory. At the same time, The Hague, residence of the Dutch government, should be taken by parachute forces operating from captured airfields. As we shall see, this latter project did not succeed. However, the "Fortress," one of the most densely inhabited parts of Europe, where city borders city, was particularly vulnerable to air attack.

What were the Allies planning during the eight months that preceded the German offensive? General Gamelin, sixty-seven years old, a highly educated man with an enviable reputation, thought and acted completely within the limitations of his World War I experience. As the German-Franco border seemed safely protected by the Maginot Line, the Belgian frontier had to be defended by the best Allied troops against a new invasion through the Low Lands. The German right wing had to be opposed by a strong Allied left wing. If the Germans were to invade Belgium and Holland, that left wing, which contained almost the whole British Expeditionary Force (B.E.F.), would advance into Belgium and take its position on the river Dyle. This would secure a large part of Belgium and leave the possibility of aid to the Dutch open, should Holland also be attacked. In that case, General Giraud's Seventh Army would advance from Antwerp to Breda and link up with the Dutch in Brabant. Gamelin's "Major Général des Armées" Georges opposed this extension and called it a dream and an adventure. Nevertheless, the action was carried out in May 1940, but led only to weakening the Allied reserve without accomplishing anything for the Netherlands.

The Allied move into the Low Countries was bound to leave the Maas section near Sedan extremely weak. It was just at this vital point that the Germans later made their breakthrough, as the French did not even have reserves available for a counterstroke.

Another basic mistake of the Allied High Command was the poor distribution of armor. Notwithstanding the warnings of Colonel Charles de Gaulle and the British expert Liddell Hart, tanks were mainly seen as a supplementary weapon to assist infantry. The massed use of the German Panzer divisions in May 1940 came as a terrible surprise.

France had only 1220 airplanes, 140 of them bombers. Considering the extreme weakness of the Dutch and Belgian air forces, the three continental countries could not match the powerful Luftwaffe, that roamed freely over Holland, Belgium, and Northern France when the offensive started. The Royal Air Force (R.A.F.), which, as it turned out later, could very well hold its own against the Germans, had only a limited number of squadrons on the Continent. The decision to save it for the battle of Britain turned out to be one of the wisest of the whole war.

Of course, all these facts were not known at the outbreak of the war. Still, there were repeated warnings of things to come.

Shortly after the beginning of the war, the British Secret Intelligence Service (S.I.S.) in The Hague was informed that a military conspiracy against Hitler existed in Germany and that members of that group wished to make contact with England. After consultation with London, two British intelligence officers, Major R.H. Stevens and Captain S. Payne Best, joined by a Dutch lieutenant by the name of Klop, met the Germans at Zutphen and later at The Hague. On the second occasion, the German group was represented by a certain Major Schaemel, who explained the goals of the conspiracy. The German High Command, he declared, wished to imprison Hitler and start peace negotiations with England and France. After renewed consultations with their superiors, Stevens and Best met Schaemel again on November 7 at the border town of Venlo and told him that they were willing to meet the leader of the German conspiracy — a general, so far unnamed — at the same place. After a delay, they were told that the mysterious chief conspirator would meet them at Venlo on November 9.

The rest of the story sounds like a very bad spy thriller. The two English officers, again accompanied by Lieutenant Klop, arrived in Venlo at 4 p.m. in a Buick. They drove to a café where Major Schaemel sat on the terrace, ostensibly waiting for his friends. When the three officers alighted from their car, they were suddenly fired upon by several men and dragged over the German frontier, which was only 125 feet away. Lieutenant Klop was severely wounded and died a few days later in a German hospital at Düsseldorf.

The two English officers were brought to Berlin and realized too late that they had fallen into a trap. Their good friend Major Schaemel was the head of the counterespionage division of the Gestapo, Major Walter Schellenberg. The whole story about a conspiracy against Hitler was a fake to lure them into captivity. Ironically, there were indeed conspirators against Hitler within the German officer corps, but Schellenberg was probably not even aware of them. He had just concocted a believable story that the British were only too ready to swallow, because the animosity of certain military circles against Hitler was well known in England. The two British officers spent the whole war as prisoners in Germany, but survived to tell their story later on.

By a strange coincidence, an attempt to assassinate Hitler at the Buergerbraeu Keller in Munich took place on November 8. The story of this very mysterious affair has never been completely cleared up. The would-be assassin was a German by the name of Georg Elser, and it is probable that the whole plot was engineered by Himmler to strengthen German morale and increase Hitler's popularity. We will not go into this story here, as it did not directly concern the fate of the Netherlands. In any case, the German propaganda now claimed that the S.I.S. was behind the plot against the Fuehrer and linked its activities to Elser, who later died in Dachau. The Dutch government vainly protested the kidnaping at Venlo. Not less than nine written complaints were sent to the Germans, for the incident clearly involved a violation of Dutch territory. The Germans left all those notes unanswered. But when Hitler attacked Holland six months later, he mentioned the Venlo affair as proof that the Dutch had acted in complicity with the British.

In fact, Hitler had planned the invasion at an earlier date. It was originally scheduled for November 12 at 7:15 A.M., but was postponed for meteorological reasons. There might have been a second one. King Leopold of Belgium had been warned of an impending German offensive by a most unlikely person, the German ambassador, Mr. Buelow-Schwante, who belonged to a group of diplomats hostile to Hitler. Another warning had come from Colonel Oster of the German counterintelligence. King Leopold thereupon immediately traveled to The Hague for consultation with Queen Wilhelmina. On November 7, the two monarchs made a joint declaration, offering to mediate peace "before the war in Western Europe begins in full violence."

At the same time, Adolf Hitler was drafting a justification for the impending attack on the two neutral countries. It is possible that the rather embarrassing coincidence made him hesitate. Obviously, nobody would believe his claims that two little countries were conspiring against Germany at a moment when they were making a plea for peace.

The offensive was postponed. Hitler's generals, who had not been happy about a major action so late in the fall, were momentarily relieved — but not for moral considerations. When Hitler told them two weeks later that his decision to attack the neutrals was final, not one of the military leaders uttered the slightest objection. They remained silent, just as they would later calmly accept the Nazi excesses in the occupied countries.

From then on the attack was postponed again and again until January 13 when it was suddenly canceled by the Supreme Warlord because of an almost ridiculous event. On January 10, Hitler ordered large air attacks on French airfields for January 14. Three days later, shortly before sunrise, the big offensive against Belgium and Holland was to begin. But on the very day he had made the decision, a German air force officer, Major Helmut Reinberger, made a forced landing near the town of Mechelen in Belgium. When Belgian soldiers approached, Reinberger hurriedly tried to burn the contents of his briefcase. The soldiers extinguished the fire and took him and his partially burnt documents to military quarters. Here the officer made a second attempt to burn his papers, but was prevented from doing so. Three days later, all German troop movements were abruptly stopped. At the same time, the Belgians deployed stronger forces at the border and called up two new classes. The German ambassador in Brussels was told by Foreign Minister Spaak that the Belgian government was now in possession of documents that contained "clear proof of an intention to attack."

Reinberger's papers did include the entire plan for Hitler's operation against Holland, Belgium, and France. The Allies were given copies by the Belgian government and then — strangely enough! — nothing was done about the whole matter. Some feared that the documents might merely be a plant, though this seemed hardly logical. In any case, the Belgians did not change their adamant position on strict neutrality. No proper staff consultations between the Allies and neutrals were arranged. Nor did the Dutch and Belgians exchange military information to any great extent. Both governments remained determined to stake their safety on Hitler's respect for international law. They were soon to cry aloud for help from the Allies, whom they had even refused proper information about their own military forces. Faced with the almost certain knowledge that Germany would attack them, the Belgians did not allow their prospective .defenders to reconnoiter the Dyle position, which was the latter's future line of advance.

The icy-cold winter of 1939-40 passed rather quietly in Holland, though the general feeling of uneasiness was growing. The war on the seas started claiming victims among the neutrals. The Dutch tanker *Sliedrecht* was sunk by a German submarine and 26 lives were lost. In November, the large liner *Simon Bolivar* struck a magnetic mine and sank with many of her passengers. Both British and German planes often infringed on Dutch air space, notwithstanding all protests. Strange incidents continued to happen on the Dutch-German border. The police detected a smuggling operation, whereby Dutch uniforms of various kinds were transported to Germany. The reason for that peculiar transaction became clear on the day of invasion.

In November, the strong concentration of German troops deployed along the frontier caused great unrest. Prime Minister de Geer tried to calm the public with a thoroughly unrealistic speech in which he claimed there was no cause for alarm. Nevertheless, work on the fortifications was continued with energy, though not always with common sense.

The army had already been mobilized on August 20. Its shortcomings were glaring to knowledgeable persons. The line along the river Maas was defended by pieces of artillery manufactured before 1900. There were no tanks, and only 26 armored vehicles in the whole army. In February, Commander-in-Chief Lieutenant General I.H. Reynders was replaced by General H.G. Winkelman.

During the eight months of that "twilight war," life in the Netherlands remained basically quite normal. There were no shortages and very few restrictions. Politically, the only shrill noises came from the extreme Right. In April, Anton Mussert declared during a press interview that in case of a German attack the Dutch National Socialists would sit and watch with their arms crossed. This caused some excitement, as it sounded very much like open treason. A few days before the German invasion, the government declared a state of martial law, and 21 persons — mostly Dutch Nazis — were interned. The most prominent internee was M.M. Rost van Tonningen, a member of the Second Chamber* of Parliament, a reputed financial expert, and a violent Nazi.

Meanwhile, the Germans had occupied Denmark almost without resistance and defeated the Norwegians and a hastily dispatched Allied force that was in no way prepared for such a difficult campaign. For the first time, it dawned on many people that sending an expeditionary force to a foreign shore was an immensely complicated enterprise, especially if the adversary had superiority in the air. Also, for the first time, the lurking danger of a fifth column was fully understood. The Germans could not have entered Norway with such ease without Quisling's treachery. A fact that later on proved to be of great importance almost went unnoticed. The Germans had won the Norwegian campaign, but they had lost a considerable part of their navy.

An atmosphere of nervousness and premonition settled over the country during the first days of May. German and Allied broadcasts outdid each other in rumors and propaganda. Both London and Berlin had established Dutch radio programs. The German High Command was busy with the last details for "Plan Yellow," the great spring offensive. It had been drastically changed since the original plan had fallen into the hands of the Belgians. On May 8, Hitler's Chief of Operations, General Jodl, noted in his diary: "Alarming news from Holland. Canceling of furloughs, evacuations, roadblocks . . . Fuehrer does not want to wait any longer."

*The Second Chamber roughly resembles the British House of Commons.

CHAPTER THREE

The Netherlands had an extremely valuable contact in Berlin. He was Colonel Hans Oster of the Abwehr, an intimate collaborator of Admiral Canaris. Oster, like his chief, was a determined enemy of the Nazi regime and a leading member of the opposition among the resistance group that had been slowly established within the Abwehr. Unlike most of his fellow officers, Oster was ready to use extreme methods for overthrowing Hitler. "It is my purpose and my duty to free Germany and the world from this plague." These words he uttered to Major G.J. Sas, the Dutch military attaché, who was his close friend.

Oster had already warned Sas in November 1939 that a January invasion of the Netherlands was impending. This prediction did not materialize, though for reasons not within Oster's knowledge. In April 1940, Oster had told Sas of the planned attack against Denmark and Norway. The information was duly passed on to Oslo, but the Norwegians simply could not believe it and considered it just part of the "war of nerves." They soon learned better, to their great sorrow.

On the evening of May 9, Oster informed Major Sas that the order for the invasion of Holland had been received. However, counter orders were still a possibility, and the two men waited anxiously until 9:30 p.m. for final confirmation. At 9:50 p.m., Oster, who had checked with the German High Command, told his friend: "This is the end. No counter orders. That swine (Hitler) has gone to the Western front. It's all over now. Let's hope we see each other again after the war." They never did. Oster was arrested in 1943 and hanged in Flossenburg concentration

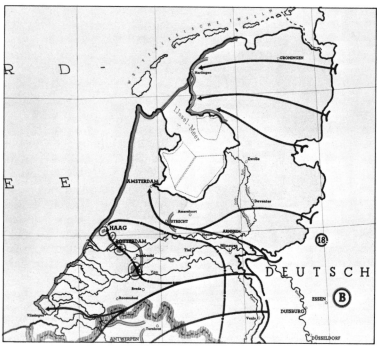

Plan of the German offensive against the Netherlands, May 1940
Library of Congress

camp a few weeks before Germany surrendered. German historians are still arguing whether Oster was a hero or a traitor.

Sas went to the Dutch embassy, informed the Belgian military
attaché, and then called the Department of War at The Hague.
After a painful wait of 20 minutes, he got a marine officer by the
name of Post Uiterweer on the phone. "Tomorrow at dawn. Hold
tight." Then Sas gave a code word that confirmed the date of the
attack. The Hague was still not quite convinced and had the
Chief of Foreign Intelligence call back: "We have heard the bad
news of Mrs. Sas' illness. Have all doctors been consulted?" Very
annoyed, Sas replied, "Why bother me again? You know it now.
She has to have an operation tomorrow morning" and hung up.

Both conversations were tapped and the leak announced to the Abwehr, Oster's own organization. The Abwehr Chief, Admiral Canaris, had the matter investigated and let it die.

There had been other warnings. A week before, a secret message from the Vatican had predicted the German offensive. Also, a strange wire, destined for an American newspaper, had been decoded in Amsterdam on May 9: "Wise willies whispering witching hour Friday dawn."

The Dutch government had already canceled all leaves of military men on May 7. At the border, great activity on the German side had been noticed during the evening, and at 9:45 P.M. — even before the message from Major Sas had arrived — a warning was sent to all commanding officers in that region. The troops in Fortress Holland were not alerted. Obviously, the Dutch High Command had never heard of airborne landings and thought it unnecessary to get them in readiness.

At 1:30 A.M., the Dutch air observation reported that numerous planes were passing over Holland. At 2:45 A.M., the last squadron seemed to have left Dutch territory in a westerly direction. No bombs had fallen yet, and some observers thought hopefully that the planes were on their way to England. But it was merely a clever deception. The planes turned around over the North Sea, and at 4 A.M. their bombs were falling on the Dutch airfields. At exactly the same time, German troops started crossing the border.

When the sun rose at 4:15 A.M. on a cloudless sky, the population woke to the roaring of planes and the thunder of antiaircraft guns. People dressed in their nightgowns and pajamas streamed into the streets and stared stupefied at the German air armada overhead. When they turned on their radios, they soon realized what was going on: parachutists landing at all the airfields around The Hague, at Waalhaven, and at the Moerdijk! The author himself, who lived at the village of Santpoort near Haarlem, was awakened from his slumber by the furious firing of the sole antiaircraft battery in that area. Three Dutch fighter planes, easily recognizable by their orange markings, rushed from the skies, seemingly in pursuit of some enemy bombers. They were the only Allied planes that the author saw during the five days of the invasion. Two days later, the Dutch air force had practically been wiped out, and the R.A.F., engaged in desperate battles over France and Belgium, could not offer assistance. Alert followed upon alert, and the horrified inhabitants of Santpoort soon noted that the Luftwaffe operated in their skies without serious opposition. People began to make preparations for the blackout, and there was still a certain mood of optimism, mainly due to complete ignorance of what modern war really meant. The landlord's daughter bravely declared that she would pour boiling water on German infantry. She never got a chance, but later was of great help to the author in obtaining forged papers.

The war was already on for two hours when the German ambassador, Count Julius von Zech-Burkersroda, asked to see the Dutch Minister of Foreign Affairs, Mr. van Kleffens. The count was one of the diplomats of an era long passed who had been left on his post by the Nazis as some sort of venerable window dressing. The poor man was completely confounded and cried like a baby. He had lived in Holland for 17 years and was overcome with shame and horror. Van Kleffens took the message from his hands and read that his government had been guilty of collaborating with England and France: "We inform you of the action of a powerful German force. Resistance is completely senseless." The note went on, promising a guarantee for the dynasty if the Dutch would not fight, and asked for direct contact with the German command. Van Kleffens said: "You will understand that this is not in accordance with our principles. We must consider ourselves at war with Germany." He then drew up a reply. The ambassador shook hands and left, still weeping. The whole conversation took only six or seven minutes.

At the same time, an even more ludicrous comedy was enacted at Berlin. The Dutch ambassador, Mr. Haersma de With, was asked to see von Ribbentrop, who handed him papers containing the same accusations against Holland and a plea to offer no resistance. The German government claimed that an invasion of the Ruhr with the connivance of Holland, Belgium, and Luxembourg was impending. The German action was only taken to prevent this aggression. The same story was later told to the press with the hypocritical embellishment that Germany was protecting Holland's neutrality against the aggressors. The Germans tried to give the impression that they had been suddenly faced with the threat of an Allied attack and merely acted to forestall it. They succeeded in completely deceiving their own people, but hardly anybody else.

At 8 A.M. a communiqué from Queen Wilhelmina was read over the radio protesting "the flagrant breach of conduct, usual among civilized nations." The people were asked to do their duty, and the Dutch national anthem, followed by the anthems of England, France, and Belgium, was played. The radio also warned the antiaircraft defense not to shoot at Allied planes. They never got an opportunity to do so, for hardly any appeared. Further announcements warned of fifth columnists and German parachutists in disguise. As we shall see, these warnings were not without justification, but they caused a tremendous number of rumors and increased the nervousness of the troops. Still, in the middle of all the confusion, life seemed to go on normally. Bread, milk, and vegetables were delivered from door to door as usual. The radio, when not announcing communiqués, intoned "La Madelon" and Dutch and English marching songs.

The Luftwaffe's first heavy blow fell on the airfields. At Bergen in North Holland, a number of Dutch fighters were destroyed with their motors running, before they could even take to the air. The three airfields around The Hague, Valkenburg, Ockenburg, and Ypenburg were first bombed, then airborne troops were landed in considerable numbers. There followed a murderous fight, especially at Ypenburg, where a number of heavy transport planes landed. Three groups of transports were shot to pieces by the defenders; a fourth one could not land because the field was strewn with the wrecks of their predecessors. In the meantime, German parachutists had come down near Delft and proceeded to Ypenburg, driving Dutch prisoners before them. The Dutch hesitated to fire on their countrymen, and the parachutists temporarily took possession of the airfield. Eventually, the Dutch drove them off again. At the small Ockenburg airfield, twenty transports managed to land, but here, too, the defenders held on. At Valkenburg, the German airborne troops and parachutists took the airstrip in the early morning hours, but by evening it was again in Dutch hands.

The successful defense of these three small airfields saved The Hague and the Dutch government. It had been the German plan to arrest the royal family and the ministers on the first day of the invasion. The first planes that circled over the city had dropped leaflets: "The city is surrounded by strong German troops. Any resistance is senseless." The failure to take the airfields had far-reaching consequences. It enabled the government to escape to England and to carry on the war with the Dutch navy and all other means available. This also provided at least some national leadership in a desperate period and gave the population the moral backbone to overcome the hardships of occupation. Hitler, who was certainly no fool in such matters, had planned it differently. On May 2, he had already given to General of the Air Force Student orders to lay his hands on the royal family. If amenable, the Queen should be treated with military honors. Otherwise, she should immediately be brought to Germany.

The battle around The Hague had yielded 1,100 German prisoners; they were immediately brought to the port of Ijmuiden and shipped to England.

Things took a very different turn at the airfield of Waalhaven near Rotterdam. After a heavy bombardment, parachute troops landed outside of the airport, while a whole fleet of transport planes disembarked about 5,000 German troops under General von Choltitz, who four years later made history by surrendering Paris to the Allies. The commander of the airfield was taken prisoner and driven toward a Dutch position that was still resisting. The Germans later claimed that he tried to make his troops surrender; but it is more likely that he was to be a human shield, a practice the Germans had already used at Ypenburg. In any case, the commander was killed by Dutch bullets.

The attack on Waalhaven succeeded quickly and gave the Germans an operational base against Rotterdam and Dordrecht. Not less than 240 landings were made on May 10, and the planes now started unloading light artillery. The German force proceeded north toward the city of Rotterdam, which was already under attack from a second group that had landed in 12 hydroplanes on the Nieuwe Maas. The Germans reached the bridges over the river, but here they were stopped by the energetic resistance of Dutch marines. Heavy fighting raged in the harbor. The large liner *Staatendam* was gutted by flames, and the Dutch destroyer *Jan van Galen* was sunk by German planes after a fierce battle. The Germans now held a foothold within Fortress Holland, but for the time being their advance was stopped.

An even more disastrous event took place at the southern ridge of the fortress. The vital Moerdijk bridges fell undamaged into German hands. Here, the German parachute troops achieved complete tactical surprise. The Dutch force that guarded the bridges had not been alerted, an almost incredible piece of military stupidity. Some of the men hastily started to put on their uniforms when the Germans were already landing. The bridges were attacked from both sides and quickly occupied. One of the German officers, who led the attack, had lived for 15 years in that region and was known to his neighbors as a great cyclist. No wonder he knew the bridges well!

When the Moerdijk disaster was announced to General Winkelman, he immediately called Gamelin and urgently asked for aid. The latter promised help and ordered General Giraud's Seventh Army to advance into Brabant. Giraud, of World War I fame, and later the protégé of the Allies in North Africa, advanced so fast that he outran his ammunition. He actually reached Rozendaal on May 12. On this day, the Dutch radio announced hopefully that the Allies had come to Holland's aid, but as we shall see, it was with too little and too late.

While all these actions were going on, the war had also started at the Dutch-German frontier. The border was only secured by comparatively weak units with inadequate artillery, as a prolonged defense of the border region was never intended. A stronger line existed behind the rivers Ijssel and Maas. All troops in that sector had the task of delaying the German onslaught and carrying out prepared destructions.

Though the border troops had been alerted in time, here, too, the Germans achieved some tactical surprise, though by very devious means. At Gennep, the Dutch guards noticed some Dutch military policemen conducting a group of German soldiers — seemingly prisoners — over the vital railway bridge. Suddenly, both "policemen" and "prisoners" started firing at the Dutch;

they were German soldiers, partly in disguise. The bridge was taken undamaged, and soon afterward a German armored train rolled into Holland. As it turned out later, some 30 Dutch Nazis, especially trained for such tasks, took part in that action. It now became clear why the Germans had organized the theft of Dutch uniforms in the preceding months.

In the south, the Germans quickly overcame the Dutch troops in the lower corner of Limburg and pushed into Belgian territory, where Fort Eben Emael fell on May 11 to a brilliantly conceived and executed attack by gliders.

The northern border provinces of Holland were hardly defended. The Dutch retreated, blowing up about 200 of their bridges; but this destruction produced fewer results than expected. In the evening of May 11, the Germans reached the Afsluitdijk, which connects Friesland and North Holland. Here the Germans finally met determined resistance. At Kornwerderzand, the Dutch held a fortified line and neither air attacks nor artillery could dislodge them. An infantry thrust over the dike was repulsed on May 13, with heavy losses, and the German artillery

German troops at destroyed bridge in Maastricht during their offensive in May 1940

was silenced by the fire of the gunboat *Johann Maurits van
Nassau*. When the Netherlands surrendered on May 14, the
Germans had still made no progress against the Dutch position.
The main German thrust rolled against the central Dutch defense, the Grebbe Line, which was reached in the morning of
May 11. The fortifications had been modernized during the
last months, but they had the same fatal weakness as the Maginot Line: Their guns pointed in only one direction. A breakthrough could, therefore, become fatal to the whole position.
Furthermore, the Germans, partly by espionage, partly by aerial
observation, were very well informed about those fortifications.
For months, German planes had photographed the Grebbe Line
from the air, and a German officer who lived at Veenendaal had
visited it a few days before the attack, naturally as a tourist.
The Dutch authorities had been careless in such matters. Another
big mistake was allowing the numerous fruit trees in the Grebbe
area to stand undisturbed — for agricultural reasons! Those trees
provided protection for the invading troops. Also, the Dutch air
force had by this time vanished from the skies, and no help from
the Allies was in sight. As a consequence, German planes freely
circled over the fortifications and directed the German artillery
fire.

The best troops of the Wehrmacht, many with battle experience from the Polish campaign, were used in this area, and
against their fanatical attacks, the defense began to falter. Wild
rumors circulated among the Dutch, and many officers became
nervous. On the afternoon of May 13, Rhenen fell; the situation
then became so critical that it was decided to evacuate the whole
position. This was carried out during the afternoon and the following night, but the retreat toward Utrecht became very dis-
orderly, and much equipment was lost.

But the real decision came further to the south in the Peel.
The troops that covered that area were particularly badly prepared; their guns were at least 40 years old. A German armored
train advanced to the village of Mill and started unloading its
troops. At the same time, General Kuechler's Ninth Armored Division began a relentless push to link up with the airborne troops
at the Moerdijk.

Two motorized infantry divisions of the Seventh French army had reached Breda on May 11, and there was a brief encounter at the Wilhelmina Canal. They were quickly thrown back by the German tanks, which were aided by strong air raids. The population in and around Breda was ordered to evacuate, and a mass exodus into Belgium followed. The French retreated toward Antwerp and only managed to throw part of their troops into the islands of the Scheldt estuary. By the evening of May 12, the German tanks had passed the Langstraat and reached the Moerdijk bridges.

Around the same time, the Dutch government wired to London that the situation had become desperate and that only immediate Allied aid could stop the Germans. On the morning of May 13, Queen Wilhelmina went on board a British warship. She had first intended to go to Zeeland, but the situation was deteriorating so fast that the ship changed course and made for an English port. Princess Juliana and her husband, Prince Bernhard, had already left on the previous evening on a British torpedo boat. The Dutch cabinet transferred all its powers to General Winkelman and left a few hours after the Queen. Winkelman was given orders to fight on as long as he felt that there was purpose in further resistance.

The communiqué that announced the flight of the Queen and the government deeply shocked both the army and the population. Only later did the people realize that Wilhelmina had made a very wise decision. But the first reaction was a feeling of being abandoned, and many Dutchmen accused her of having saved her own skin and left her people to face the enemy. This first emotion gradually passed when it was realized that a captive government would have been a great asset to the Germans.

But certainly the event was very bad for morale. Still, resistance continued and the Germans, who needed their troops elsewhere, became nervous as rumors of British landings persisted. In fact, only a few destroyers had landed to help in carrying out certain destructions.

The obvious way to break into Fortress Holland was to storm the bridges over the river Maas at Rotterdam and take the city. With Rotterdam in German hands, General von Kuechler's Panzer divisions could advance north toward The Hague and Amsterdam. But by the evening of May 13, the German forces were still held at the Maas bridges, which lay under heavy fire. That evening, the German commander in the Rotterdam sector received the following telegram: "Resistance at Rotterdam has to be broken at all costs. If necessary threaten destruction of the city and carry it out."

General Schmidt, the recipient of that fateful wire, replied that he needed air force support for a breakthrough. On the next morning, General Kesselring, who commanded the Second German Air Force, could not make contact with General Schmidt. Thereupon, he called Goering and had — as he later declared himself — "a long telephone discussion which lasted for hours" with the supreme commander of the Luftwaffe. Kesselring was aware of the possiblility that the city would perhaps surrender under the threat of air bombardment. In that case, the air attack could even affect the Germans on their march; but Goering didn't seem worried and ordered the air strike for 1:20 P.M. The more conscientious Kesselring ordered the German squadron leader to watch for signals from the ground. At 10 A.M., he finally made contact with the Germans at the Maas bridges and was informed that the city had been asked to surrender. It was then decided that red flares should be fired from the Norder Island on the river if the attack was to be canceled. That information was also transmitted to the bomber squadron, which was already loading at Bremen. Its commander should also maintain radio contact with the Second Air Force and with the German troops on the ground. If red flares were sighted, a secondary object on the Dutch coast was to be attacked.

At the same time, three German officers under a white flag appeared on the Maas bridge and asked to be taken to the Dutch commanding officer. They were blindfolded and driven to Colonel Scharroo, the garrison commander, to whom they handed a German ultimatum. The document threatened complete destruction unless the city surrendered within two hours. The colonel was asked to delegate a plenipotentiary for signing the surrender. The message was not signed. Scharroo was in no mood to capitulate, but called General Winkelman and asked for instructions. The latter decided that Scharroo should first get in contact with the German officer who was responsible for the unsigned ultimatum. Perhaps Winkelman was afraid of some act of treachery. The Germans were constantly dropping leaflets all over the country that urged the Dutch to end their resistance, and German radio transmitters tried to spread confusion. The Germans claimed later that Winkelman was just playing for time. It has also been said that no international law exists that makes it mandatory to sign an ultimatum. It seems that both the German and the Dutch commander were unaware of this.

It was 11:45 A.M. A Dutch officer, Captain Bakker, was sent with the Germans to find out whether the ultimatum was genuine. At the same hour, about 100 German bombers at Bremen took to the air.

At 12:15 P.M., Schmidt and Bakker met at an ice-cream parlor at the left bank of the Maas. General Schmidt was told that an ultimatum had to be signed and agreed to issue a new one. He timed the expiration of the second document at 4:20 P.M. and correctly informed the Second Air Force to cancel its air strike.

But when the two men left the ice-cream parlor, the roar of the approaching Heinkels was already audible. The general ordered firing of the red flares, but they were only noticed by the left wing of the squadron, which turned off and bombed the secondary target. The right wing—by intent or oversight—started to unload its bombs on the center of Rotterdam. A German observer described the event with marked enthusiasm: "The approach is like on maneuver, quiet and secure. The planes are searching systematically for their targets. Soon the center of Rotterdam is burning at many places. Within a few minutes the center is enveloped in dense black and sulfur-yellow clouds. The bombers are flying quite low over the city. A splendid picture of invincible strength." It was, in fact, a very easy task. No adversary in the air and not a single antiaircraft gun fired from the ground. It was a windy day, and the flames spread with terrible speed while thousands of inhabitants fled through the burning streets.

The radio contact with the troops on the ground did not function. The planes unloaded all their bombs and returned to

Bremen, where they were loaded for a second air strike. This second bombardment did not occur, as the city had surrendered in the meantime. The planes were called back by a radio message. For years — even after the war — it was believed that 30,000 persons had perished in the attack. This was greatly exaggerated, but the truth was bad enough: 900 persons killed, several thousand injured, and 78,000 made homeless! Among the buildings destroyed were 21 churches and 4 hospitals.

Rotterdam was not an open city and, therefore, not protected by any international law. Nobody was ever sentenced at Nuremberg or elsewhere for having ordered the air strike. Of course, it should never have taken place while negotiations for surrender were going on. The Germans claimed that it was really all accidental and blamed the Dutch for delaying tactics. But it is all too probable that the attack would have transpired under any circumstance. Even if Colonel Scharroo had authorized Captain Bakker to sign an instrument of surrender, it would still have been too late. The first ultimatum expired at 12:30 P.M., and exactly one hour later the planes started unloading their deadly freight. They had already left their airfields at 11:45 A.M., and it is difficult to see why things should have gone differently if General Schmidt had received a formal surrender in that ice-cream parlor. He tried to stop the attack anyway. When Colonel Scharroo finally surrendered the city at 4 P.M., he told General Schmidt that he considered the bombardment before expiration of the ultimatum as a breach of faith. The General replied: "Colonel, I understand your bitterness."

An hour later, General Winkelman ordered the Dutch army in Fortress Holland to lay down its arms. Right after the news of the Rotterdam disaster, the announcement was issued that Utrecht was threatened by a similar fate. The destruction of a second large city was more than the unfortunate commander in chief could stomach. At 4:50 P.M., he issued the following order to all commanding officers: "Germany has bombed Rotterdam today, and Utrecht is threatened with destruction. To save the civilian population and prevent further bloodshed, I believe to be justified to order the troops under your command to stop fighting."

The surrender, which was signed on the next morning by Winkelman and von Kuechler at Rijsoord, did not include the troops in Zeeland that were still fighting side by side with the French.

Those troops kept resisting until May 17, when the Germans shelled the old historic town of Middelburg on the island of Walcheren. The French General Mittelhauser, who had been sent by Gamelin as liaison officer to Winkelman, arrived too late to meet the Dutch commander and returned to his superior without having achieved anything. The French front had collapsed near Sedan, and the Germans were already advancing on Laon. This completely unexpected disaster forced an Allied retreat in Belgium. The Seventh French Army, which only a few days earlier had entered Dutch territory, had to pull back in a hurry. Antwerp fell on May 18. A mixed Allied force still held out at the Terneuzen-Ghent Canal, and a last small corner of the Netherlands, Zeeuwsch Vlaanderen, remained a battleground until May

Hermann Goering (left) inspecting destruction at Rotterdam after the Dutch surrender, May 1940

Library of Congress

23. By then, the Germans had reached the sea near Abbeville, and the whole Allied force in Belgium was encircled. Four days later, King Leopold of the Belgians surrendered the remnants of his army and his person, a fateful decision that later cost him his throne.

For the great majority of the Netherlanders, the war had lasted only five days. The greater part of their navy had not been in home ports when the invasion occurred and was spared until another enemy faced them in the Java Sea two years later. The air force had been practically destroyed except for a few planes that managed to reach British soil.

A small number of soldiers and civilians also escaped to England. The harbor of Ijmuiden was filled with refugees on the day of the capitulation, but very few got away. The port was partly blocked by a liner, that had struck a mine and other ships that the Dutch had sunk themselves. Of the smaller warships, the destroyer *Jan van Galen* and the gunboat *Johan Maurits van Nassau* were sunk fighting bravely, and so were a number of other small craft.

The Germans, content with the Dutch capitulation, did not intern the army, though they could have done so according to military law. However, they felt that at that time it was wiser to have the Dutch troops disarm and demobilize. Officers had to sign a pledge not to take up arms again. Those of the army of the Netherlands Indies, which were still at war with Germany, refused and were interned. A few weeks later, General Winkelman and several other high officers were also declared prisoners of war and carried off to Germany.

The losses of the Dutch army had been comparatively slight: only 2,100 dead and 2,700 wounded. The civilian population's casualties were hardly lower. The exact German losses were never published. The heaviest casualties were suffered by the Luftwaffe, which had lost not fewer than 525 machines in that brief campaign.

CHAPTER FOUR

The average Dutchman, after hearing of his country's capitulation, felt a mixture of anger and relief. It took a few weeks until the initial shock wore off. By then Belgium had surrendered, the British Expeditionary Force (B.E.F.) had been embarked at Dunkirk, and France was on the verge of collapse. The first emotion over the military defeat passed gradually. If the renowned French army could not resist the German onslaught, who could blame little Holland, with its peacetime army and its obsolete equipment, for giving in so quickly? A prolongation of the struggle would only have caused more casualties and destruction without changing the course of events. At that time, few Netherlanders felt like fighting against hopeless odds. Resistance had been offered *pour la gloire des armes* and that was enough.

Many people were not yet aware that their world had turned upside down. Until May 14, 1940, they had been free citizens of one of the world's oldest democracies. They could assemble and talk as they wished, travel all over the world, and spent their money anywhere without restriction. Their political and religious rights had been granted for centuries; they were time-honored privileges that were taken as self-evident. For those very few who had been watching the European scene since 1933 with mounting alarm, the German invasion and occupation was no great surprise. Some of them like the poet Menno ter Braak, aware that they had now fallen into the clutches of limitless tyranny, took their lives.

The man on the street was grieved and startled, but not desperate. Many people seemed to live in a strange state of euphoria, hoping for speedy liberation, though no real cause for such optimism existed. However, the great majority of the Dutch never lost the feeling that this was just a passing, though unpleasant, phase that would end as suddenly as it had begun. In many, this confidence, which in the summer of 1940 seemed almost unrealistic, clearly had religious roots. Hitler was an evil, godless man, and wrong could never defeat right. This somewhat naïve but deep rooted feeling — a heritage no doubt from the sixteenth century struggle against Spain — never left the hearts of millions of ordinary, otherwise quite sober, people. This granite spirit, persistent and for the greater part quite unheroic, proved to be the strength of a country that had been easily defeated by overpowering might of arms.

Of course, there were men who took a far less sanguine approach to the whole situation. They felt that at least for the time being the Germans were in full control and that it was wise to kiss the hand one could not bite. Most of these people did not like what had happened, but were ready to accept realities. They were somewhat encouraged by the fact that the German occupation in those early days was far from unbearable. The German soldiers kept excellent discipline and were told by their officers — sometimes in the presence of Dutch civilians — to behave with reserve and politeness. There were no drunken brawls or noisy celebrations that are so often the outward show of conquest. In fact, many Dutchmen who had read about German atrocities in Poland in their newspapers were now skeptical and believed such stories wildly exaggerated. German officers always behaved with decorum, nobody was killed or raped, and Germans, quartered with Dutch families, were often friendly and helpful. The occupation of Fortress Holland took place almost without incident. At Rotterdam, the German General Student was severely wounded by a stray bullet, but the German officers in charge kept their heads and prevented serious bloodshed. As it turned out, the general had been accidentally shot by one of his own men. During those first weeks, it seemed that Holland could almost continue its peaceful life under German occupation. Soon, theaters and movies opened again — the latter, of course, with German films only — and restaurants and night clubs did excellent business with the occupation troops. The Germans, having quickly noticed that many goods that were scarce at home were plentiful in Holland, filled the stores. A common joke these days was the story of the British spy in German uniform who was immediately recognized and arrested because he carried no package.

If a large number of Dutchmen were depressed but compliant, a small group was openly enthusiastic. When German troops marched into Amsterdam, they were greeted at the Berlage bridge by members of the N.S.B. with "Sieg Heil" and "Heil Hitler." The party organ, *Volk en Vaderland*, condemned the flight of the royal family and praised the Germans as a "young nation" that was liberating Europe.

The attitude of the N.S.B. during the brief compaign had been more than doubtful. The Dutch authorities had arrested a number of them, together with most German civilians, as a preventive measure.

Enough fifth columnists remained to do a lot of harm.

Several years later, while living under a false name, the author quite accidentally met a Dutchman who had taken part in the organized smuggling of Dutch police uniforms to Germany. At the time of this encounter, the man was an officer in the S.S. Of course, he was quite unaware that he was talking to a member of the resistance. He was later killed in action during the British advance of 1944. As already mentioned, some traitors took part in German *coup de mains* on Dutch bridges. Others served the Germans as propagandists by spreading rumors and confusion. There were also several cases of open treason within the army. Colonel Mussert, the brother of the N.S.B. leader, was shot by two fellow officers when he tried to have tank obstacles removed. Others were very quick to surrender to the Germans.

The leaders of the N.S.B. added fuel to the talk of treason by immediately embracing the cause of the invader once the fighting was over. Some were moved by ideological motives; many others felt that an excellent opportunity had arisen to get jobs that under normal circumstances were completely out of their reach. The Germans — as previously in Norway — were delighted with the Dutch "quislings," but were somewhat cautious in making them masters of the country. They were sensible enough to realize that the Dutch Nazis were a small party that consisted at least in part of extremely doubtful elements. In Norway, the appointment of the Quisling government had done more harm than good to the occupying power. Therefore, it was decided to make use of the N.S.B., but to put real power into more trustworthy hands.

Here the Germans made their first critical mistake. A purely military occupation — as in Belgium and northern France — would have been far less obnoxious to the Dutch than political rule by a National Socialist proconsul. Perhaps the hope to "integrate" the Germanic Netherlands completely into the Reich played a certain part. Here the Nazis were deluded by their own propaganda. They believed that Nordic countries like Denmark, Norway, and the Netherlands would be easily absorbed into their "greater Germany." During the first years of occupation, German propagandists constantly talked about racial affinity, common blood, and similar slogans. It took them a long time to realize that this type of voodoo appealed to very few people. The Dutch had been an independent nation since 1572 and were not easily moved by pan-germanic ideas that had no roots in their own history. Such appeals worked in Austria, the Sudetenland, and the German-speaking parts of Poland. They were bound to fail in Holland, where democracy and Christianity were far more deeply entrenched.

In any case, Hitler decided to put the Netherlands under a "Reichskommissar" who would wield the supreme power and be under direct control of Berlin. This did not exclude the possibility of forming a Dutch Nazi government at a later date.

The man who now became the most absolute ruler of the Netherlands since the infamous Duke of Alba (1567) had been a little known attorney in Vienna until he suddenly became Austrian minister of the interior in February 1938. From that day on, he became notorious as the man who engineered Austria's *Anschluss* into the Reich.

Arthur Seyss-Inquart had been known in Vienna for "national sympathies." In the strange idiom of the decaying Austrian republic, that meant that he was a Nazi, though a respectable one, and not of the radical wing. In fact, he was a practicing Catholic and had not been involved in subversive activities against the Austrian government, which had banned the Nazi party in 1933. When the Austrian Chancellor Kurt von Schuschnigg was pressured into an "agreement" with Hitler, one of the conditions was the appointment of a "nationally minded" minister of the interior. Seyss-Inquart was suggested for the job, and Hitler agreed after some hesitation. A few days later, the new minister made a carefully worded speech in which he defined the rights of the Austrian National Socialists. Swastikas and party uniforms started appearing in the streets. After this promising start, Seyss-Inquart traveled to Germany to pay respects to his Fuehrer.

Later on, he claimed repeatedly that he did not favor complete absorption of his country into the Reich. Perhaps he did believe that Hitler would grant the Austrians an independence of sorts under a Nazi government of their own; but when he learned of Hitler's true intention, he willingly made himself a mere tool. On Austria's last day of independence, March 11, 1938, he remarked characteristically, "I'm only an historical telephone operator." In any case, on the evening of that eventful day, Seyss-Inquart found himself suddenly chancellor of Austria. He had superseded poor Schuschnigg, who had trusted him to the last and did not understand that a former fellow officer and good Catholic could also be a traitor. That chancellorship was of brief duration since Austria became a German province only a few weeks later. Comparatively little was heard of Seyss-Inquart for about one year. Then he was made deputy governor general of occupied Poland. By May 1940 he was clearly ready to take over a more prominent job.

Outwardly, Seyss-Inquart looked insignificant. He limped from a severe injury suffered in World War I and was a monotonous, uninspiring speaker. Of all the Nazi leaders who were later sentenced in Nuremberg, he seemed to be the most colorless. Nevertheless, he was very intelligent, well read, and a great lover of music. According to Nuremberg records, his I.Q. was 141, ranging just below Dr. Schacht's, Hitler's financial wizard.

48

Arthur Seyss-
Inquart
World War II
Collection of
Seized Enemy
Records,
National
Archives

His loyalty and obedience toward his Fuehrer were unlimited.
Many Dutchmen hoped that an Austrian ruler would not be
quite as bad as a German. They had a disappointment coming.

Seyss-Inquart took office at the historic Knights Hall at The
Hague on May 30. In a windy speech, he declared that Holland
and Germany were bound by common blood, but that it was not
his intention to force the Nazi creed on the Dutch people. In
a separate communiqué, the Netherlands were assured that their
laws would remain valid "as far as possible." Judges, civil servants,
and other functionaries were admonished to obey the German
regime.

Seyss-Inquart had brought with him four deputies. Three of
them were of little importance, but the fourth, the man in charge
of security, deserves full attention, as he was destined to play a
decisive role.

Hanns Albin Rauter, like his superior, was an Austrian. But un-like his chief, he came from the radical wing of the Nazi party. This group contained a number of fanatics, among others the odious Ernst Kaltenbrunner, who became head of the Central Bureau for Security during the last phase of the war. Rauter fled to Germany after the ill-fated Nazi coup-d'état against Chancellor Dollfuss in 1934 and became a leading member in the Austrian Legion, an armed organization of Nazi exiles. They returned triumphantly to their homeland in 1938, and Rauter quickly advanced in the S.S. until he was appointed as "Higher S.S. and Police Chief" for the occupied Netherlands. His rank was equal to that of a general. As such he was in complete control of the complicated German security apparatus that comprised the S.D.,* the Gestapo, the regular and military police, and various special, uniformed Dutch auxiliaries that later came into being. Except for the army, navy, and air force, Rauter came to dominate the whole intricate system that soon was to control life in the occupied Netherlands.

During the first phase of the occupation, Seyss-Inquart hesi-tated introducing German Gestapo methods into Holland. How-ever, the power of his subordinate grew from year to year, and soon the country was ruled exclusively by police terror. Very characteristic is the history of German jurisdiction in the Nether-lands. One of Seyss-Inquart's first ordinances referred to the es-tablishment of German courts. The task of these courts was to handle all offenses against the occupying power in the widest sense. A Dutchman accused of an offense against a German or even against another Dutchman serving the invader became sub-ject to German jurisdiction. In the beginning, German courts maintained at least a semblance of correct procedure. The ac-cused was represented by counsel of his choice, interpreters were present in court, and the public was admitted. In fact, not all judges were Nazi, but they were often exposed to pressure by Rauter's S.D. Even an acquittal did not always help the ac-

*The S.D. (Sicherheitsdienst) was originally a subdivision of the S.S., but later became the controlling police agency for Germany and occupied Europe.

cused, for he could immediately be rearrested. Later on, special military courts took over most political cases. Only German attorneys were admitted, and the trial became a mere farce, for the defendant was often refused the opportunity to speak.

But in 1940 the war in the Netherlands was still predominantly a paper war. As soon as bombs stopped raining on Rotterdam, there began a rain of decrees. In the first place, it was forbidden to show the national flag or the orange flag of the royal house. Nevertheless, a vivid demonstration took place on June 29 on the occasion of Prince Bernhard's birthday. The mayor of The Hague, Mr. de Monchy, coolly signed an address of congratulation for the prince and was promptly dismissed from his office.

The next step was to regulate distribution of food, and soon afterward of shoes, textiles, and soap. It quickly became very clear to everybody that enormous amounts of goods of every type were constantly shipped to Germany. Ironically, this gave even a certain justification to the black market, which started to grow in proportion to shortages. It could be claimed that in this manner the goods at least remained in Holland. However, those who transacted such business were rarely fired by patriotic considerations.

A number of political measures followed. First, the biggest labor union was placed under a Dutch Nazi commissar. Then the Socialist and Communist parties were dissolved and their property put under custodianship of Rost van Tonningen. This gentleman had been interned and transported to Zeeland during the May fighting. From there, his guards had brought him to Calais, where he was liberated by the Germans. The former party newspapers now fell under his control. One of the directors committed suicide after seizure of his newspaper.

The remaining political parties were in a difficult position. It was already clear that they would be eventually disbanded as in Germany and Austria. This would leave the Dutch Nazis the only political party. The first appointments made by Seyss-Inquart immediately made it obvious that they were given preference without the slightest consideration of ability.

It was at first attempted to form a committee from the six surviving parties. However, the two conservative Protestant parties*
declared that they could not sign any manifesto that did not
proclaim allegiance to the House of Orange. This was immediately rejected by the Germans.

Finally, a new organization was formed under the name of the
"Netherlands Union." It was headed by the Royal Commissioner
for Groningen, J. Linthorst Homan, Professor J. E. de Quay, and
a high police functionary, L. Einthoven. This triumvirate published a communiqué that asked all Dutchmen to join in the new
task of reorganizing the country under the changed circumstances
of the occupation. The main points of that manifesto were:

1. National cooperation on a broad political front.
2. Social justice.
3. Freedom of religion.
4. Strengthening of Holland's position within Europe.
5. Close cultural relations with South Africa and the Flemish-
   speaking parts of Belgium.

There were several sentences in the text that sounded very nationalistic. The occupying authorities were assured of the loyalty
of the signers. However, most citizens rightly assumed that this
was just lip service. A large number of people† joined in the hope
that the organization at least might not be national socialistic and
would be given a measure of recognition by the Germans.

The men who founded the "Netherlands Union" were undoubtedly patriots and filled with the best intentions. They were
courageous enough to oppose some facets of national socialism,
like the persecution of Jews. However, they were politically
naïve, and believed that some sort of cooperation with a totalitarian power might be possible. Perhaps this was because none of
these three well-meaning men was actually a professional politician. The Netherlands Union existed about one year, then came
to an inglorious end. It was simply dissolved by the Germans.

*The Christian Historic Party and the Antirevolutionary Party.

†At one time the "Netherlands Union" had 800,000 members.

52

Meanwhile, the opposite camp had troubles of its own. The Dutch are, and have always been, a very sectarian nation, and even the comparatively small percentage of outright Fascists was split in three groups. The more moderate elements, who called themselves the "National Front," gathered around a man by the name of Arnold Meyer, whose main program proposed a future union between the Netherlands and the Flemish-speaking Belgians. As we have seen, similar ideas had also seeped into the "Netherlands Union." In practice, nothing ever came of it, as the majority of both nations showed not the slightest inclination for such an artificial fusion.

A smaller group of extremists, which went under the name of N.S.N.A.P.,* was in favor of complete integration of the Netherlands into the "Great German Reich." This was in clear contradiction to the program of the N.S.B., the party of Anton A. Mussert.

Born 1894 in the western Netherlands, Mussert lost his parents at an early age. Acording to the recollections of a Dutch writer,† he must have been a most insufferable boy. He studied engineering, and at the age of 33 became chief engineer at the Public Works Department in the province of Utrecht. He married his aunt, who was 15 years his senior, a match for which he was often held up to ridicule. As we have already mentioned, Mussert became the founder and leader of the N.S.B., and though not a particularly forceful personality, he maintained his leadership of the party until the day when he was arrested for high treason by the Netherlands' government (1945).

A heavy-set, balding man, who slightly resembled Mussolini, Mussert was neither a great orator nor of superior intellect. Under normal circumstances, he would have remained the rather pedestrian chief of a small right-wing party. During the May campaign, he had been hiding out in the house of a friend in the village of Huizen, as he — quite rightly — feared being imprisoned. When fighting was over and the country occupied, Mussert presented himself to his countrymen as their once and future

*National Socialist Nederlandse Arbeiders Partij.

†Pierre van Paassen: *Earth Could be Fair.*

Mussert (right) receives a birthday gift from his German protector Fritz Schmidt.

Library of Congress

54

leader. Soon he proposed to Seyss-Inquart that a Dutch government be formed consisting of members of the N.S.B. The Reichskommissar politely declined. The Austrian quisling eyed this Dutch counterpart with a certain condescension. The N.S.B. at that time had only 30,000 members, and Seyss-Inquart was far too clever not to realize that they represented only a small segment of the nation. Besides, there was no reason for hasty decisions. Such questions could be safely settled when the war ended.

So certain were the Nazis of having won the war that the position of the Netherlands at the coming peace negotiations was already discussed. These were the days when German soldiers marched through the streets singing "Wir fahren gegen Engelland."* Indeed, many small events seemed to predict a speedy expedition across the English Channel. The Dutch harbors were filled with canal and river barges, that had been given concrete floors for the transportation of armor. Also, they were equipped with collapsible ramps to act as sally ports and as gangways for men and vehicles. A great number of tugs were assembled to drag the barges toward Britain's shore. This accumulation of craft in Dutch ports, especially at Rotterdam, was of course known to the British, and the Royal Air Force became more active over Holland. In September, all foreigners were suddenly expelled from the coastal zone. It was also noticed that German troops were training for invasion at the seashore.

The Dutch, an old seafaring nation, watched these preparations with a great deal of skepticism. When the invasion did not materialize, rumors rose that the Germans had actually made an attempt and been defeated with heavy losses. These stories were entirely false, but they were widely believed at that time. By October, it became clear that Britain could not be overcome and that the world was in for a long war.

*"We are sailing against England." During 1940 the most popular German marching song.

CHAPTER FIVE

During the winter of 1940-41, the Dutch population hoped, grumbled, and listened to the B.B.C.* For the first time since May 10, the news was not exclusively bad. The stubborn British were not only resisting Hitler's air attacks, but had even won a smashing victory in the Libyan desert. Mussolini's invasion of Greece had proved to be an embarrassing failure. American aid to Britain was on the rise, and Franklin Delano Roosevelt, who was considered a great friend of the Netherlands, had been re-elected President.

The British radio broadcasts — especially the speeches of Churchill and Queen Wilhelmina — were the ray of hope for a vanquished and harassed nation. In July, Radio Orange, a daily transmission in Dutch, was introduced with an address of the Queen. The German authorities immediately made it an offense to listen to foreign broadcasts. But they realized very well that any effective control was simply impossible because there were more than one million radio sets in the country. Soon people who were caught listening to the B.B.C. were sent to concentration camps, but this never deterred others from tuning in. Mimeographed sheets of important news were circulated. The systematic Rauter began urging that all radio sets be confiscated. However, for the time being, Seyss-Inquart rejected the idea because of the adverse effect such a step would have had on the population. After all, this would indicate that the Germans were afraid of British propaganda. He also hoped that his own men

*British Broadcasting Company.

on Radio Hilversum* would prove equal to that challenge. Indeed, he had won at least one effective propagandist, Max Blokzijl, previously a journalist with the conservative newspaper, *Algemeen Handelsblad.* A man of sharp wit and considerable eloquence, he became the foremost preacher of the Nazi gospel in Holland. Called "Lying Max" by the patriots, his program, "Burning Questions," was nevertheless widely listened to. Another novelty on the air was a political cabaret, that not without humor ridiculed the Allies and their supporters. In the first phase of the war, both sides still used farce and jokes as a weapon.

The Dutch Nazis in particular were the constant object of the sometimes bizarre humor of their adversaries. Members of the N.S.B. were under obligation to sell the party newspaper. They were often serenaded by young men with a mock song following the tune of a well-known military march, "Let it be known that we're traitors."† Incidents between Dutch Nazis and Loyalists multiplied, especially in workers' districts. Propaganda marches of Nazis in working-class quarters in Rotterdam were greeted with a rain of bricks. In September, a violent street battle took place in The Hague, during which a member of the N.S.B. was killed. He was buried with great ceremony, and the newly appointed attorney general, Dr. R. van Genechten, made the funeral speech. The latter was another of the new men, now gaining prominence. He was a Belgian and had belonged to the so-called Activist party, which collaborated with the Germans in World War I. Under death sentence for high treason, he escaped to the Netherlands and tried unsuccessfully for a professorship at the University of Utrecht. Van Genechten became a fanatic Nazi and successively plenipotentiary for education and commissioner for the province of Zuid Holland. A completely unbalanced person, he had to seek psychiatric help in 1943 and even tried to commit suicide. After the liberation, he was arrested, and this time he succeeded in hanging himself in his prison cell.

*All Dutch radio programs were transmitted from the town of Hilversum.

†The original tune goes: "Let it be known that we're tough boys." ("En dat wij toffe jongens zijn, dat willen we weten.")

The Germans were not overly impressed by such supporters, though the Dutch Nazis eagerly proclaimed that the future belonged to Germany and never ceased to revile the former Dutch government and the royal family. In imitation of their masters, a paramilitary organization called W.A.* was formed, and later the Netherlands S.S. However, the latter became quickly a German auxiliary unit that had to swear an oath of allegiance to Hitler, not to Mussert. In fact, the Netherlands S.S. felt no loyalty to its own country at all and openly advocated annexation. This was contrary to Mussert's ideas, who saw clearly enough that such a development would leave him at best with the office of Gauleiter of a new German province.

This split in the Dutch Nazi party was also due to personal disputes. The radicals were sponsored by Rauter, who despised Mussert and called him "that little Philistine." As Rauter had ready access to the Reichsfuehrer of the S.S., Heinrich Himmler, his influence was considerable and often overshadowed that of Seyss-Inquart, who at least formally was his superior. The latter took a more cautious view and was willing to give Mussert a certain amount of aid, but thought little of the N.S.B. leader's ability. As we shall later see, Mussert tried to obtain concessions from Hitler personally, but without any measure of success.

The only German in office who stood above all these party matters and petty intrigues was the commander of the armed forces in Holland, General of the Air Force Friedrich Christian Christiansen. He had been an aviator during World War I, later an officer in the merchant marine, and finally, a protégé of Goering in charge of all German Air Force training schools. Christiansen was no radical Nazi and could have had a moderating influence on the situation. However, like many correct German officers, he lacked the strength of character to act according to his views. Outside of purely military affairs, his voice was rarely heard.

*Weer Afdeling. (Defense Division.)

So, for all practical purposes, the Netherlands was to be governed for five years by two Austrian Nazis with very little experience in the practical ways of government. Neither of them had the slightest interest in the people they ruled, nor did they possess any deeper knowledge of its ways and customs. The whole regime has a fine model in German literature: The Landvogt (prefect) Gessler in Schiller's *Wilhelm Tell*, who forces the people to pay reverence to his hat on top of a pole. Seyss-Inquart merely replaced the hat by the swastika.

Of course, Seyss-Inquart fully realized that to rule the country, the cooperation of the Dutch government apparatus was required. The ministers had left, but their deputies remained. At the top of each department stood a secretary-general whose function was similar to the undersecretaries in the United States. These were the men who had to carry out the policies of the invader.

In 1937, the Dutch government prepared secret instructions regarding the conduct of affairs in case of foreign occupation. These directives were extremely vague and left the decision to serve practically to the individual officer. They were admonished to continue their work if the nation's welfare were to be served. They should resign if their service would mainly aid the enemy and its war machine.

It is clear that those instructions under the actual conditions of 1940 were of doubtful value. In total war, almost every governmental action to some degree advances the invader's interests. The ways and means of a Nazi occupation were in no way foreseen in 1937, and no consideration had been given to the possibility that the aggressor would not honor the rules of war.

The Dutch civil servants were consequently faced with a situation without clear instructions or precedent. Understandably, most of them stayed at their desks.

As always, Seyss-Inquart, well aware that his cadre of pro-German officials was quite limited, proceeded cautiously. Some officers, like the secretary general of defense, who were obviously hostile to the occupying power, were dismissed. The same fate befell all Jewish civil servants in November 1940, among them the President of the Supreme Court, L.E. Visser. This was completely in violation of Dutch law, and the court itself was expected to protest, but it remained silent. At least two Dutch universities showed far greater courage. A group of professors first petitioned Seyss-Inquart not to introduce anti-Jewish legislation. When this was ignored, both teachers and students rallied to a vigorous protest.

At the famous old University of Leyden — founded in 1575 during the war of independence against Spain — Professor R.P. Cleveringa bitterly denounced the German action and highly praised a dismissed Jewish colleague. When Cleveringa ended his address, the students went on strike. The Germans reacted immediately. They closed the university for the duration of the war. Cleveringa was arrested and remained in jail for eight months. A strike of students also took place at the Institute for Technology at Delft. This university remained closed until April 1941. Then classes were allowed to resume, for the authorities had a certain interest in graduating young engineers. The other higher schools of learning made no strong protest and remained open for a time.

Another group of officials slated for increased attention were the mayors. The powers of a mayor in Holland were considerable, for he headed the local police force and the administration of public records. The latter were of foremost importance as they contained complete data on every single citizen. Consequently, the administration of every city, town, or village was responsible for the distribution of ration cards for food, textiles, and coal. The Germans realized early that here lay the artery to the whole population. A man without personal documents and ration cards in wartime woud be like an outcast in his own country. Nobody had ever thought of that fact before the occupation, and the Germans found all files in perfect condition. The Dutch administration had always been famous for its orderliness.

Naturally, the Germans also had access to the police files, which contained complete information on all foreigners residing in Holland. Many of them were refugees from the Nazi regime, and their personal data now fell into the hands of the Gestapo. For the time being, little was done about the matter, except for expelling these people from the coastal zone. Because of the key position of the mayors, Seyss-Inquart was eager to remove those who were known to be Dutch patriots and replace them with members of the N.S.B. or persons inclining toward collaboration. Subsequently, the mayors of most larger cities were slowly dismissed and superseded by such individuals. Some of the new mayors had no qualification at all for their office and jokes about those incompetent city fathers abounded. A typical story was told of a member of the N.S.B. who bitterly complained that he hadn't been made a mayor yet, whereas one of his friends, Mr. Janssen, was already burgomaster of a beautiful village. He received the reply: "Sorry, we had to give preference to Janssen. He can read and write."

A similar situation arose with the police service. Shortly after the occupation of Holland the Germans organized their own police apparatus. Its most important part was the Security Service, or S.D., which concerned itself with all offenses of a subversive or political nature. The Secret State Police (Gestapo) was actually a part of this giant organization that, like an enormous spiderweb, covered all of German-controlled Europe. Its center was in Berlin, where Reinhardt Heydrich had become its powerful chief. The S.D. soon began to hire Dutch undercover agents, so-called V-men. The Security Service in Holland stood under Rauter's command. His deputy until 1943 was a professional German police commander, Dr. Wilhelm Harster.[*]

Aside from the S.D., the Germans had their own executive police troops, generally called the "Green Police" because of the color of their uniforms. They became identified with police terror and were soon hated and feared by the Dutch population. Their methods were entirely different from those of a normal police force in a civilized country. They always acted with the utmost brutality, and soon stories about atrocities committed by these

[*]Harster is serving at present a long prison term in Germany as a convicted war criminal.

police bullies abounded. They were even feared by the German soldiery, though the army also had its own military police.†
One of Rauter's first acts was to increase the Dutch police forces, mainly by demobilized soldiers. He realized that his reserve of German policemen was limited; therefore, a strong Dutch force of reliable caliber was necessary. The old Dutch police administration underwent a thorough reorganization, whereby all services were centralized and subjected to the secretary general of justice. Furthermore, Rauter soon instituted a new police school at Schalkhaar in which new recruits were to be trained according to German principles. These men later gained a very evil reputation.

However, the greatest part of the Dutch police consisted of good patriots who were averse to working for the occupying power. Their position was far from enviable. Most of them — like the far greater number of Dutch civil servants — were decent men, loyal to their country and the royal family. Of course, they had been brought up to obey their superiors and to perform their duties in an orderly manner. They had grown up in a state in which law and order were respected. Civil rights of all citizens were a century-old tradition. They had a reputation for being strict and meticulous, but police brutality was almost unknown in Holland. Now they suddenly found themselves servants of a foreign dictator and forced to act against their own compatriots. If they refused, they were faced with the loss of their jobs and possibly even worse consequences. During the first years of the occupation, most of them obeyed orders, often unwillingly. Victims of Nazi persecution were sometimes warned in advance by well-meaning policemen. In the later phase of the war, many joined the resistance.

The judicial system remained almost undisturbed until 1943. However, as we have already mentioned, this was only in regard to nonpolitical affairs. All defendants who were accused of activities directed against the occupying power were tried by German courts if they were not sent to a concentration camp

†The German M.P. went under the name of "Feld Gendarmerie." Their presence was little noticed during the first years of occupation.

without any legal procedure. This left only that part of the jurisdiction in Dutch hands that did not concern the Germans.

In his inaugural speech, Seyss-Inquart had promised not to
interfere with Dutch political life. He kept that promise for
exactly seven weeks. Then came a wave of arrests during which
a number of politicians was seized and interned in the notorious
German concentration camp of Buchenwald. This was motivated
by the internment of German civilians in the Netherlands Indies,
where they were considered enemy aliens. Among the Dutch
politicians imprisoned was the former Minister of Justice
Goseling. He died after eight months in the camp. At the same
time, the suppression of political parties began, though at first
it was only directed against those of the Left. The more conservative elements were spared for the time being, perhaps because
the German administration hoped for their collaboration. In fact,
Hendrick Colijn, Holland's most renowned prewar statesman,
was received by Seyss-Inquart. Shortly afterward Colijn published a pamphlet, "On the Border Between Two Worlds," that
recommended limited cooperation with Germany, provided that
the monarchy would be retained. It appears that Colijn, who was
seventy-one years old, was thoroughly confused by the events;
after a few weeks, he repudiated his proposal, which had evoked
many protests from his own party. Thereafter, he kept in the
background, and little was heard of him until he was arrested and
taken to Germany in 1941, where he died three years later.

As already mentioned, the new regime had placed the largest
labor union under a Nazi commissioner. This was the N.V.V.
(Nederlands Verband van Vakverenigingen), which was predominantly Socialist. Some staff members resigned, but the
majority carried on. The two denominational unions — one Protestant and one Catholic — were at first allowed to pursue their
activities undisturbed. Right after the capitulation, the Germans
started an intense propaganda drive to induce workers to go to
Germany. Dutchmen, willing to work in the Reich, were promised good wages, pleasant working conditions, and regular
vacations. As many men were unemployed due to demobilization
and war events, a certain number went on a more or less voluntary basis. Soon pressure was used by withholding unemployment

benefits from those unwilling to go. Until 1942 no one was actually forced to relocate to Germany. Prices and wages were at first frozen; later, moderate increases were granted. A new charity organization, Winterhulp Nederland, was organized, copying the German example. It met with almost complete failure, though the support of many Dutch officials had been enlisted. Refusal to join in that National Socialist charity drive was a frequent and not very dangerous form of protest.

Another new institution was a German type of labor service originally introduced to act as a sort of manpower pool for demobilized army personnel, with the task of repairing war damage. Its first commander was a Major J.N. Breunese, not a Nazi. Later, compulsory labor service for all Dutch boys at the age of 18 was decreed. After one year, it became clear that the organization was to be Nazified. Thereupon, Breunese resigned.

All these measures were bound to annoy particularly the working class, which was most affected by rationing, unemployment, higher costs of living, and destruction of their party organizations. Also, it soon became known that those wonderful jobs in Germany consisted often of hard and unpleasant work in armament factories. The mounting forced export of foodstuffs and cattle to Germany was another source of anger. Incidents multiplied. At the Wilton shipyards, a number of workers were arrested for alleged sabotage. It also was rumored that the Germans intended to force the deportation of dock workers from Amsterdam. A growing atmosphere of hatred against the invader was noticeable, especially in the big industrial cities. A German police report mentioned "a dangerous anti-German and anti-N.S.B. attitude." Under those circumstances, any minor incident could provide the spark that would lead to a violent explosion. It was the W.A. that finally threw the match into the powder keg.

CHAPTER SIX

Early in February 1941, the black-shirted bully boys of the
W.A. started causing trouble in The Hague, Rotterdam, and
Amsterdam. The Dutch police, under order to protect the hooli-
gans "in the interest of the Netherlands," remained inactive. The
W.A. followed the example that Nazi stormtroopers had set in
Germany. In Rotterdam, an office of the "Netherlands Union"
was smashed to smithereens. In Amsterdam, the terror was mainly
directed against the Jews, who were dragged from streetcars
and restaurants.

The large Jewish district in the north of Amsterdam and
the adjoining working-class neighborhood became the scene of
violent clashes. Small action groups* — both gentile and Jewish
— retaliated against the Nazis. Seyss-Inquart's deputy in Amsterdam, Boehmcker, ordered the W.A. to stay out of the Jewish
quarters, but was not obeyed. On February 10, 40 men of the
W.A. — got into a heavy fight with Jewish action groups. Several
Nazis were injured and one of them killed.

This was exactly what the more radical elements of the regime
had waited for. Rauter sent a provocative report to Himmler
in which the dead W.A. man was claimed to have been bitten
through his jugular vein. The Jewish quarter was guarded by
Dutch police while the Germans started chasing "terrorists."
One week after the aforementioned fight, the "Green Police"
raided an ice-cream parlor in the Van Woustraat, which
was frequented by action groups. In the ensuing battle, the

*Those groups were called Knokploegen (K.P.) That name was
later also used by other resistance organizations.

64

Germans were drenched with acid. The owners of the ice-cream parlor were arrested and one of them later executed.

On February 22 and 23, the German police entered the Jewish quarter and arrested 425 young men below the age of 35. The prisoners were treated with the greatest brutality in full view of the population. Red posters appeared on the walls in which the public was informed that the arrests were made in retaliation against the attack on the police and that the prisoners would be transported to a concentration camp in Germany.* The brutal acts committed by the German police brought the excitement in Amsterdam to a fever pitch. A few days before, there had already been considerable unrest, both in the streets and in the harbor. The dock workers were mostly Socialists and Communists, and their bitterness against the German occupation regime, which had dissolved their parties, now found additional fuel.

The initial action came from Communists, who were well organized and had capable leadership. From November on, they had been secretly publishing a newspaper, *De Waarheid,*† and constantly attacked the Nazis, even though at that time the Germans still had their famous nonaggression pact with the Soviet Union. On February 22, a Saturday, when the news of the arrests spread, the Communists decided that the time for a protest strike had come. Thousands of pamphlets were mimeographed, urging a one-day work stoppage in protest against the illtreatment of the Jews. Furthermore, the text called for wage increases and higher unemployment benefits. The gentile population was encouraged to help the Jews and resist the W. A.

The authors of those leaflets must have been surprised at the tremendous success of their appeal, especially since the majority of the people who took part in the strike were far from being sympathetic to communism. But here, for the first time, was an issue that went far beyond party or self-interest. By Tuesday

*They were indeed shipped to Mauthausen in Austria. None of them survived.

†*Waarheid* means truth. This is also the name of the Soviet newspaper, *Pravda.*

noon the big harbor of Amsterdam lay idle. At the same time, all municipal traffic stopped. Streetcar conductors, after some hesitation, left the cars in their sheds or returned them after a brief run. Of course, as traffic came to a standstill, the news of the strike quickly spread through the city. German soldiers stared incredulously at the spectacle. No German worker had ever dared to strike since the advent of the Hitler regime in 1933. Later in the day, a number of other workers in municipal and private enterprises went on strike. The center of Amsterdam was filled with people excitedly discussing the situation and urging more men to join the work stoppage. The few streetcars that were still circulating were forced back to their terminals. Demonstrations occurred all over the city. The Dutch police made no great effort to disperse the crowds.

It so happened that Seyss-Inquart was in Vienna on February 25. His Amsterdam deputy, Boehmcker, who must have been a very astonished man on that winter morning, urged Mayor de Vlugt and the commissioner of the Dutch police to break up the strike. The burgomaster had posters printed in which a curfew was announced and demonstrations in the streets were prohibited. The tone of that manifesto was not very convincing. The last sentence read: "If all cooperate, we shall end todays confusion with united efforts." However, the curfew was obeyed, and no incidents took place during the night.

But now Rauter took action. German police units were assembled and marched into the city. On Wednesday morning, the Germans declared a state of siege. As this was a privilege of the military, the order was signed by General Christiansen. He ordered that work be resumed on February 27. All political parties in the province of North Holland were prohibited from any activity, including the wearing of uniforms, which meant that the W.A. had to stay home for the time being. Of course, all demonstrations remained forbidden, and drastic penalties under German military law threatened any striker or agitator.

Wednesday the strike still persisted and even spread to Haarlem and Zaandam. Angry crowds prevented the streetcars from running, but in the afternoon, policemen were stationed next to the conductors, and service was resumed. Municipal plants and offices returned to work, as the employees were threatened with dismissal. However, other factories went on strike and the general situation was still very confused.

By noon, Rauter's police and S.S. troops arrived in great numbers and fired ruthlessly into the crowds. Seven people were killed and 45 wounded. Two more persons were shot in Zaandam. This was the end of the February strike. On Thursday morning, the workers returned to their jobs.

The original appeal to the workers had only spoken of a one-day work stoppage as a way of protest. In fact, the strike had lasted two days and most participants felt that further extension would only lead to a senseless massacre, as the strikers were unarmed and no match for Rauter's police forces. The workers had clearly shown their anger and protest. They were not in a position to cripple the German war effort. Such action only became possible years later when the Allies were already at the gates.

As an act of defiance the strike was a success. The participants felt pride and relief to have challenged the invader. Sympathy with the strikers was almost general throughout the country.

The February strike also marked the point of no return. During the first eight months of the occupation, a tolerable relationship with the occupying power was still a possibility. The Germans had destroyed that chance by sponsoring the N.S.B. and forcing their ideas on an unwilling population. A purely military occupation might have caused less antagonism.

The German administration was undoubtedly aware of the situation. The contemptuous "Holland will annex itself" — a remark allegedly made by Bismarck under very different circumstances — was rarely heard from now on. For several months, the German authorities followed a more cautious line. At the same time, the pressure against every type of resistance was quietly increased. About 100 persons who had taken part in the strike, most of them Communists, were arrested. The city of Amsterdam and several smaller towns were fined. Those fines were levied like taxes from inhabitants of the higher-income group. Mr. de Vlugt, the mayor, who had shown little eagerness to suppress the strike, was replaced by a former marine officer, E.J. Voute, of pro-German leanings. Also the towns of Haarlem, Hilversum, and Zaandam were put under the rule of new burgomasters. One of them had been dishonorably discharged a few years earlier because of treasonable utterances. Soon afterward, the secretaries general for justice and finance were dismissed and their posts given to Dutch Nazis. That so many Dutch officials remained loyal to their legal government caused the German authorities to place more and more members of the N.S.B. in such positions. This again led to an increasing struggle within Dutch ranks, as many citizens bitterly resented the promotion of persons whose only claim to fame was a membership card of the N.S.B. More and more people started talking about "hatchet day," the day of reckoning with the Dutch Nazis. A widely told story described a man going into a hardware store and asking to buy a hatchet. The owner replied: "I am sorry, they are all sold out. How about a piece of lead pipe?" This was merely talk, but it showed the gulf that was constantly widening between the Loyalists and the supporters of the "New Order."

In one respect, the strike was a grave warning to the Dutch. The studied ferocity of the German police troops discouraged any further open uprising. Even to the bravest person it had become clear that it was hopeless to fight disciplined, well-equipped soldiers with bare fists. No further open demonstrations took place in Amsterdam for the rest of the war, not even in the spring of 1943 when strikes were widespread all over the country. Resistance had gone underground and operated after dark or behind closed doors. The Dutch, with their long tradition of honesty, square dealing, and moderation, were slow to learn such methods.

Probably no other country in Europe is so unsuited for action against an occupying military power as the Netherlands. In 1940 about nine million people populated a small area of 33,000 square miles. The country is flat and possesses excellent road and rail communications, with practically no inaccessible regions. While Yugoslavian and Greek partisans could always find refuge in their mountains, difficult for motorized troops to penetrate, the Dutch resistance worker was not favored by geography. Even France, Norway, Poland, and Czechoslovakia offered some natural shelter to desperate men who were willing to brave the enemy in the hills and forests and carry out "hit and run" raids. No such national redoubt — to use an expression coined by Dr. Goebbels — existed for the Netherlander. He could find no other refuge than a city apartment, an attic or a basement, at best a remote farmhouse. The Germans, on the other hand, had all the advantages of an extensive net of roads, railways, and rivers. Therefore, they could move their troops at great speed all over the country. The few less densely inhabited regions would be easily controlled by comparatively small forces of soldiers and policemen. Forests cover only 7 per cent of the Netherlands, and they can be easily penetrated by infantry.

The German and Belgian borders were heavily guarded, and clandestine traffic was extremely difficult. Escape routes to Belgium played a certain part in the later phase of the war, but they could only be used by small groups of men who knew the frontier region very thoroughly. The coastal area was closely patrolled from the beginning of the occupation. In 1941, access to the coast was forbidden to civilians. Later, the chain of German fortifications, which became part of their "Atlantic Wall," made any approach from the rear almost impossible. In front of those forts and redoubts lay the sea, which had become practically inaccessible to the Dutch. All harbor areas were under strict control. Only the port of Delfzijl in the north provided a tenuous contact with neutral Sweden, and as we shall see later, was used by an underground group until 1943.

Clearly, contact between Dutch resistance organizations and the Allies was bound to be extremely difficult. During the first year of occupation, an occasional British seaplane might land on Dutch waters. In one case, a particularly daring agent was put ashore by dinghy after seven unsuccessful attempts.

At the beginning of the occupation, young Dutchmen frequently tried to reach England by boat. During the whole war, only 200 succeeded. After May 1941, the province of Zeeland, the Frisian islands, and the isles South of Rotterdam were off limits for all Dutchmen except the inhabitants of that region. When, in April 1942, the coastal zone between Den Helder and Hook van Holland became a restricted area, further escapes were indeed impossible. There still remained the long escape route through Belgium and France to Switzerland or Spain. This meant crossing three heavily guarded borders.

The author and his wife were once approached by a smuggler who had overheard a few of their remarks on a crowded train and figured — not without justification — that they might be interested in leaving the country. A meeting at a small railroad station was arranged, and the man offered to guide his prospective clients safely to Switzerland for a price of Hfl. 10,000. (When told that such a sum was not available, he quickly dropped his offer to Hfl. 3000.) His whole behavior was somewhat reminiscent of the bandit Sparafucile in Verdi's *Rigoletto,* and the author decided to reject the proposed deal. The man could well have been a German agent. After the war, a number of cases became known in which would-be fugitives were guided right into the hands of the Gestapo.

Until November 1942, some people managed to cross into unoccupied France and reach the Pyrenees on foot. From there, they could try to cross the Spanish frontier across the rugged mountains. After the occupation of southern France, this, too, became increasingly difficult.

Because geographical conditions were so unfavorable, Dutch resistance was practically thrown upon its own resources until the Allies had regained control of northern France and Belgium.

But geography was only one of the difficulties encountered. Equally important was that the country was completely unprepared for a struggle against the Nazi war machine. In the first place, every tradition of conspiracy and insurrection was lacking. Writers and poets liked to raise memories of the heroic fight against Spain (1568-1648) and resistance against Napoleon (1806-13). This sounded very good, but modern total war provides few parallels with those events. The technique of an underground struggle cannot be learned from history books. In fact, for many generations no similar situation had occurred; therefore, the Dutchman of 1940 — unlike the Belgians or Yugoslavs — had absolutely no experience with foreign occupation. In addition, he was the product of a relatively well-to-do country with fewer hates and frustrations than the poor but tough farmer or shepherd in the Balkans, who, after all, had little to lose.

By nature and tradition the Dutch had strong family ties, and their approach to modern life was generally conservative, whatever their political conviction. Radicalism and fanaticism of any kind never found very fertile ground in the Netherlands. This was undoubtedly one of the reasons why national socialism could not take root. The membership of the N.S.B. rose during the war to about 50,000* but a goodly number of these persons were merely opportunists, mockingly called the "bread N.S.B." On the other hand, the underground movement, notwithstanding all persecutions, was slow to adopt terrorist methods. Assassinations did not take place until 1943. During the first years of the war, resistance newspapers and pamphlets were comparatively moderate. At first they mainly urged non-collaboration with the enemy, aid to Nazi victims, and opposition against the N.S.B. Gradually, when the struggle became fiercer and bitterness against the oppressor rose, acts of violence became more frequent.

We have already mentioned that the Germans found the Dutch administration in excellent condition. Nobody had thought of destroying official records in case of military occupation, with the result that they fell undamaged into German hands. The Gestapo inherited extensive data files and had no trouble securing any information desired. It was easy to study files on every citizen, his business, his bank accounts, his religious and political affiliations. Besides, there were sufficient informers, both Dutch Nazis and German residents, who could be useful in digging out facts about suspicious or hostile persons. This tremendous pool of information later turned out to be a terrible disadvantage to the resistance. In fact, destruction of files became such an important issue that even the aid of the Royal Air Force (R.A.F.) was demanded in several instances.

It is difficult for people who never lived under a dictatorship to fully apprehend the enormous importance of personal papers. Soon after their arrival, the Germans established a new system of identification cards. Every citizen above the age of fifteen was required to carry his card at all times, and controls, especially in trains, stations, and public places, were frequent. The card

*Mussert claimed at his trial that his party had 80,000 members, but this figure was not verified.

contained all personal data, a photo, and the fingerprints of the bearer. A person without a proper identification card was subject to immediate arrest.

The second vital document for each citizen was his ration book. It contained small stamps for each type of food, textiles, shoes, and coal. The stamps were issued every month. Until the summer of 1943, distribution of the stamps took place in a rather leisurely way, with little control.

Aside from these two documents, there was a whole system of permits for countless purposes. Businessmen had to fill out interminable forms for distribution of raw materials. In the later period of the war, almost everything depended on some sheet of paper, as, for example, possession of a bicycle or the right to leave one's home after curfew.

This whole system contributed to the difficulties of the resistance movement. However, it also lead to innumerable forgeries and later on to frequent attacks on rationing and public registration offices. One of the large underground groups maintained a regular office for forging documents.

At the beginning of the occupation, practically no one was available who had even the slightest experience with underground or intelligence work. In consequence, many of the early resistance fighters were completely unsuited for such work and were soon caught by the German Security Police. Many courageous and dedicated people lost their freedom and even their lives because they acted without the necessary caution. To show the Nazis open defiance or comtempt led quickly to imprisonment or made the person in question conspicuous. The Germans soon prepared lists of hostile elements and later drew on them for hostages. It took a long time till the men of the resistance learned their perilous jobs.

Though some small resistance groups started functioning as early as 1940, anti-German activity was first and for all an attitude and only later became a real movement. The initial reaction was emotional, not political. Most early joiners had little conception of military intelligence work or systematic sabotage. That resistance was a way of contributing to the Allied war effort was only learned gradually and painfully.

Of course, it is tempting to speculate what would have developed if the Germans had maintained their correct attitude of military occupation of the first weeks. It is not likely that they would have won the sympathy and willing collaboration of the population. However, it is a long road from mere aversion to actual fighting resistance. If the Germans had not interferred with the politics and civil rights of the Dutch, they would have been able to govern the country with far less difficulty. By trying to Nazify Holland and sponsoring the N.S.B., they earned the bitter hatred of the vast majority. In the end, they were regarded with a fierce and desperate rage that will leave its traces for many years to come.

From the German point of view, it would have been far easier to govern with moderation. Granted that in the words of St. Just, "one cannot rule without guilt," there was no necessity to oppress a small nation of generally quiet and law-abiding citizens. It would have been none too difficult to gain their resigned indifference. The two countries were far from being hereditary enemies. Even nationalistic Germans who hated Frenchmen and Poles cannot have felt any similar emotions toward the Dutch. The latter disliked the Germans as invaders and arrogant bullies, but large-scale resistance would have been far less prevalent if the regime had proved less oppressive.

In the last analysis, it was the blind and ferocious tyranny of a totalitarian dictatorship that determined the course of events. Most Dutchmen saw in the attempt to force a totally foreign ideology on their nation a deep disrespect for all their traditions, rights, and interests. Under such circumstances, all propaganda about kinship and Germanic brotherhood was pure waste of effort. Besides, it became soon obvious that those strange protectors practiced legalized plunder to a degree previously unknown.

In the summer of 1940, the German authorities started moving foodstuffs and raw materials in large quantities to the Reich. Only a six-months' supply to keep industry going was left in the Netherlands. The exports to Germany doubled in value versus those of 1938. By the end of the year, the country was practically integrated into the German war economy. Later on, various special requisitions followed, such as the forced delivery of copper and silver coins. When the war with Russia began, many surplus metal goods and stores of winter clothing were also confiscated. In the summer of 1942, the German police suddenly deprived about 100,000 persons of their bicycles, the most common vehicle of transportation in Holland. Naturally, this type of spoliation, which mainly affected the average citizen, increased resentment, as it was considered sheer robbery.

The first organized resistance group was already formed in the summer of 1940, though at that time few people were aware of it. This organization called itself Order Dienst* and was known by the initials O.D. Most of its members were professional military officers, and the group was organized along military lines. Politically, it was conservative and its official goal was to maintain law and order in case of a German collapse. In 1940, this did not sound too realistic, but clearly the leading members were optimists.

Such expectations for the future aside, the O.D. did engage in military espionage. The leading officers of the Dutch intelligence service had left with the government. No wireless transmission sets or secret codes were left behind. Nothing had been prepared to set up intelligence networks. The British Secret Intelligence Service (S.I.S.) had a branch in Holland, but the personnel had left in such a hurry that a suitcase with important information remained behind and fell into German hands. Therefore, all clandestine contact between Holland and England was at a complete standstill in the summer of 1940. It became necessary to rebuild the whole net of intelligence.

The first attempt was made in August 1940 when a Dutch navy officer, Lieutenant L. van Hamel, was dropped near Leyden. Van Hamel had distinguished himself at Dunkirk. His orders were to establish contact with several independent groups that were to gather and transmit reports to England. Many of his contacts refused to cooperate, but he finally succeeded in setting up four groups for intelligence purposes. He had brought one wireless set with him, and three more were built in Holland. When trying to return to Britain in October 1940, van Hamel

*Order Service.

was arrested in Friesland, sentenced to death, and executed. One of the groups he had developed grew into the Intelligence Service of the O.D. and kept transmitting to England until 1942. Some reports were also smuggled through ports in western France. This was the beginning of military intelligence work in the Netherlands, an operation that later led to great losses of lives.

Illegal bulletins and newspapers were another sign of beginning resistance. The first were messages and chain letters, handwritten or typed, later mimeographed and printed. Shortly after the capitulation, a small group that called itself Geuzen* started giving out secret newsletters. The earliest surviving bulletin dates from May 18, 1940. It was written by a Haarlem teacher, Bernard Ijzerdraat, who was the leader of the "Geuzenactie." This group also engaged in minor acts of sabotage, but was soon caught. On March 4, 1941, Ijzerdraat and 14 others were sentenced to death because of sabotage committed at a shipyard in Rotterdam and executed by a firing squad. They were the first group of Dutch patriots to die in that manner.

Another secret group, which called itself the Committee for the Free Netherlands, was also short-lived. It published an open letter to Seyss-Inquart and several communiqués; but all members were arrested after a few months of activity. A publication called *Bulletin,* which was distributed in the province of Utrecht, fared somewhat better. It was published from June 1940 to August 1941. However, its circulation was very small.

The first underground newspaper of real importance, *Vrij Nederland,* was initially published as a mimeographed sheet on August 31, 1940, Queen Wilhelmina's birthday. The editors were a Calvinist group who had first circulated declarations of General Winkelman concerning the bombing of Rotterdam. Most of them were arrested in March 1941, but the paper survived, and from December on it was printed.

The second larger publication, which started out in 1940 and survived the war, called itself *Het Parool,* "The Watchword."

*The expression dates from the war of independence against Spain. "Geus" like "Yankee" was originally a derogatory name. The Dutch rebels adopted the name out of defiance.

Its founder was Frans J. Goedhart, a Socialist newspaperman who wrote under the name of Pieter t'Hoen.* The paper started as a newsletter; in fact, the name *Parool* was only used from February 1941 on. A few months later, it appeared in regular print and quickly became one of the foremost underground publications.

We have already mentioned the Communist newspaper *Waarheid* (Truth) that appeared at first as a mimeographed sheet in Amsterdam. Before the German attack on the Soviet Union, *Waarheid* condemned the war as "imperialist conflict," but, nevertheless, was fiercely anti-Nazi.

There were also several clandestine papers that addressed themselves mainly to university students; but they played only a minor part during the first two years of the war. During that whole period, circulation of underground newspapers was still small. Still they reached a considerable number of people, as they were handed from one man to another and were frequently retyped by voluntary helpers. As they consisted only of a few pages, they had little space for discussion of politics and limited themselves mainly to attacks on the German administration and the N.S.B. Some also attacked the "Netherlands Union" because of its professed willingness to collaborate with the occupying power. The resistance considered this "Union" only as a "lackluster opposition," and its speedy demise was not regretted.

During the spring of 1941, attempts to resist the German regime were still isolated, emotional, sometimes immature. The main aversion of most patriots was still directed toward the N.S.B., which was now clearly a German handmaiden. Its leaders outdid themselves in Byzantine praise of the Fuehrer, who was busy demolishing Greece and Yugoslavia. Once more it was *"la guerre fraîche et joyeuse."* But as in 1940, when victory in Norway proved to be a setback in disguise, the successful Balkan campaign postponed the invasion of Russia for about five weeks. It was, as Field Marshal von Rundstedt remarked years later laconically, "a very costly delay."

*This means Peter the Chicken and refers to a Dutch writer of the eighteenth century.

CHAPTER SEVEN

Turning on one's radio in wartime frequently brings surprise and excitement. However, few people expected anything sensational on June 22, 1941. Though it was generally known that Hitler was massing troops in the east, the sudden onslaught on the Soviet Union — less than two years after concluding a non-aggression pact! — came as a shock to the average citizen of occupied territory. It was far less of a surprise in England. In fact, the British government seems to have been much better informed than their counterparts in Moscow. As in May 1940, the Germans destroyed a good part of the enemy air force in the first hours of attack. Hitler's surprise tactics in the west were repeated on an even larger scale in the east.

The Soviet Union had never been very popular in the Netherlands. No diplomatic ties between the two countries existed. Communism had not been a serious danger, but it was completely incompatible with the ideas of the vast majority. The Socialists rejected it just as wholeheartedly as the denominational parties, though for other reasons. The single paladin of the Soviet Union was the small Communist party, which controlled in 1939 about 3 per cent of the electorate. It had been dissolved by the German authorities on July 20, 1940 and promptly went underground. We have already described its part in the February strike in Amsterdam. The Germans were well aware of Communist activity and arrested 600 party members almost simultaneously with their invasion of Russia. However, the three national leaders of the party were not apprehended. A small left-wing splinter group under H. Sneevliet, whose ideas imitated those of Trotsky, continued its activity until 1942. Sneevliet was arrested and executed by the Germans. It is interesting to note that Radio Orange honored him as a martyr, and the national anthem was played in his memory after the execution. The case is symptomatic. The struggle against the oppressor united the most divergent elements.

The general attitude in Holland followed closely that of Winston Churchill: "If Hitler invaded Hell, I would at least make a favorable reference to the Devil in the House of Commons." Two days after the attack on Russia, Queen Wilhelmina declared that the Dutch government followed the same line as their British ally. Fighting Hitler was the mutual task. The Germans reacted by conficating royal property and removing all pictures of the Queen and her family from public buildings. From now on, she was always referred to as "Wilhelmina von Oranje-Nassau," meaning that she had lost all royal prerogative. Probably, somebody in the Department for Propaganda remembered that Louis XVI became simply "Louis Capet" during the French revolution. However, the historical parallel was out of focus. Louis had been deposed by his own people.

The first weeks of the war in Russia were accompanied by a wave of propaganda. It followed two main directions. In the first place, the Soviet regime was depicted as a monstrous tyranny, and stories of atrocities of all kinds abounded. Predictably, they made little impression in a country in which German jails and concentration camps took their daily toll. On July 10, a conference of Dutch journalists was informed that during one week all newspapers had to publish photos of atrocities on their first page. Papers that did not do their duty were threatened with heavy penalties. Since the Dutch press was by then almost completely controlled by Dutch Nazis, they all published the assorted horrors. The effect on the public was negligible.

The second appeal of German propaganda was directed toward young Dutchmen, who were exhorted to join ranks with Germany and its allies to fight the Bolshevists. Until June 1941, "plutocractic England" had been the object of attack, and in a somewhat tortuous way the Dutch people were now informed that communism, not capitalism, was the main enemy. Both systems — invented and run by Jews — were basically the same and served only the subjugation of Germanic nations. As the Dutch were already enslaved by the Germans, only a very limited number of young men swallowed the bait. The N.S.B. seconded the German appeal with enthusiasm and provided most of the volunteers. They got support from an unexpected ally. Lieutenant General H.A. Seyffardt, a former chief of the Dutch general staff, founded a Netherlands legion for combatting Bolshevism. That legion was supposed to fight under its own Dutch officers, but actually the commander and most officers were German. Seyffardt was not a member of the N.S.B. His appeal was mainly directed to former Netherlands army personnel. He met with very limited success, but the government in London and the resistance angrily branded him a traitor. Nemesis caught up with him in 1943.

At about the same time, a Dutch volunteer unit of the Waffen S.S.* was formed, the S.S. Standarte Westland. It consisted of members of the Netherlands S.S., which has already been mentioned.† Later, on the Netherlands Legion was dissolved and integrated into the Waffen S.S.

Altogether 12,000 Dutchmen took service in these units during the full duration of the war. Many of them saw action on the eastern front and about 3,000 never returned. Most Dutch combatants were dedicated Nazis; others joined out of a sense of adventure. For a nation of more than nine million inhabitants, the figure of volunteers was not impressive.

The Dutch Nazis were now actively engaged in war against the Allies. While the Dutch Navy and a small number of soldiers were fighting side by side with the British, Netherlanders had taken military service with the enemy. Sometimes, the rift ran straight through families, one brother fighting in the German and one in the Allied armies.

From January 1941 on, the N.S.B. was openly subsidized by the Germans, ostensibly for the purchase of uniforms. Temporarily at least, Mussert seemed to gain influence. One of Seyss-Inquart's deputies, Fritz Schmidt, eagerly promoted Mussert's

*The Waffen S.S. was the military branch of the S.S. In the latter part of the war, they were practically on equal footing with the German army.

†See page 57.

80

interests, much to the annoyance of Rauter and the radical S.S. group.

Mussert was probably well aware that strong factions within the German government hoped for complete annexation of the Netherlands. Perhaps there were even more far-reaching schemes. After the war, Dr. Felix Kersten, Himmler's private masseur, a therapist of sorts, claimed that the Reichsfuehrer S.S.* had seriously considered transplanting the whole Dutch population to the east. Kersten alleged that he had talked Himmler out of that monstrous plan. Though his story sounded none too probable, he was awarded a high distinction by the Dutch government in 1950 for wartime services to the Dutch nation. Possibly, a vague project regarding such a mass deportation was indeed contemplated. It is a definite fact that plans for transferring Dutch settlers to the Baltic countries were drawn up but never realized. For that project a so-called East Company was set up in Holland, but due to the turn of the tide on the Russian front, it never accomplished anything.

By October, the walls of Dutch cities were plastered with posters proclaiming the speedy fall of Moscow and calling for new volunteers to take part in that glorious venture. During the whole summer, the Dutch people had been bombarded with propaganda. Perhaps the strangest episode was the so-called V-campaign.

The original idea came from two Belgians who were working for the B.B.C. Resistance men in Belgium were known to paint the letters R.A.F. on walls and fences to encourage their compatriots. It was then resolved to adapt the letter V for victory as a common symbol. It had the advantage that it could be scribbled on very quickly. The deputy editor of the B.B.C., who called himself "Colonel Britton" and commanded a large following among listeners on the continent, decided to play that card to the full. His first call to write a V on every wall in occupied Europe was made in January 1941. By April, the B.B.C. service, broadcasting to the Netherlands, took up the lead and encouraged patriots to paint that magic sign wherever possible.

*Himmler's official title.

A musical touch was added to the campaign by starting the broadcasts with the first measures of Beethoven's *Fifth Symphony,*° which are easy to knock on a door or a window. By the summer, the V was all over Holland. The German propaganda now decided on a counterblow. They adopted the V themselves and suddenly the streets were cluttered with pamphlets, proclaiming that V meant victory for Germany on all fronts. V's were painted on walls and sidewalks in large orange letters. In the field of propaganda, Dr. Goebbels was not easily outdone.

Of more importance were a number of political actions taken during the summer. In the first place, all surviving political parties were dissolved. The ill-fated "Netherlands Union" survived a few more weeks, but it was completely muzzled as its publications and insignia were already prohibited. By the fall, the N.S.B., which had commanded only 4 per cent of the votes in 1939, was the only legal party.

The denominational unions had so far lived on sufferance, but were now put under a Nazi commissioner. Thereupon, almost all union officials resigned. The members were urged to join the newly constituted Netherlands Labor Front, but few did, and the whole organization never achieved any real influence. For all practical purposes, Dutch labor had no functioning representation for the last four years of the war. The workers, never very kindly inclined toward the Nazis, turned increasingly hostile. Slowdowns and sabotage became more frequent. German supervisors did not always realize what was happening and complained about "those stupid Dutchmen" who never did anything efficiently. Especially in the large Philips plant at Eindhoven, where much war equipment was produced, and in the Limburg coal mines, low output became the order of the day.

Another type of opposition began to make itself felt in 1941. The churches raised their voices against the policies of the invader.

Of the Christian denominations, about 60 per cent were Protestant. The Dutch Reformed Church,† which is similar to the

°Equals the Morse sign for the letter V (short—short—short—long).

†Nederlands Hervormde Kerk.

Presbyterian Church in the U. S., was the largest of the various groups. The whole history of the Netherlands is closely connected with the development of that congregation that had originally developed during the struggle against Catholic Spain and later became the state religion. The House of Orange and many upper-class families belonged to the Dutch Reformed Church.

At the end of the nineteenth century, a group of more orthodox Calvinists receded from the old organization and formed their own "Reformed Churches."* Though this congregation was comparatively small† and consisted mainly of "little people," it became an extremely active and principled element in the spiritual life of the nation. Many of their prominent members were in politics, and the Church itself often guided the faithful in matters of public concern.

The Catholics, though a minority of the total population, were the largest religious group in the Netherlands because the Protestants were divided into so many sects. Like the more orthodox Calvinists, the Roman Catholic Church exerted great political influence. Trade unions and many educational institutions were often guided by the episcopate. Long before the war, members of political organizations opposed to the church were barred from receiving the sacraments. Naturally, this included National Socialists.

These facts must be understood in order to evaluate the position of the churches under the occupation. The Dutch clergy of both denominations almost universally took the stand that it was their duty to speak out plainly and clearly on matters of conscience. The Dutch Reformed General Synod stated in July 1940 that Christian ideas had to be upheld against National Socialist doctrine.

With the churches coming into conflict with the occupying power, opposition against National Socialism became more widespread. German appeals that all Christians should join in the struggle against Bolshevism were in vain. To the faithful,

*Gereformeerde Kerken.
†About 8 per cent of the population.

both totalitarian doctrines were manifestly false. But the Russians were far away and Communists in Holland no immediate threat. Therefore, the fight against Naziism received precedence, though at first mainly in the spiritual field. Both Protestants and Catholics correctly affirmed that a compromise with any type of totalitarian dictatorship was not possible. The Dutch Reformed Church made the issue very clear: Communism and fascism were incompatible with the Christian concept. Cooperation with the Nazis was out of question. As far as German measures were concerned, the church reasserted the words of the Bible: "We must obey God rather than man."

The first problem that brought the churches in conflict with the occupying power was the treatment of the Jews. As early as October 1940, the Protestant churches raised their voices in protesting dismissal of Jewish civil servants. The Catholic church instituted a fund for special emergencies that was mainly used to help Jews, later also for other persecuted persons. During the first years of the occupation, the churches constantly tried to stem the anti-Jewish measures by appeal and protest. But all efforts, including a personal interview between leading churchmen and Seyss-Inquart, proved fruitless. However, the attitude of the churches encouraged many persons to assist their hunted countrymen. The Catholic episcopate, which had a valiant leader in the Archbishop of Utrecht, Dr. J. de Jong, forbade its communicants to take part in manhunts organized by the Nazis. This restriction included not only Jews but also labor draftees and veterans threatened by reinternment. A Catholic policeman or civil servant who cooperated with the Nazis was considered to act under duress only if in danger of being shipped to a concentration camp, but not through fear of losing his livelihood. People who lost their jobs because of such civil disobedience were financially supported by the churches.

The resistance of the churches had great influence on institutions of learning, as several of them had religious affiliations. When the German authorities demanded a loyalty pledge from university students, the faculty advised them not to sign. At the Catholic University at Nijmegen, only two students signed. The occupying power also made several attempts to interfere

84

with church services. It was an old tradition to pray for the
sovereign, and Sunday services of the Dutch Reformed Church
always included a prayer for Queen Wilhelmina. Seyss-Inquart
tried to stop this custom, but the church refused, though it willingly — perhaps not without a little self-righteousness — included
another prayer for the occupying authorities. In Catholic chapels,
the hymn "Lord, Safeguard Our Queen," was sung regularly
throughout the occupation.

The mounting Nazi terror did not spare ministers of religion.
A considerable number of them were arrested. Forty-three Protestant preachers and 49 Catholic priests lost their lives during
the war, mostly in concentration camps. About their treatment,
we shall quote a witness who watched the following incident
in the notorious camp of Vught:

> I was talking to Father N. of The Hague, who has been imprisoned
> for eight months because he refused to marry an S.S. man and
> his girl friend. Suddenly one of the most feared S. S. leaders ap-
> proached. "Hey, you," he says to the priest, "you can sing, can't
> you?" Father N. answers calmly, "Yes." "All right, now sing some-
> thing from Mass and do it fast!" The priest pales but firmly shakes
> his head. "You don't want to, you dirty bastard?" yells the villain.
> "I'm only allowed to sing Holy Mass in front of the altar," the
> priest replies quietly. In the next moment, he received a blow in
> his face. "Now pray!" orders the sadist. "That I will do and also
> pray for you" answers Father N. and he starts slowly reciting the
> Lord's prayer. The rascal turned around and left.°

Vught and Amersfoort were the most feared concentration
camps in Holland. For years, they were scenes of all the horrors
human minds can conceive. Amersfoort, which was later also
used as a transit camp for prisoners to be shipped to Germany,
had a particularly sadistic commander, K.P. Berg.† The unfortunate prisoners were not only starved and beaten, but constantly subjected to the most disgusting humiliations.

The camp at Vught was used for men and women; some of the
°B. Voeten: *Doortocht* (Contact, Amsterdam, 1946).
†Executed for war crimes in 1949.

inmates were employed as forced labor in nearby factories. For a time, it also served as a transit camp for Jews. Vught became the stage for one of the worst atrocities of the whole occupation, when 72 women were locked into a small bunker because they had ill-treated a treacherous fellow prisoner. When this horrible prison cell — comparable to the Black Hole of Calcutta* — was opened on the next morning, 10 women had suffocated and several had gone insane. That was even too much for Rauter, who was hardly very sensitive in such matters. The camp commander responsible for this revolting incident lost his job and was sent to the eastern front. But cruel treatment of prisoners continued until the camp was finally liberated in the fall of 1944.

There was a third camp at Ommen, that was mainly used for black marketeers but also for the overflow from ordinary prisons. When stories about maltreatment of inmates began to circulate, a few judges from Amsterdam decided to investigate the camp personally by visiting it in disguise. They wrote a report on their findings, sent it to Seyss-Inquart, and requested the secretary-general of justice to close the camp. This was actually done in 1943. The courageous initiative of the judges produced success.

Many political prisoners went to the regular jail at Scheveningen near The Hague, which soon was called with wry humor "Orange Hotel." Treatment in that prison differed, depending on the guards and the offense of which the prisoner was accused. Sometimes, persons suspected of espionage or sabotage were tortured for days, for example, by having their hands tied behind their back and then attached to a pole in such a manner that their feet did not touch the ground. Then the prisoner was beaten with rubber truncheons on his breast, abdomen, and genitals. "Milder" forms of torture consisted of incarceration in cold, dark cells, exposure on cold winter days in the prison yard, or "cold bath." Outside of the prison in the dunes was the place of execution. After the war, a great number of bodies were dug up from unmarked graves.

By the summer of 1941, mass arrests and executions became more frequent. Some resistance groups, especially the O.D.,

*An incident from the war in Bengal (1756).

fared very badly during that period. A large number of their leading members were caught by the German police, and 72 were later executed. Among those sentenced to die were several army officers and policemen.

For the first time, aid for the resistance from abroad became more active. In the fall of 1940, a number of students from the University at Leyden had managed to escape to Sweden. They left aboard Dutch freighters that were transporting chemicals from the port of Delfzijl. Unfortunately, one of the young men was rash enough to broadcast his adventures over Radio Boston, with the result that the Germans became more watchful. Still, Delfzijl remained a center for intelligence work. Information was smuggled to the Dutch Consul-General at Stockholm via the skippers. A Delfzijl physician, Dr. A.L. Oosterhuis, managed to open a real channel of information by collecting information for Radio Orange and sending it to Sweden. In this way, London received for the first time Dutch underground newspapers and other material by boat and plane. Although this "Swedish route" was slow and cumbersome, it enabled Oosterhuis to furnish some vital information to the Dutch Government regarding German intelligence agents. In July 1943, Oosterhuis and all his helpers were arrested by the S.D., and henceforth the connection via Sweden was cut off.

Meanwhile, one of the student escapees, S.E. Hazelhoff Roelfsma, suggested a daring plan. He knew that German officers generally gave Friday night parties at a hotel on the seaside promenade of Scheveningen. A gentleman in evening dress, perhaps a little tipsy, might make his way from a landing craft right into that boisterous party without arousing suspicion.

It was certainly a highly original idea, but it proved full of grave dangers. The British motor boat had to approach the Dutch coast unseen in the darkness during curfew. At a short distance from the Scheveningen beach, the supposedly intoxicated party boy had to get into a dinghy. Then he was to be put ashore smelling of brandy and hopefully babbling out some drunken tale if challenged by a German sentry.

It took eight attempts to carry out this fanciful scheme. Finally, in November 1941, an agent, Pieter Tazelaar, was put ashore.

His orders were to contact a prominent Socialist politician and smuggle him out of the country. In this he did not succeed. The S.D. got wind of the plan, and the politician, Dr. Wiardi Beckman, was arrested while waiting for transport at Scheveningen. He later died in a concentration camp. Tazelaar managed to escape and eventually reached Switzerland, accompanied by a member of the O.D. The two young men succeeded in returning to England.

The first week of December 1941 was one of the most eventful ones of the whole war. On December 3, General Guderian's tanks had arrived at the Tula-Moscow highway in a last desperate attempt to reach the Russian capital. They were stopped, and three days later the Soviet counteroffensive broke loose in icy-cold weather. For the first time, the German army had to retreat, and the roads west of Moscow were littered with abandoned tanks, trucks, and guns. At about the same time, the Germans suffered a second setback at Rostov in the south, and for a few days Marshal Timoshenko was the most popular man in Holland. Then, on December 6, came the news of Pearl Harbor, which was greeted with understandable satisfaction. With the United States in the war and the Germans suffering heavy losses in Russia, a wave of optimism developed. Such optimism waned when the extent of the first Japanese successes became clear. By the end of the year, they were already advancing on Singapore. The superiority of the new enemy on the seas and in the air boded ill for the Netherlands East Indies, which were in the first line of defense. With their great colonies in peril and oppression at home mounting, the year 1941 ended for most Dutch families on a dismal note. The words of the conqueror of the Indies, Jan Pieterszon Coen, "Do not Despair!" were widely quoted.

CHAPTER EIGHT

The Dutch government arrived in London in disarray. During the months of the "phony war," no preparation had been made for a possible transfer of government in case of German attack. Even after the events in Denmark and Norway, the matter was not given close consideration. The result was a hasty evacuation on board a British destroyer. The ministers and a few civil servants settled at Grosvenor House Hotel. Later on, they moved to Strelton House. The refugees who had left Holland on the eve of the capitulation were a mixed group of hapless people. The Queen was at first the guest of the English Royal Family at Buckingham Palace.

Nevertheless, the government did not come to London empty-handed. The Netherlands still prossessed three great assets: their colonies, the Royal Navy, and the merchant fleet. The Netherlands' East Indies were a mighty source of raw materials. Curaçao and Aruba were imporant because of their oil refineries, and Surinam had its bauxite mines.

The navy was almost intact. Only the *Jan van Galen* and several smaller units had been lost. Its four cruisers, eight destroyers, and a number of minesweepers and submarines were a welcome addition to the British Royal Navy, which was soon to face a desperate struggle on the Atlantic and in the Mediterranean. Both the navy and the merchant fleet were integrated under British command and played their part in the Allied effort. They suffered heavy losses and maintained Holland's tradition of a seafaring nation of rank.

Of the air force, only 27 planes of the marine service had survived the disaster. About 250 men, aviators and ground personnel, escaped to England and were later integrated into the 320th squadron of the R.A.F. It took part in the invasion of France.

Only small fragments of the Netherlands' Army managed to reach Britain, altogether about 1000 men. A larger group had made it to Dunkirk, but was eventually taken prisoner by the Germans. The troops in England were a hodgepodge of various services, badly demoralized. "Run-away-troops," an officer called them, "a big mess!" Eventually, a Dutch unit, the Princess Irene Brigade* was formed, retrained, and later completely reorganized. Under its commander, Lieutenant Colonel de Ruyter van Steveninck, the Brigade was sent to France in August 1944 and fought successfully until the end of the war.

The history of governments-in-exile has rarely been a very happy one, and the London expatriates were no exception. Its particularly unfortunate start was due to the weakness of Prime Minister D.J. de Geer. It soon became obvious that de Geer did not believe in Allied victory and wanted to negotiate with Hitler. The other ministers objected vehemently, and on September 3, 1940, de Geer was discharged from his office by Queen Wilhelmina. He was appointed to study the financial status of the Netherlands East Indies and left for Lisbon in November. Once on neutral territory, de Geer informed the Dutch government that he wished to return to Holland. Despite the protests of his former colleagues, he requested a visa from the German authorities, who were, of course, delighted to grant it. Back home, the ex-prime minister published a pamphlet, "Synthesis in War," in which he advised his countrymen to collaborate with Germany. The German occupation regime endorsed the booklet, but it was almost ignored by the population and sharply refuted by the resistance. After this episode, de Geer faded into oblivion until he was brought to trial by the postwar Dutch government.†

*Princess Irene, born in 1939, was the second daughter of Crown Princess Juliana.

†He was tried in 1947 and sentenced to one year in jail, with three years' probation, for assistance rendered to the enemy.

When de Geer left England, Minister of Justice Pieter S. Gerbrandy became his successor. A law professor, Gerbrandy was a man of limited outlook and ability, but he had one quality that made him suitable for his job: a deep, almost religious belief in victory. He quickly restored the prestige that the government had lost by de Geer's defection.

We need not review all the changes that occurred in the Dutch government during its stay in England. The loss of the Netherlands East Indies in 1942 led to a reconstruction of the cabinet, whereby Lieutenant Governor H.J. van Mook became Minister of Colonies, the last man to bear this title.[*]

The activities of the government-in-exile were greatly hampered because during the first years of its existence, it was almost completely cut off from the home country. Information from occupied Holland was scanty and slow. This put the government in the unenviable position of an absentee landlord who lacks information on his property. One of the foremost tasks of the cabinet was to influence morale at home and give the people a certain amount of guidance. In July 1940, it was given facilities to broadcast to the Netherlands as the first foreign government on British soil. This was mainly Gerbrandy's achievement since he maintained good connections with the B.B.C. as a former chairman of the Dutch Advisory Broadcasting Council. Radio Orange started functioning on July 28, 1940. Later, a second service, the "Brandaris,"[†] directed mainly to Dutch seamen on Allied vessels, was started. The two stations were combined in 1942.

The biggest morale builder for the Dutch nation was undoubtedly Queen Wilhelmina. For more than 40 years, she had ruled her country in peace and relative prosperity, and once the initial shock of her flight to England was over, her prestige rose very high. The Germans were perfectly aware of that, and even the great propaganda chief, Dr. Joseph Goebbels, worried about it.

[*]In 1945, the department was renamed. Van Mook's successor was minister of overseas territories.

[†]The Brandaris is a famous lighthouse on the Frisian island of Terschelling.

Wilhelmina,
Queen of the
Netherlands
*Library of
Congress*

Wilhelmina was sixty years old when she had to leave her kingdom. She had been very pretty as a young queen, but now she was a gray, stern, heavy-set woman, all dignity but no charm. Her private life as the spouse of an insignificant German princeling had not been altogether happy.*

History is full of exiled queens, but very few played their part so well. Her radio addresses were extremely effective because she knew how to speak with aplomb and sincerity.

*Her husband, Prince Hendrik von Mecklenburg-Schwerin, died in 1934.

Had Wilhelmina lived in the Middle Ages, she would have fought for her realm with the same tenacity as that fifteenth century amazon, Jacoba, Countess of Holland, Zeeland, and Hainaut.* It is characteristic that, aside from the N.S.B., no opposition against the monarchy developed in the five years of occupation. Wilhelmina was universally accepted as the symbol of national independence and survival. Pins and pendants were made from coins bearing her picture, and many people displayed orange flowers as a silent demonstration until forbidden to do so by the authorities. To the Germans, the loyalty of the Dutch to their royal family was a constant source of anger. The Dutch attitude towards the cabinet in London was more restrained; it was respected without ever becoming very popular.

Crown Princess Juliana and her two small daughters moved to Ottawa, Canada, and remained in the background, though she also occasionally broadcast to the Dutch people. Her husband, Prince Bernhard of Lippe-Biesterfeld, though a German, had from the first day on expressed complete loyalty to the Netherlands and had become surprisingly popular. This was no small achievement for a man with a thick German accent.

Clearly, it was one of the main tasks of the exiled government to maintain contact with occupied Holland. Broadcasts to the Dutch people could only be meaningful if the originators of such messages were well informed about events in the country. During the first three years of war, this was a most difficult problem. Sometimes grave mistakes were made that gave the listeners a sense of unreality. For example, in October 1941, after an R.A.F. raid on Rotterdam harbor, the inhabitants were told to leave that neighborhood. As most of them earned their livelihood there, this advice was rather pointless. The incident led to a conflict within the cabinet, and two ministers resigned. On other occasions, instructions or appeals broadcast from London were too vague or altogether impossible to carry out. This situation improved when secret channels of communication were

*Jacoba (Jacqueline) of Bavaria, at one time also Duchess of Gloucester, spent her life in a desperate struggle against Burgundy (1401–1436).

opened that gave the government a better understanding of conditions in the occupied country. Considering all the obstacles, it must be said that Radio Orange did a fairly good job. Temporarily, an allegedly independent station, which called itself "The Fly Killer,"* was operated. Its broadcasts were sent out from London, but pretended to come from a secret transmitter on Dutch soil. For a while, they found a great number of raptured listeners, but eventually the originator, a Dutch journalist, ran out of material and the broadcasts had to be discontinued.

A more permanent propaganda was the dropping of newspapers from aircraft or balloons. From April 1942 on, a monthly bulletin, "The Whirlwind," was regularly dispatched to Holland. In the latter part of the war, large quantities of a small, daily newspaper, *The Flying Dutchman,* were dropped by the leaflet squadron of the Eighth U.S. Air Force.

In July 1940, a special intelligence service (C. I. D.) was set up by the Dutch Government under the direction of F. van't Sant, who was Queen Wilhelmina's private secretary and had some experience in this type of work. Of course, this organization depended completely on the S.I.S. During the first years, the latter was none too eager to pass on military information to the Allies. Therefore, the Dutch authorities in England were sometimes poorly informed about events abroad. As we shall see later, this lack of knowledge had very unfortunate consequences. The various offices, active in espionage and sabotage matters, operated quite independently, and cooperation was none too good. For a period, the Belgian section of S.I.S. was given the task of building an underground network in the Netherlands, but did not pass on its information to the Dutch. It must be admitted that the British Secret Service was overwhelmed with work and clearly had a hard time with its many Allies, most of them quite inexperienced in intelligence work.

C.I.D. was not a very successful operation. It dispatched about a dozen secret agents to Holland, most of whom were quickly caught by the Germans. Van't Sand resigned in the

---

*In Dutch "De Flitspuit," actually a small spray gun for destroying insects.

summer of 1941. A new office (M.V.T.) was founded under Colonel M.R. de Bruijne to recruit underground agents and to render advice to British intelligence. There seems to have been a great tendency on the part of the Dutch government to organize new agencies without affecting the actual situation. Often conflict and competition erupted between those offices. They were directed by brave army and marine officers who were not suited for carrying out intelligence operations. This situation didn't improve until 1944. In the meantime, many valuable men were sacrificed.

On the British side, the Special Operations Executive (S.O.E.) was responsible for sabotage and underground activity on the continent. This organization acted independently from the much older and highly respected Secret Intelligence Service (S.I.S.) We shall describe the actions of S.O.E. in the Netherlands in the next chapter.

As the end of 1941 drew near, the political situation in the Far East became tense. For a long time, there had been a growing awareness of Japan's designs on French Indochina, Malaya, and the Dutch East Indies. Now France and the Netherlands were defeated and powerless, and the British were engaged in a mortal struggle for sheer survival. In 1940, Japan had concluded the Tripartite Pact with Germany and Italy, which bound it to enter the war if the U.S. should actively intervene. The Japanese also forced the weak Vichy government to grant them air bases in Indochina and actually occupied that country. The threat to all of Southeast Asia was now obvious. The Americans reacted with economic sanctions, and the British and Dutch governments took simultaneous actions. This meant that Japan was cut off from its vital oil supply in the Netherlands Indies. From this moment on, war became very probable because of Japan's oil shortage, which left her with the choice of abandoning her conquests in China and Indochina or taking military action against the U.S., England, and the Dutch East Indies. Summer and autumn passed with uneasy and ineffective negotiations between Washington and Tokyo. The State Department had little illusions about the outcome. Cordell Hull told the British ambassador on November 29, 1941, that "Japan may move suddenly and with every possible element of surprise." Indeed, she did.

The decision to attack was taken by the Japanese cabinet only two days later. On the next day, Churchill informed the foreign secretary: "A Japanese attack on the Dutch possessions may be made any time." He was still uncertain how the U.S. would react to such an act of aggression. The great surprise was not that Japan went to war, but that it attacked the United States. To many men, the December 7th attack seemed an almost suicidical action. On the next day, both the English and the Dutch declared war on Japan. Perhaps the man most surprised about Pearl Harbor was Adolf Hitler.

From then on, events followed each other with dazzling speed. On December 25, Hong Kong fell to the Japanese. The weak British forces in Malaya could not stop the invaders, who had complete superiority in the air. Dutch submarines sunk a number of troop ships, and four Netherlands air squadrons were thrown into the battle. Together with British Hurricanes unloaded at Singapore, they did much damage to the enemy, but the Allied forces were so inferior in quality and training that they could only resist by constantly giving ground. By the end of January, the British had been forced back into Singapore Island after blowing up the causeway that connected it with the mainland. The siege soon turned out to be a hopeless affair, with one million people pressed together within a radius of three miles, lacking proper water and food supplies. On February 15, the exhausted troops surrendered. The fall of Singapore sealed the fate of the Dutch East Indies.

The Japanese pressed their attack relentlessly through the island maze. After occupying the Philippines, the oil-rich island of Borneo, then Celebes and Ambon were overpowered. By establishing new air bases and remaining always under protection of their aircraft carriers at sea, the Japanese outnumbered their adversaries on every occasion. The small Dutch garrisons on the widespread island belt were beyond rescue. Java, the center piece of the Dutch Indies and of the Allied defense, came under air attack from mid-February on.

The Allied High Command was fully aware that it stood on

the eve of disaster. With Singapore lost, the successful defense of Sumatra became practically impossible. Time was too short to enforce that enormous island, which had only a small garrison. Meanwhile, Bali and Timor were occupied by the Japanese, whereby the air link with Australia was disrupted. There was nothing to be done but to fight it out with the insufficient forces available. General ter Poorten, the Dutch army commander, declared somewhat grandiloquently, "that it was better to die on one's feet than to live on one's knees."*

The Netherlands Indies were ill prepared for the Japanese onslaught. Since the homeland was in bondage, the army had very limited resources to call on. In Java, there were only three weak Dutch divisions plus some native auxiliaries of very doubtful value. The Allies enforced these troops with a British contingent and a U.S. regiment of field artillery. The northern shore of Java is 800 miles long, and obviously that limited force was far too small for a successful defense. The greatest part of the Netherlands' air force had already been sacrificed in the struggle for Singapore. Of the remaining 10 air squadrons, only a part was serviceable. There were also about 40 R.A.F. planes that had been withdrawn from Singapore and a few American fighters and bombers. Much of the Dutch navy had been destroyed piecemeal during smaller engagements in the Straits of Makassar and Lombok. Only two cruisers, *De Ruyter* and *Java*, and two destroyers, *Kortenaer* and *Witte de With*, remained. To this scanty force were added the slightly damaged American cruiser *Houston*, the British cruiser *Exeter* and the Australian cruiser *Perth*, plus four American and three British destroyers. This was the total force that opposed the approaching Japanese. A second British squadron, which was short on fuel, was withdrawn through the Sunda Straits and did not take part in the final engagement.

General Percival Wavell, the Supreme Commander in the A.B.D.A. area† had arrived in Batavia on January 10, 1942,

*The phrase was borrowed from a speech of La Passionaria during the Spanish Civil War.

†American, British, Dutch, Australian.

but quickly realized that only a rear-guard action could be fought with such slender forces. The Japanese took Borneo, with its important refineries at Balikpapan, though with the loss of five transports. On February 14, Japanese airborne troops were dropped at Palembang on the island of Sumatra, and were soon aided by a powerful invasion by sea. This decided the fate of that large island and placed the Allied troops in Java in a most precarious position. Wavell correctly decided that sending more troops to Java would only increase the coming disaster and ordered an Australian force, which was still at sea, to Burma. He wired to Churchill: "Anything put into Java now can do little to prolong the struggle. . . . I hate the idea of leaving these stout-hearted Dutchmen and will remain here and fight it out with them as long as possible if you consider this would help at all." Churchill declined and ordered Wavell to leave, which he did on February 25.

All Allied naval forces were then entrusted to Admiral Helfrich of the Dutch navy. The four cruisers and nine destroyers under the command of Admiral Karel Doorman sailed from Soerabaja to intercept the Japanese. An attack against a superior fleet, undertaken without any fighter protection, was sheer suicide. In the first engagement, Doorman lost two of his destroyers, and the British cruiser *Exeter* was struck in the boiler room. She was ordered back to Soerabaja, protected by the last surviving Dutch destroyer *Witte de With*. Next, the destroyer *Electra*, attacked by three Japanese destroyers, was sunk. The four Allied cruisers kept firing at the enemy in a confused fight during the ensuing darkness. One more destroyer struck a mine and sank; another one, with almost no fuel left, had to be withdrawn to port. This left the four cruisers with neither air protection nor naval escort. Around midnight, Doorman on the *De Ruyter* sighted two Japanese warships. He signaled, "I attack, follow me." Shortly afterward both his flagship and the *Java* were hit by torpedoes and sank quickly. Some survivors were picked up later by a hospital ship. Doorman himself perished with the *De Ruyter*. The *Perth* and the *Houston* disengaged, refueled at Batavia, then attempted to pass through the Sunda Straits. They ran straight into the Japanese invasion fleet, which

The Dutch cruiser *De Ruyter* in action

Library of Congress

was disembarking troops at the extreme western end of Java. After sinking two transports, both cruisers were lost.

The damaged *Exeter*, escorted by two destroyers, tried to pass the Sunda Straits and reach Ceylon. However, the three ships were spotted by the Japanese and attacked by far superior forces. They were sunk by overwhelming gunfire. Only the surviving American destroyers, their torpedoes used up, managed to slip through the narrow Bali Strait under the cover of night and escaped.

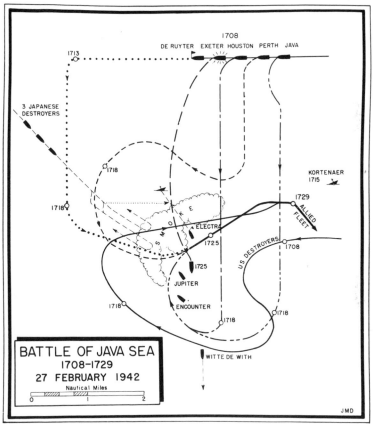

The battle of the Java Sea, February 27, 1942

U.S. Navy Photograph

With the Allied fleet destroyed, Java lay open to the invader. A desperate effort to replenish its wasting air strength was undertaken by the U.S. aircraft tender *Langley,* but it was sunk by Japanese air action. Another transport carrying crated airplanes arrived too late. The big island had to be defended without further naval or aerial support, a hopeless task.

The Japanese invaded Java from three sides, and as they possessed complete air superiority and soon also outnumbered their adversaries on the ground, the end could not be delayed very long. The Allied troops were driven back toward the city of Bandung, which had been considered a very strong defense position. But organization broke down completely. Soon the "fortress" was flooded with fleeing, hungry, demoralized troops and hapless civilian refugees. Exposed to constant air attacks, the situation soon became untenable. On March 8, Governor-General T. van Starkenborgh-Stachouwer, surrendered all Allied forces to the Japanese. Lieutenant-Governor H.J. van Mook* and 14 members of the administration left for Australia, on the day before the capitulation so that some sort of token government service in exile could be maintained for the East Indies.

For the Dutch government in London, the fall of the East Indies and the loss of almost the whole navy was a terrible blow. With the exception of the small colonies of Surinam, Curaçao, and Aruba, the overseas empire had been lost, though at that time few people realized that the loss was to be permanent. For Holland itself, the events in Asia were depressing, expecially for those who had relatives in the Indies. By the summer of 1942, most Europeans in the Dutch Indies were interned. The conditions in those tropical internment camps were quite horrible, and a great number of persons died. The uncertainty about the fate of their next of kin was another heavy burden many Dutch families had to carry during the last three years of the war.

*After World War II, van Mook played an important part in the liquidation of the Netherlands East Indies. He correctly foresaw that Indonesia would gain its independence.

CHAPTER NINE

Napoleon's contention, "A spy at the right place is worth 20,000 soldiers at the front," has never been contested. During World War II, espionage reached proportions that would have amazed even the artful Fouché! *

Like Bonaparte, Hitler occupied most of Europe and held it in an iron grip. To receive military and political information from the closely guarded continent was vital to the Allies. The willingness among the oppressed to work against the occupying power was almost unlimited. But, as many found out to their disappointment and sorrow, espionage may be an activity for gentlemen — according to the chief of German military intelligence in World War I — but definitely not for amateurs.

Technically, the work of intelligence agents had greatly changed. The old cloak-and-dagger romanticism — if it ever really existed — had been replaced by collecting military data and passing it on by wireless. Transmitting secret information to England became a most important task for Allied agents. The Germans were concentrating on catching the wireless operators by using direction-finding devices. We shall not try to discuss the technique in detail, but a few basic explanations are necessary.

Naturally, messages were always sent in code. Wireless sets were at first clumsy, primitive affairs, that weighed about 65 pounds. By 1942, the British Secret Service was able to equip its operators with smaller equipment that was easier to hide.

*Napoleon's minister of police. He had been a terrorist during the French Revolution. Fouché is rightly considered the originator of the secret police.

The possibility that an agent would be caught and forced to transmit reports by the enemy was always considered. For this reason, all operators were given so-called security checks. These consisted in certain small mistakes or peculiarities that the agent used in his telegrams. If those minor errors were missing, the receiving agency would know that something was amiss. Moreover, experienced wireless operators recognize each other when they have been in contact for any length of time. Just as an individual will recognize a correspondent's familiar handwriting, so will a wireless operator get accustomed to his partner's way of wiring. Therefore, it was not easy to replace one man by another without the party on the other side noticing the change. It followed that it was in the interest of the Germans to "turn around" Allied operators.

Most agents sent from England to Holland were directed by the Special Operations Executive (S.O.E.). The task of these agents was to make underground contacts, stimulate acts of sabotage, and supply military information. The British intelligence agencies planned at an early stage of the war to set up organizations for assisting the Allies when invasion of the continent began. At that time, strategy was still geared to comparatively small scale assaults, which would be supported by armed uprisings in Western Europe. The concept of a mass invasion, as it actually took place in 1944, had not yet been considered.

A small-scale landing in France during the fall of 1942 (Operation Sledgehammer) was actually under discussion, but it was later canceled and replaced by the ill-fated raid on Dieppe.

In most cases, agents were dropped in pairs, one man a trained wireless operator, the other a sabotage expert. The first pair was put ashore by motorboat in September 1941. During the first months, those operations suffered from poor preparation. The organizers had insufficient knowledge of the actual situation. Naturally, the German-controlled radio broadcasts were listened to in Britain, and the Dutch newspapers reached London via neutral countries. But a multitude of small details abounded that could hardly be known to the intelligence officers or was simply overlooked. For example, some of the agents were given Dutch silver coins, that had been out of circulation for months.

Two of the men wore identical hats, ties, and raincoats of a very poor quality because it was assumed that there was a shortage of textiles. That masquerade only made them conspicuous. The wireless sets were packed into suitcases of a size only manufactured in Britain. Even more serious, the men wore wrist watches that could not possibly have been purchased in Holland. The gentlemen of the S.O.E. were clearly well-meaning but inexperienced men. They had the ill fortune to encounter a formidable adversary.

Abwehr III f, the German counterintelligence agency in The Hague, was run by an officer of the highest ability and imagination, Lieutenant Colonel Hermann Giskes. An excellent organizer, Giskes moved coolly and systematically, the very antithesis of the Gestapo brutes. With his counterpart at the S.D., Joseph Schreieder,* he maintained a more or less uneasy cooperation. Schreieder, a small, bald-headed Bavarian, was a first-class criminologist.

The drama started to unfold in February 1942 when a wireless operator by the name of Willem van der Reyden was arrested. Interrogated by Giskes, van der Reyden became talkative and supplied a great amount of information on codes. However, he did not reveal his security checks, and when the Germans used him for wiring to London, there was no reply. A few weeks later, a new Allied transmitter was located in The Hague. This led to the arrest of Hubert Lauwers, who operated the set, and of Thijs Taconis, the companion sabotage agent. The latter had already made contact with the Dutch resistance. However, that particular O.D. branch of the underground had been penetrated by an agent of the Abwehr.

The Germans acted with great circumspection. At first, the radio transmitter, operating under the code R.L.S., was carefully watched and all data collected. When Giskes knew all he wanted, he had the persons involved promptly arrested so that no news of the event could possibly be reported to En-

*After the war, Schreieder was tried for alleged war crimes. He was acquitted and served as prosecution witness at the trial of his superior Rauter and of General Christiansen.

gland. His plan was to absorb R.L.S. into his own organization and to use it for counterespionage. When radio operator Lauwers was captured, his complete secret code for deciphering wires fell into the hands of the Abwehr. All R.L.S. transmissions that had been taken down before were now an open book to the Germans. Giskes' next step was to induce Lauwers to work for the Abwehr. He promised his captive that neither he nor any other enemy agents would be tried by a military court if Lauwers would only consent to cooperate. The prisoners were treated correctly and no brutal methods were used. After some hesitation, the captive agreed to use his set on behalf of the Abwehr. He could do so without acting contrary to his orders, simply by withholding his security check.

On March 12, 1942, a start was made with what became later known as the "Englandspiel." Since it operated under the code word "Northpole," it has also sometimes been called the "Northpole game."* Lauwers' way of transmitting should have shown his partners that he was no longer at liberty. But the incredible happened; S.O.E.-Dutch replied. When a request was made to drop another pair of agents and additional equipment, London complied. At first, both Giskes and Lauwers, with very different emotions, thought that this was some clever fake. But on March 27, two more agents were parachuted into Holland with their supplies. Of course, they promptly fell into the hands of the Abwehr. From now on, the Germans possessed a direct channel to S.O.E. and were able to manipulate further operations.

The technique of "turning around" radio transmitters was used frequently during World War II. The Englandspiel is by no means the only example of this kind of counterintelligence work. The most celebrated case concerned Roman Czerniawski alias Armand, a Polish officer, who seems to have worked for the British and German intelligence with his famous mistress Mathilde Carrée ("La Chatte"). In another case, the Germans succeeded in using the two chiefs of an extremely successful Soviet

*Giskes himself described his experiences after the war in a book, *London Calling Northpole*. The code word "Northpole" was Giskes' idea.

espionage net, the so-called Rote Kapelle, for transmissions to Moscow. However, no real success crowned those efforts. The Allies also organized similar "games." What is remarkable about "Operation Northpole" is that it existed for two years and yielded tremendous results.

Early in April, S.O.E. ordered Taconis — for weeks a German prisoner — to contact another pair of agents who had just been parachuted into Holland. They and their contacts were again arrested. Among those men was another wireless operator, H.J. Jordaan, who despite heavy pressure refused to admit that a security check had been assigned to him. However, he had asked London shortly before his arrest for permission to train a Dutch operator. Unaware of Jordaan's plight, London replied, "instruct new operator in use of security check." It was now clear that Jordaan had told a false story, and he finally broke down and divulged the desired information. This enabled the Abwehr to open a second channel of wireless communication.

Now the Englandspiel was running at rocket speed. More and more agents were sent over and fell into the well-prepared trap. The process of deception functioned without a hitch. On clear nights, Giskes' Dutch V-men would assemble at an indicated, lonely spot and signal to the approaching planes with red searchlights arranged in a triangle. The planes would then drop the agents or release large containers filled with arms, explosives, and other sabotage materials. Some planes carried up to eight containers of several hundred pounds of material. The agents were welcomed by the reception committee, congratulated for their successful journey, and invited to a sumptuous meal with drinks. Of course, they confidently told their new friends about their orders and experiences in England. Then they were suddenly arrested and gleefully informed that they had been betrayed by their superiors in London. In most cases, that severe shock was sufficient to break down their resistance. The interrogation went on for hours, sometimes for days, and the Germans generally got the information they wanted.

So confident was the S.O.E. of its success in the Netherlands that they decided, with approval of the Dutch government-in-exile, to set up an armed underground organization by their agents. Seventeen groups of 100 men each were to be formed in different parts of the country. They were to be armed by droppings and trained to destroy bridges, railroad junctions, etc. at the right moment. On June 27, 1942, G.L. Jambroes, the first agent-organizer, arrived, and as his landing had been announced over the contaminated channel, he was immediately arrested. He was followed by 35 additional agents — one of them a woman — * who all suffered the fate of their predecessor. The constant flow of resistance organizers, which went on until May 1943, presented a peculiar problem to the Germans. It became necessary to announce some successes of the sabotage agents. In the long run, it proved impossible to feed London invented stories. Therefore, Giskes decided to have a few acts of sabotage committed by the Abwehr itself. On several occasions, railroad lines of minor importance were blown up. In August 1943, a barge loaded with aircraft parts sank in Rotterdam harbor after a great explosion to the jubilation of the onlookers. Who could have guessed that it had been sabotage faked by the Abwehr? Such small incidents did not seriously hamper the German war effort, but proved effective in providing real news for S.O.E.

A particularly interesting illustration of the way Giskes operated was the so-called attack on the radio transmitter at Kootwijk, which was used to direct submarines. In July 1942, the sabotage group under Taconis received detailed orders from London to destroy the antennas. As we have seen, poor Taconis had been a prisoner for several months, and of course, no resistance squad had ever been formed under his direction. Giskes wired back that the transmitter was poorly guarded and that the radio masts could be destroyed without great difficulty. On August 9, London ordered Taconis to action. Giskes waited for two days, then announced to S.O.E. that the plan had failed because of land mines. The resistance group had been fired upon by the guards and had lost three men. All this was pure invention. To make the deception complete, a report appeared in all daily newspapers that "criminal elements" had tried to blow up

---

*Beatrix Tervindt, trained to aid downed pilots. She was one of the few survivors of the Englandspiel.

a radio transmitter, though without success. If London received Dutch newspapers, they would find the confirmation of the attack right there in print. In fact, S.O.E. later announced that Taconis would be decorated for bravery. Giskes must have been greatly amused when he was given that piece of news over his secret channel. The unfortunate hero and his friends were at that time in a German prison at Haaren. However, Giskes stuck to his promise; they were well treated, and the tragedy that followed later was not of his making.

Another very clever way of deceiving London was practiced by occasionally helping stranded Allied aviators. R.L.S. would inform S.O.E. that a British pilot had been hidden in Holland and requested confirmation if the man in hiding was actually on record with the R.A.F. The data submitted by the Abwehr were always correct. Of course, London would confirm that the man in question was genuine. He was then smuggled out of the country by Abwehr agents. Some of these men reached England via Spain and praised the Dutch resistance to the skies. They had, of course, been told that their mysterious helpers were the men of "Operation Northpole."

A far more serious consequence of the Englandspiel was the infiltration of the real Dutch underground, of which no less than 400 members were rounded up in connection with R.L.S. The arrest of so many Allied agents gave the Germans the opportunity to penetrate leading resistance circles. A notorious Dutch V-man, A. van der Waals,* managed to contact the National Committee, which formed a sort of high command. It consisted of prominent politicians who were to pave the road for the Dutch government-in-exile. Van der Waals offered them his services for transmitting news to London, then betrayed the committee and its affiliated groups to the Germans. The members were arrested and interned at St. Michielsgestel. As in many other countries, the Germans often spared the lives of important personalities, perhaps with an eye on later exchanging them or using them as hostages. This seems to be the explanation for the strange fact that some of Nazi Germany's most famous adver-

*Tried and executed as a traitor after the war.

saries, like Leon Blum, Paul Reynaud, and Kurt von Schuschnigg, survived the war as Hitler's prisoners. Also peculiar was an official communiqué declaring that van der Waals had been assassinated, ostensibly by the resistance. This report was completely untrue and soon recognized as false. The news of the betrayal of the National Committee reached London via Sweden* and caused great uneasiness in Dutch government circles. Other signs that there was something wrong multiplied, but S.O.E. continued dropping arms to their nonexisting secret army until October 1943.

Perhaps the Englandspiel would have gone on for even a longer period, but in August 1943 two of the arrested agents made a daring escape from their prison in Haaren, which was negligently guarded by Netherlands S.S. men. After hiding for a while in Holland, they managed to reach Switzerland and sent telegrams to London warning that the plans of S.O.E. had completely gone astray. The wily Schreieder, who almost lost his job because of the two escapees, informed London that the men had defected and were now serving the German security police. He had correctly foreseen that his prisoners would contact S.O.E. and wished to counteract their warnings. He almost succeeded. When the fugitives finally reached Britain, they were suspected of working for Germany and temporarily imprisoned. However, by January 1944 the horrible truth of "Operation Northpole" dawned on the men who had organized it.

By then, the Germans were operating 14 secret transmitters to London, but no further droppings of agents and arms occurred. In the meantime, three more men escaped from Haaren. They were eventually recaptured and two of them were shot while allegedly trying to escape.†

In February 1944, Admiral Canaris, chief of the Abwehr, was suddenly deposed. That honorable and competent officer had been one of the most ardent adversaries of Adolf Hitler.

---

*See page 86. The report was made by Dr. Oosterhuis.

†These two men were recaptured by the Germans with the aid of the notorious Christiaan A. Lindemans, the so-called "traitor of Arnhem."

He was later imprisoned and executed. The Abwehr was then subordinated to the R.S.H.A. (Reichssicherheitshauptamt), in other words, to that sadistic monster Ernst Kaltenbrunner. The captured Northpole agents were transported to Germany, and most of them perished after inhuman tortures at Mauthausen. Lieutenant Colonel Giskes' promise to treat them as prisoners of war was completely ignored. Giskes, now far from popular with the S.D. and its new boss, an incompetent by the name of Erich Naumann, was helpless. He had tried to fight a gentleman's war and ended up as the subordinate of a gangster.

Of the 54 agents captured, only 7 survived. Furthermore, 12 British bombers were shot down while delivering materiel. Of the latter, 15,000 guns and a large quantity of other arms fell into German hands. Far worse was the great damage done to the Dutch resistance, which lost 400 men by arrests as a consequence of the Englandspiel.

During the first months of 1944, contact over the contaminated channels became less and less frequent. Giskes realized that the game was up, and with a last sarcastic gesture he chose to end it once and for all on April 1, 1944. This last telegram is worth quoting: "Lately you are trying to do business in the Netherlands without our assistance. We think this rather unfair in view of our long and successful cooperation as your sole agents. But never mind, whenever you will come to pay a visit to the continent, you may be assured that you will be received with the same care and result as all those you sent us before. So long." Understandably, there was no reply.

It had been the ultimate hope of the Abwehr that they would eventually learn the date of the invasion via their secret channels. In that expectation, they were disappointed. It could very well have happened. The intended destruction of the transmitter at Kootwijk was part of the preparation for the raid on Dieppe. A similar order, previous to the invasion in Normandie, might have put the Germans on the alert.

The full facts of the Englandspiel became known in Holland only two years after the war and caused great excitement and consternation. A number of newspapermen and politicians of the lunatic fringe claimed that the Dutch agents had been intentionally sacrificed by perfidious Albion. Though this accusation made very little sense, the Dutch government ordered a thorough investigation by a parliamentary commission. After a long, detailed study and interrogation of all surviving persons in both camps, its conclusion was rather anti-climactic. The tragedy was caused by "serious mistakes" within the S.O.E.-Dutch organization in Britain. There was not the slightest evidence of bad faith or wilful betrayal. Negligence, overconfidence, and grave underestimation of a very shrewd opponent were the cause. Probably the worst error was the lack of any control on the agents who were sent to Holland.

Within the gigantic struggle for Europe, the Englandspiel was only a minor episode. The lesson it taught was well learned in Britain, and during the last year of the war, cooperation with the Dutch underground greatly improved and booked successes. It is interesting to note that almost all intelligence organizations on both sides committed very grave errors. Human failure is just as frequent in that field as in other, more conventional professions.

CHAPTER TEN

While the Dutch resistance fought, suffered, and grew, one segment of the population was overtaken by a frightful cataclysm. During the years of 1942 and 1943, the Jewish inhabitants of the Netherlands were almost exterminated.

At the beginning of the occupation, Jews numbered about 140,000. The Jewish community had a long and honorable history. Many Jews had settled in Holland during the sixteenth century when the Holy Inquisition drove them from Spain and Portugal. They prospered in the tolerant religious climate of the young republic and received full civil rights at the time of the French Revolution. Until 1935, there was no anti-semitism of a political nature. Certain social boundaries were observed, but those existed also between Protestants and Catholics. By and large, Jews in Holland lived the normal life of all other citizens. Unlike Germany, where almost all Jews were distinctly middle-class, a great number of skilled and unskilled workers inhabited Holland, especially Amsterdam. On the other hand, many Jews of considerable wealth lived there also, and a fair proportion were prominent in the sciences, the arts, and the theater. We have already mentioned that the supreme court justice was a Jew, and some were also active in politics.

With the rise of Nazism in Germany an influx of refugees began. Their number increased in 1938 after the events in Central Europe and the severe persecution in November of that year. The attitude of the Dutch government and of the great majority of the population was sympathetic, and a public collection for the victims in 1938 proved a great success. However, at the same time the N.S.B. increased its anti-semitic propaganda. By the end of 1938, the government practically barred further immigration, partly because the new arrivals were mostly penniless and a potential burden, partly also out of fear of annoying Germany. In 1939, refugees who had no means and no working papers were interned at a newly built camp, Westerbork, in the province of Drente. Altogether, there were 15,000 refugees and about 10,000 other foreign Jews in Holland when the country was overrun. On the night of the capitulation, a few hundred Jews succeeded in escaping by boat. There were also a number of suicides.

During the first eight months of the occupation, the German authorities proceeded with a certain reluctance. In Berlin, the war was considered won. Perhaps the expectation of a speedy peace and the future position of the Netherlands East Indies played a part in that cautious approach. However, all Jewish civil servants were dismissed by order of the permanent secretaries of the various departments. The latter protested twice, but in vain.

The next step was a complete registration of the Jewish population. When the new identification cards were issued, the Jews found that theirs had been marked with a large "J." The full consequence of that measure was not then understood. In fact, during the first phase of the occupation, many Dutch Jews naïvely believed that the Germans would only persecute the refugees.

We have already narrated how the N.S.B. got into the act of Jew-baiting and how those events led to the first mass arrests and the strikes in Amsterdam. About the same time, the Germans took a very important step: They established a Jewish Council; its task was to control the Jewish community. The function of dealing with individuals was thereby transferred to a Jewish organization.

Previously, some Jewish organizations under the leadership of the former chief justice, Lodewijk Visser, had declared that Jews should not collaborate with the Nazi authorities. However, the Germans had no difficulty in finding men who were willing to accept a leading part in the new council: Abraham Asscher, an industrialist, and David Cohen, professor of ancient history at the Municipal University of Amsterdam. Both men had a record of charitable activities. Cohen had been chairman of a committee for aid to refugees. According to the German leadership principle, the two chairmen were entrusted with almost dictatorial power. Their first function was to persuade the Jews of Amsterdam to stop fighting the N.S.B. on the streets. They did so, despite grave misgivings in various circles. Farsighted men like Justice Visser predicted that any kind of collaboration with the Nazis was reprehensible and could only consist in carrying out a destructive policy against the Jews themselves. Professor Cohen, a pure pragmatist, brushed these warnings aside. Others claimed that the Jewish Council tended to give more protection to the well-to-do at the expense of the poor.

It is likely that Asscher and Cohen originally believed that they were performing a humanitarian task by becoming a sort of intermediary between the oppressor and the persecuted. Like many other Dutchmen, they were extremely naïve and had no conception of the true nature of national socialism. By becoming collaborators, they were turned into instruments for the extermination of their own co-religionists. From its inception, the Council assumed a double function. It did assist Jews in legal and financial difficulties, provided educational programs, and later supervised distribution of food. But — far more important — it became an agency to direct the Jewish community according to German policies. As it was the goal of the Nazis to destroy the Jews, the Council grew into the odious role of a sub-Gestapo with far-reaching powers. In fact, it sometimes almost mirrored the actions of the N.S.B., which performed somewhat similar services for the invader. The only way one can excuse the policy of the Jewish Council is to remember that it had to work under extreme pressure and hoped against hope that the war would end before the Germans could complete elimination of all Jews. That ultimate goal was not yet clearly visible in 1941. But events in Germany, Poland, and other occupied territories boded no good. A man like Cohen, with plenty of experience in refugee aid, could not have remained unaware of what was going on elsewhere.

There followed a flood of anti-Jewish measures that mainly served to isolate the Jews and break up their basic means of

114

The concentration camp at Mauthausen, Austria

existence. They were barred from all public places. Their business establishments were first registered, then put under Nazi administrators, and finally sold. In a similar way, Jewish real estate was disposed of. More and more professions were forbidden to them. A former Jewish bank was turned into a sort of agency for confiscation. It became the recipient of all Jewish bank accounts, which were then blocked. The owners were only permitted small monthly withdrawals. All this went on slowly and systematically without much noise.

The outrages of the N.S.B. against the Jews had been stopped, but in June 1941 the German police suddenly arrested 230 young men. Like the group imprisoned in February, they were shipped to Mauthausen. By the end of the year, their families had been informed that they had all died.* From that time on, the word

*There was, in fact, one lone survivor of the first group. He had remained in Buchenwald for "medical experiments."

"Mauthausen" became synonymous with certain death. The Germans used it again and again as a threat, and the fear that this camp inspired drove many Jews to obey the orders of the occupying power.

It sounds somewhat ironic that Rauter, when on trial for his life, declared that he was disturbed by the "high mortality" at Mauthausen. It is true that no larger groups were sent there after June 1941. As we shall see, other destinations were just as unhealthy.

In April 1941, a sinister young man by the name of Dr. Erich Rajakowitsch° appeared in Amsterdam. He had arrived on orders from Heydrich to organize a central agency for Jewish emigration. This sounded innocent enough. At that time, the whole Western hemisphere was still neutral, and a limited emigration of Jews seemed possible. However, the new agency granted only a handful of permits to leave Holland. By fall the emigration office was a large organization with many employees and began to register all Jews. People with valid visas flocked to the Jewish Council in the hope of receiving exit permits. But strangely enough, the central agency went on registering people who had neither a visa nor any chance of obtaining one. The applicants had to fill out innumerable forms and outline all their possessions. When the U.S entered the war, it became obvious that emigration had then become quite impossible. But still the activity of the agency went on.

The prospective emigrants would have learned the truth if they could have seen Dr. Rajakowitsch's correspondence with other German agencies. The term "emigration" was gradually replaced by "resettlement." The decision for the "final solution of the Jewish problem" was taken by Hitler during the summer of 1941. The actual orders were apparently given to Heydrich — but only verbally. On January 20, 1942, the latter convened a number of S.S. leaders at Wannsee and informed them of Hitler's plan. It meant, clearly and simply, that all Jews under German dom-

°Rajakowitsch was tried in 1965 before an Austrian court but escaped with a short prison term. The Netherlands government is still charging him with war crimes but could not obtain his extradition.

ination should be transported to the east and killed. The details of such an enormous operation had still to be worked out. Of course, they were not made official, but quite a number of persons in high positions knew exactly what was transpiring.

During the winter of 1941-42, grim rumors of terrible atrocities in Eastern Europe started circulating. The B.B.C. repeatedly mentioned that Polish Jews were being massacred by means of movable gas vans. Most listeners simply refused to believe such reports and hopefully considered them Allied propaganda.

However, by the spring of 1942 it became clear that far more radical measures against the Jews were afoot. In the first place, a new regulation placed unemployed Jews into labor camps in Eastern Holland. Due to many dismissals, there were about 8,000 unemployed. The Jewish Council, through its weekly publication, put great pressure on those people to obey all instructions. Next, Jews were forbidden to travel or to move without a special permit. In several small towns, Jews were suddenly rounded up and either forced to move to Amsterdam or directly transported to the old refugee camp at Westerbork. At the same time, Jewish children had to leave regular public schools. Each edition of the *Jewish Weekly* published by the council brought new decrees. On May 2, 1942, all Jews were ordered to wear large yellow stars with the word "Jew" imprinted on them. From that moment on, the Jews were living in a virtual prison without walls. That last debasement caused deep anger among the gentile population. For a few days, the unfortunate outcasts received many proofs of sympathy. Some non-Jews even started wearing the Star of David; but when the German police arrested such persons, the movement quickly died away.

Within the next weeks, a special curfew for Jews was announced; their bicycles were taken away, and they were barred from using public transportation. Then came the decisive blow. In June 1942, the heads of the Jewish Council were informed that Jews would be transported to Germany as forced labor. However, it soon became known that the real destination was camps in Poland.

All Christian churches vehemently protested against the deportation order. They also announced that the protests would be read from the pulpit on the subsequent Sunday. Thereupon, the German authorities threatened immediate deportation of all converted Jews. The Protestants desisted, but Archbishop de Jong refused to be intimidated and had his message read by priests in every single Catholic church in Holland. Seyss-Inquart — allegedly a practicing Catholic! — carried out his threat and had all Catholic Jews included in the deportation. Among the victims was Edith Stein, a nun and a well-known Catholic writer.

The first transport was ordered to depart on July 14, 1942. The persons assigned to it had been simply informed by mail. Many did not turn up, but the German police arrested 750 hostages. Eventually, 6,000 Jews were shipped to Westerbork during the month of July.

In the meantime, Fritz Schmidt, one of Seyss-Inquart's deputies, whom we have already mentioned as an eager promoter of Mussert, made two speeches in which he described the future fate of the Jews in the most vigorous terms. It was now perfectly obvious that deportation meant unmitigated slavery, if not worse. From the German point of view, this was a mistake, because more Jews refused to report at the station where the trains for Westerbork left. The result was further pressure on the Jewish Council, which was compelled to publish an extra issue of its weekly, announcing arrest and shipment to Mauthausen for those refusing to obey orders. There followed another wave of arrests. Nevertheless, the turnout continued to be poor, and by the beginning of September, the Germans decided on a change of tactics. Calling up persons by mail was maintained in the provinces, but in the big cities the Jews were rounded up by night raids. This proved a very simple operation, especially in Amsterdam, where most Jews had been forced into virtual ghettos. After curfew, whole streets were encircled by police and the inhabitants loaded into trucks and transported to the assembly point, a former theater. There was practically no resistance; most people packed their belongings and complied. At the check point, the prisoners were screened, whereby personnel of the Jewish Council gave a limited amount of aid by providing meals, informing relatives, and sometimes trying to obtain delays. Then the captives were taken to the railroad stations and went by train to the transit camp. Basically, it mattered little if Jews obtained written orders or were hauled from their homes; their fate remained the same. Those found hiding were interned in separate barracks at Westerbork, but in the last analysis, they did not fare much worse than the rest.

A good part of the dirty work was left to the Jewish Council and to the Dutch police. The latter employed mostly young recruits of Rauter's police school at Schalkhaar for this brutal activity. They had been thoroughly indoctrinated and could be trusted by the Germans. The Jewish Council, whose personnel steadily increased, did all the paper work. Exemptions from deportation, which in 1942 were still frequently granted, had to be processed through the council. The German authorities realized that the deportation of more than 100,000 persons would take at least one year. They were none too concerned about priorities as they knew perfectly well that delays for certain groups would only be temporary. At the beginning, all personnel of the council and those working directly for German enterprises were exempted. Several actions were undertaken to save at least segments of the Jewish population. The Secretary-General for Internal Affairs, K.J. Fredericks, a well-meaning collaborator, managed to get a reprieve for 400 Jewish intellectuals, mainly university professors. They were not brought to Westerbork but to a small camp at Barneveld. They were later deported to Theresienstadt in Czechoslovakia, where there was at least some chance of survival. Another list was composed by a certain Dr. Calmeyer, who was a subordinate of Seyss-Inquart. This category encompassed Jews who claimed gentile ancestry. Even stranger was the case of the Portuguese Jews. That group submitted a memorandum asserting that they were actually a non-Jewish, Mediterranean race and should be allowed to stay in Holland. That claim was just as nonsensical as the entire Nazi race theory. The German authorities studied it earnestly until 1944 and finally deported the claimants. The only Jews permanently exempted were those married to Aryans. These remained in the Netherlands, but the men were threatened with sterilization. The churches took violent issue with this order and called it "the logical end result of an anti-Christian doctrine which supports human extermination." A few hundred sterilizations were actually carried out, but, seemingly, Seyss-Inquart got second thoughts about the subject and let the whole matter drop.

About 8,000 men who had originally gone to Dutch work camps were also deported with their families. Gradually, the pretense that Jews were being sent away as forced labor was relinquished. Inmates of hospitals, insane asylums, and old age homes were deported. No one in his right mind believed that they could serve the German war effort.

The majority of the deportees went first to Westerbork. That transit camp was like a waiting room for patients who have to undergo an operation, almost certainly to be fatal. The conditions were more than strange. It was not a concentration camp in the usual sense. The camp commander, a handsome graying S.S. officer, Albert Gemmeker, acted with restraint and decorum.* He sponsored a Jewish theater and cabaret and greatly enjoyed himself at those shows, like a Roman emperor at gladiatorial games. He could hardly be in doubt about the ultimate fate of "his actors." The administration of the camp was completely in the hands of a small group of German refugees who had been interned by the Dutch Government before the war. They had a — perhaps understandable — resentment against the Dutch inmates and were mainly interested in saving their own necks. Both the Jewish Council and the ruling clique at Westerbork opposed any resistance and served their German masters with great efficiency. The decision as to when a person was to be deported rested largely with the camp management and led to ghastly patronage and corruption. To remain in Westerbork became a sheer fight for survival.

The average prisoner at Westerbork, who had neither money nor connections, had little chance of remaining longer than a few weeks. Each transport to Poland consisted of 1,000 to 1,200

---

*Gemmeker was tried as a war criminal, mainly for executing four escaped prisoners. He was sentenced to 10 years imprisonment, the court having considered his otherwise correct behavior.

persons crammed into freight trains. Altogether 93 trains left Westerbork and two more were sent from Vught, which harbored only a small number of Jewish prisoners; 60,000 Jews were deported to Auschwitz and 34,000 to the extermination camp of Sobibor. About 9,000 went to Theresienstadt and Bergen-Belsen. When Westerbork was eventually liberated by Canadian troops in April 1945, 900 prisoners were still in the camp. No transports left after the fall of 1944.

The fate of Jewish deportees in Auschwitz and similar camps has so frequently been described that we can be very brief. On arrival there was a superficial selection by German camp physicians. Those considered unsuited for hard labor immediately went to the gas chamber. The rest were put to work in the camp and in adjoining factories of Krupp and I.G. Farben. Sickness, ill-treatment, and hunger soon reduced their numbers. Those who became unfit for work were again subject to selection and extermination. Of the Dutch Jews sent to Auschwitz, only 500 (less than 1 per cent) returned after the war. In Sobibor, there were almost no survivors at all. Only 19 persons somehow remained alive; 2,400 individuals survived the other camps. The total number of Dutch Jews imprisoned by the Nazis and returned after the surrender was somewhat below 4,000 (less than 4 per cent). The final figure of 100,500 fatalities does not include Jews who were killed in the Netherlands or committed suicide.

In what ways was it possible to escape the ordeal? Most Jews desperately tried to stay in Holland by obtaining jobs with the Jewish Council or by some other type of exemption. At one time, the Council had 15,000 at its disposal. In May 1943, the Germans had thinned the ranks sufficiently to start deporting the Council employees. The co-chairmen were simply told to designate 7,000 of their staff for the "labor draft." It is sad to report that they complied. Most of the persons did not obey the order to report for deportation, but it was then far too late for any chance of organized resistance. Those parts of Amsterdam that still harbored Jewish inhabitants were sealed off by police, and loudspeaker vans announced that recalcitrants would be shipped to Mauthausen. The Germans had no difficulty meeting their quota;

most victims were completely demoralized by fear and months of uncertainty and humiliation. In September 1943, the last remaining Jews were rounded up, including the two council chairmen who were sent to Theresienstadt and survived the war. By October, the liquidation of Dutch Jewry was practically complete. There remained only the people in hiding to deal with.

About 22,500 Jews decided to resist the German commands. Of those, about 2,000 managed to gain safety by secretly leaving the country and reaching Switzerland or Spain. Some also succeeded in hiding in France or Belgium. They could only try to escape individually or in small groups. A Zionist youth organization, with the aid of some non-Jews, managed to save 320 of its members. Both leaders of that group, a Jew by the name of S. Simon and a Christian, J. Westerveel, lost their lives, the former by suicide, the latter by a German firing squad. Due to the great difficulty in reaching neutral territory, this kind of escape was mainly undertaken by younger people. It is difficult to estimate how many were picked up during their secret journey.

The only other means to survive was to go underground. The Germans called such persons "U-boats" (submarines); in the lingo of the Dutch resistance, they were referred to as "divers." About 20,000 Jews, mostly with forged identity cards, tried to disappear among the Dutch population, but 60 per cent were subsequently arrested, either denounced by informers or victims of careless gossip or other circumstances. The rate of survival would perhaps have been higher had the Dutch underground movement been better organized in 1942. However, at that critical period, it mainly consisted of small local groups unequally spread throughout the country and hardly equipped to assist such a large number of persons. Many Dutch families showed great courage in taking fugitives into their homes. If caught, the hosts were almost invariably sent to a concentration camp. At the war's end, only about 4,000 Jewish adults and about the same number of children were still at large.

A small number of "divers," who did not look conspicuous and carried acceptable papers led, outwardly at least, a normal wartime life. Of course, they were always in peril of being found out and arrested. As razzias and controls on roads and trains multiplied, dangers lurked at each corner. But for the majority of Jews in hiding, even that hunted existence was out of the question. They had to vanish completely and spend the rest of the war hidden in a basement, an attic, or some other voluntary prison. If they had stayed at their previously legal residence, they could never risk being seen and perhaps recognized by hostile or indiscreet persons. How perilous that existence was is evidenced by the following incident. A gentleman struck up a conversation with children playing in a street at The Hague. Suddenly, one little boy said proudly: "Sir, we have a Jew in our attic." The man happened to be a good patriot and asked for the boy's address. He then warned the parents that the child's chatter might easily endanger their hidden lodger and themselves.*

Living under such circumstances created strange and unusual problems for the person in hiding and his hosts. Many "divers" had no ration book, but in the latter part of the war, the resistance did a tremendous job in supplying the underground population with the necessary coupons. The forced and permanent presence of one or several strangers in a household often caused all kind of minor conflicts. Sickness or death of the "diver" was a disaster. Sometimes the bodies of deceased persons were found in the streets without any documents and with all possible marks of identification carefully removed.

People who had taken refuge in the country, especially in small villages, had the advantage of better food and healthier living conditions. But newcomers were bound to be noticed in places in which inhabitants knew each other and where the manner of speech greatly differed from the city dweller's vernacular.† Children adapted to such situations faster than adults. Jewish children, who were hidden in Friesland, could not understand their parents when reunited with them after the war. Nor did the bewildered parents understand the language of their offspring!

*The best description of what life in hiding was like is still found in the famous *Diary of a Young Girl* by Anne Frank.

†Dialects in the Netherlands differ considerably. For example, the Brabant idiom is similar to Flemish. Frisian, spoken in the north, is a separate language.

The author spent the period from May 1942 to May 1945 as a diver, though not in hiding. He can therefore speak of his experiences, but only with the awareness that others could give somewhat different accounts of their existences. Some survivors later complained that their hosts were mercenary and only tried to take advantage of their precarious situation. Undoubtedly, some people had bad luck. However, the author was assisted by a number of persons who never asked for more than the normal rent, though they risked their own liberty for harboring a man with forged papers. His first contact with the resistance was a former colonel of the Netherlands navy, a man who saved the life of about 30 people during the war. It was this unassuming hero who helped the author and his wife to their first "underground home," two attic rooms in an Indonesian lady's house at Oegstgeest near Leyden. Soon afterward other friends contributed identification documents on which the bearer himself made some minute alterations. Next, a job was procured at a chemical company run by a young businessman who was a prominent member of the L.O., the Calvinist resistance organization. The author kept this position during most of the war, notwithstanding manhunts, railroad controls, and the constant danger of betrayal.

Living under a false name with forged documents was a strange experience for an otherwise perfectly normal, law-abiding citizen. Every policeman became a potential enemy, not to mention the almost omnipotent S.D., with its ubiquitous spies and informers. One learned certain tricks, for example to walk always on the left side of the street, so that a German bicycle police party could never approach from the rear. One had to be particularly careful in trains — the job meant daily commuting! — after having once narrowly escaped from an S.D. control that moved from car to car. Dangers lurked everywhere. After May 1943, possession of a radio set meant serious risk, but that voice from the B.B.C. in London was almost the only ray of hope and as necessary to the underground worker as narcotics to the dope addict. One learned to live a sort of split existence, half-normal citizen on the job, half-outcast, hunted, endangered, but with the persistent will to survive.

The enormity of the holocaust in the Netherlands was not due to the attitude of the Christian population. In their majority, they condemned the anti-Jewish measures and tried to render assistance to the victims wherever possible. That there were any Jewish survivors at all must be credited to the work of the Dutch resistance and to the courage and humanitarian spirit of individual Christians.

The adventures of the author's wife present a good example of the general attitude of many Dutchmen. After living for two years with forged documents, she was apprehended by German S.S. agents during a train control and imprisoned at the Scheveningen jail. When that prison was evacuated on D-day, she managed to jump off a riding train during the night. Severely injured, she was found by railroad workers who, despite the great risk involved, gave her immediate help. She was first hidden in the home of one of the laborer's, whose wife, a nurse, gave her first aid. Then she was transferred to a farmhouse, where she remained hidden for three weeks while a physician regularly attended to her injuries. After her recovery, she was "adopted" by the doctor's family and remained in his home until the end of the war. Altogether, about a dozen persons, among them a local policeman, were instrumental in saving her life. All these were ordinary citizens, acting right under the nose of the German occupation troops and without the slightest expectation of any financial advantage.

Sometimes extreme recklessness was more successful than caution. The author knew of a man in hiding, carrying badly forged papers, who had the audacity to purchase a sailboat that he used freely on the Kaag, a group of small lakes near Leyden. He figured correctly that the German police would never search for Jewish fugitives among outdoor sportsmen.

Nevertheless, a large number of Jews were thrown back on their own resources because no proper organization to aid them existed in 1942. Neither the Allies nor the Dutch Government in exile could render any real support. The railroad, leading from Westerbork to Germany was never bombed and the freight trains carrying human cargo arrived regularly at their terminals in Auschwitz or Sobibor. The deportations took place during a period when the Allied air forces were straining to hit more vital targets.

The resigned and compliant attitude of many Jews has been commented upon by many observers. They often showed dignity, but little fighting spirit. Individuals did join Dutch resistance groups, but the great majority remained submissive to the policy of the Jewish Council. They were in no way equipped for a life and death struggle with a merciless enemy. The argument that they were without training, let alone weapons, for such a terrible emergency is certainly valid. Even so, it is amazing that more than 100,000 persons could be rounded up by a comparatively modest police force without any attempt at resistance.

Most Jews had no pertinent knowledge of what was in store for them at the extermination camps. Human nature does not easily relinquish hope. Many Jews expected a difficult life in Poland, but not ruthless liquidation. The Germans nourished these more optimistic expectations by forcing the inmates of Auschwitz to write reassuring postcards to Holland. They estimated correctly that it would be unwise to drive their prospective victims to utter desperation.

Another cause for compliance was the sheer incredibility of the Nazi behavior toward the Jews. Even after the war, many persons could hardly comprehend the horrid details. Moreover, the policy of liquidation was completely absurd from a military point of view. In 1943, after the disasters at Stalingrad and North Africa, Germany strained every muscle to regain its superiority. Millions of workers were forcibly mobilized all over Europe, and railroad space was at a premium. Aside from the possessions of the deportees, the Nazi war machine gained absolutely nothing from their mass slaughter.

The question of the guilt of German authorities in Holland became the subject of several war crime trials. Both Seyss-Inquart and Rauter pleaded ignorance regarding the ultimate fate of their victims. Those statements found no credence with their judges. It is questionable if they were informed of all gory circumstances, but this is hardly pertinent. Clearly, they couldn't have cared less. Nothing indicates that they would have acted otherwise had they possessed full knowledge of the extermination procedure. One of the participants in the Wannsee conference, Eberhard Schoengarth, later became commanding officer of the

S.D. in Holland and seems to have talked rather freely. We can safely assume that at least Seyss-Inquart and the higher echelons in the S.S. were very well aware of the true facts. General Christiansen had no part in the deportations.

The treatment of the Jews increased Dutch aversion to Nazi methods and ideology. Even indifferent persons were disgusted by the brutality against women and children and the forced evacuation of hospitals and homes for the aged. The Dutch were too civilized a nation to condone such cruelties, but the protest of the churches and many other organizations were to little avail. The property of the deported Jews was seized by the German authorities and shipped to the Reich by a Dutch transport company. This was just one further step in the general plunder of the country.

Day by day, the population had to witness scenes of utter degradation like the following, which was described in the diary of a gentleman from Rotterdam: "A woman, her sick husband, and her three weeks old baby were hauled from their home. The woman carried a bag filled with rice for feeding the baby rice water during the transport. The German who had arrested her took away the bag, tore it open, and poured its contents upon the ground."

Shakespeare's words seem to fit that scene well: "No beast so fierce but knows some touch of pity. But I know none, and therefore am no beast."

CHAPTER ELEVEN

Hitler was at the zenith of his power by the summer of 1942. In Russia, the Panzer divisions were driving toward the Volga and reached Stalingrad on August 23. Further to the south, the Germans were penetrating the Caucasus region and threatening the important oil wells of Grozny and Baku. In North Africa, the Eighth British Army had suffered a severe defeat and was desperately defending the gate to Alexandria. Their vital air and marine base at Malta reeled under the constant attacks of the Luftwaffe. Even more serious, the Allies were in acute danger of losing the battle of the Atlantic, as the U-boats were sinking 700,000 tons of shipping per month. In Southeast Asia, the British had abandoned Burma and merely succeeded in extricating their battered forces minus their materiel. Only in the South Pacific were the Allies scoring successes; the Japanese were twice defeated by the U.S. Navy in the Coral Sea and at Midway Island. In Europe, few people realized the importance of those naval victories.

Everybody was talking about the "second front," and at least in the war of nerves the Allies were successful. The constant threat of invasion forced the German High Command to maintain 40 divisions in Western Europe. Except for beating back the raid on Dieppe in August and other very minor commando actions, this large force was completely idle. Work on fortifications was starting everywhere from the North Cape to the Bay of Biscay.

For the Dutch people it was a black summer. The occupation regime became more and more oppressive. In July, a large number of persons were arrested as hostages and brought to St.

Michielsgestel. The consequences became clear very soon afterward.

On August 7, an explosion occurred at a railroad overpass in Rotterdam just prior to the passage of a military train. The damage was negligible. As the sabotage attempt was directed against the Wehrmacht, General Christiansen as the supreme commander in the Netherlands demanded execution of 20 hostages. A communiqué was published threatening the shooting of "a number of hostages" if the culprits were not apprehended within two days. At least in this case the S.D. acted with more common sense than the army command. Their master sleuth, Schreieder, warned that he was sure to catch the dynamiter and that execution of hostages was superfluous. As we shall see, he was entirely correct. But it was felt that waiting would be bad for prestige, and so it was finally decided to execute five prominent hostages. The churches protested as usual and again were ignored.

The five doomed men were awakened shortly after midnight on the critical day and told that they were to die. They were permitted to see one of their relatives and a minister of their church before their execution. The men died very bravely with the shout: "Long live the Queen! *Oranje boven!*"* Two of the men were personally well known to the Queen and had been intentionally chosen to hurt her feelings. As Schreieder had predicted, the man who had placed the explosive charge was arrested two months later. He was a Communist, and when asked if he felt any regret for the hostages, he replied calmly that his only regret was not to have derailed the train with all its German passengers. The shooting of "bourgeois reactionaries" did not bother him at all. Of course, he too was executed. Clearly, fanaticism was now on the rise. This was the fruit of Seyss-Inquart's policy.

The taking of hostages is an ancient custom, but only Germany has practiced it to any extent in the twentieth century. According to international law, the killing of hostages is considered a war crime. On the basis of two cases, the American Military Tribunal at Nuremberg decided after the war that shooting of hostages was permissible as a last resort under certain circumstances.

---

*"Orange above all!"—the old acclamation of the Royal House.

Christiansen claimed later that he was under orders from the O.K.W.* to execute hostages, but considered the whole action "inhuman and in conflict with the laws and customs of war." If he really felt that way, it is astonishing that he made no effort to prevent the executions.

A somewhat similar affair took place several months later in the town of Haarlem. A German medic had been assassinated by persons unknown. In that case, the Germans executed 10 persons — among them the Chief Rabbi of Haarlem — as a reprisal. These victims were not taken from the aforementioned group of hostages, but were simply chosen from the inhabitants of Haarlem. This was the common practice in future similar incidents.

Another event that caused great indignation was the treatment of professional Dutch army officers. They were under obligation to report regularly to the German authorities. On such an occasion, they were suddenly all arrested and shipped to a P.O.W. camp in Poland. The action was undertaken in a particularly treacherous manner. The reporting officers had been told to buy two-way train tickets to the place of inspection to lull them into a false security. When they had gathered, they were taken prisoners, and waiting relatives were told to go home. In this way, 2,000 commissioned officers were reinterned. Very likely, the fear that these men would play a major part in future resistance was the reason for that measure. It almost coincided with the first mass execution; 72 men of the resistance — many former members of the Dutch army — were sentenced to death by a German military court and shot.

All these actions were a daily reminder to the average citizen that at any time he could fall victim to extremely ruthless measures by opposing the occupying power. During the same period, food rations were reduced, bicycles were confiscated, and mounting pressure was exercised on workers to go to Germany.

It was this last piece of German legislation that affected the greatest number of people. At first, all unemployed persons under the age of forty were compelled to register. Then German

*Oberkommando der Wehrmacht (Supreme Army Command).

task forces started combing Dutch factories for men who would be useful in armament plants in the Reich. Workers who refused to relocate were placed in labor camps or simply transported to Germany. The labor draft became more and more an outright deportation, and the railroad stations were often filled with weeping women and children who saw their husbands, fathers, and brothers depart to a very uncertain future. From the spring of 1942 on, the R.A.F. became quite active. Cologne, Essen, and Bremen were attacked in heavy night raids, and the Netherlands became accustomed to the monotonous drone of British bombers after dark. It is debatable if these air raids achieved very much, but they certainly gave courage to the inhabitants of the occupied countries. Until the summer of 1944, air raids actually constituted the sole Allied presence in Western Europe. Military targets in Holland were also attacked: the Limburg coal mines, the steel furnaces at Velsen, the Philips factories at Eindhoven. The number of victims of the air war was rising.

All over Europe, the war became more fierce and merciless. In the southeast, the Germans were harassed by partisans, and in Czechoslovakia the bloodthirsty Heydrich received some of his own medicine when his spine was severed by Czech bullets. The reprisal massacre of Lidice clearly showed the world what Nazi retaliation meant.

The Dutch officials who had remained at their desks came under mounting pressure. As there were not enough Dutch Nazis available, a number of important positions were still filled by men of the "ancient regime." Admittedly, their situation was difficult. If they resigned, their jobs would be given to members of the N.S.B. If they stayed on, they still could delay or circumvent at least some German regulations. Of course, this meant a certain amount of collaboration. The constant German demands for more Dutch labor put the loyal civil servants in a very uncomfortable position.

The secretary general of internal affairs, K.J. Frederiks, represented the typical plight of a Loyalist in distress. We have already mentioned that he tried to protect a group of Jewish professors. Like many others, he reasoned that he could prevent greater evil by remaining in office. This he did until the fall of

1944 when he went into hiding after an attempt was made on his life. Frederiks followed the line of reasonable collaboration with the Germans, though his loyalty to his country and Queen cannot be doubted. To the labor draft and the recruitment of workers for German fortifications in Holland, Frederiks gave his cooperation and sometimes succeeded in obtaining minor concessions. Naturally, he soon came under fire from the government in exile, and even more so from the resistance. In particular, a proclamation against sabotage signed by Frederiks and two other secretaries caused great indignation.

From an ethical point of view, the behavior of men like Frederiks was, of course, wrong. Their actions were unprincipled and mainly dictated by expediency. Their intentions were good, and it is true that at least on some occasions they modified or weakened brutal measures. Also, it is to their credit that they adamantly refused to remain in office if Mussert were appointed head of a Dutch Nazi government. This attitude probably influenced the Germans against such a step.

After the war, the authorities took a very lenient view toward that type of collaboration.* This was in part because the original instructions, which should have guided the actions of civil servants, were far from clear. In 1943, Bosch Ridder van Rosenthal published a commentary on the old directives in the clandestine press and the government-in-exile endorsed it via the B.B.C. Van Rosenthal, a former high official and a resistance leader, declared that any cooperation in assisting the labor draft, the requisition of goods, arrests, deportations, and the taking of hostages was forbidden. This was all very well, but it came too late and did not materially change the situation. The majority of civil servants continued to adapt themselves to the existing situation. When Germany's chances of winning the war decreased, willingness to collaborate gradually waned. However, barricades are rarely built by bureaucrats. The various branches of the Dutch administration functioned until the end of the occupation.

*A parliamentary commission criticized the secretaries general for some of their actions. However, the government in exile was also blamed for failing to instruct them in an adequate manner.

Mussert's hopes of eventually being entrusted with the powers of government were high in 1942, but they were in vain. By the end of that year, he was received by the Fuehrer and politely told that he was considered the leader of the Dutch nation, but that the actual forming of a government by him would be inopportune. In practice, this was a clear rejection. He could call himself "the leader" to his heart's desire, but he gained neither power nor influence. He was permitted to form a political secretariat that was supposed to consult with the German authorities on important measures. Practically, this new agency achieved nothing of consequence.

Besides the completely submissive attitude of the N.S.B. and the more or less unwilling cooperation of the bureaucracy, a third

Himmler (center) on a visit to Holland, talking to Mussert. Rauter is on the left behind Himmler.

Library of Congress

type of German camp follower existed. Like the girls who hung around army centers, they were basically prostitutes, though of a somewhat different caliber. They wished to enrich themselves by doing business with the Germans. Such people always flourish in times of war and occupation. Most of them were not Nazi sympathizers; they would just as happily have dealt with the Allies.

The building of fortifications on the Dutch coast gave such entrepreneurs excellent opportunities. New contracting firms, which undertook to construct Germany's Atlantic Wall, came into existence. Also a number of existing manufacturers saw no reason to object to German orders.

As the situation became worse, many decent and patriotic businessmen were forced to do at least some work for the Germans. Refusal could mean closing of their business and deportation to Germany for their employees. Like the bureaucracy, the business world by and large accepted its part in the new order of things. Loyal Dutchmen consoled themselves by giving the occupying power very poor service, closing their eyes to sabotage, and using raw materials distributed for "Wehrmacht Orders" for their own private customers. The Dutch are old hands in the art of trading and eyed the situation soberly. Generally, the Dutch businessman followed the example of the Abbé Siéyès, who, when asked what he did during the French revolution, calmly replied: "I remained alive."

A consequence of the increasing shortage in foods, fuel, and clothing was the growing black market. Clandestine butchering became very prevalent, and practically everything, from cigarettes to shoes was subject to illegal barter. Since any ethical element — as for example in Britain — was lacking, black marketeering reached enormous proportions. Very few people had qualms about patronizing the black market because there was a general feeling that "the Germans would take it anyway." Occupation policy is rarely favorable to economic morality.

The atmosphere of gloom that lay over the Netherlands was suddenly lifted in November 1942. On the fourth day of this month, Rommel's Africa Corps was in full retreat. The free world had a new hero, a thus far unknown and somewhat ec-

134

centric British general: Bernard Law Montgomery.* Four days later the Allies, landed in French North Africa. The Germans hurriedly occupied southern France and Tunis, thereby greatly extending their overstrained communications. They controlled almost all of Europe just when their empire started to crumble. The biggest crack so far appeared on November 19. A two-pronged Russian offensive encircled the Sixth German Army at Stalingrad, which was then trapped between the Volga and the Don. Hitler ordered General Paulus to hold his ground at all costs. An effort to relieve the besieged failed. They kept re-sisting desperately until February 2, 1943, but it was clear that they were doomed. As a consequence, the Germans had to pull out of the Caucasus and Kuban regions. Their chances to reach the great oil wells of the Soviet Union were lost forever.

Those events had a decisive influence on occupied Holland. The probability that the Allies would sooner or later attempt invasion in the west had grown almost to certainty. Hitler's whole policy had always been directed toward eliminating his adversaries one by one. The spectre of war on two, perhaps even on three fronts was very real. However, the Fuehrer was still confident that any cross-Channel operation could be repulsed, with heavy losses. In November 1942, his whole force in the west, including Denmark and Norway, amounted to 45 divisions and more than half of the Luftwaffe. One year later, he had 50 divisions in France and the Low countries and another 18 in Scandinavia. It is a little known fact that the industrial war machine of Germany was far from running at full capacity until February 1942. In that month, Albert Speer was named minister of arms and munitions. That great organizer succeeded in doubling the monthly output of arms within one year. But it was the disaster of Stalingrad that put the screws on productive capacity. The occupied countries were to feel the change.

It was then to be total war — *"la guerre à l'outrance."* What this meant became clear in the early spring of 1943. All non-

*Montgomery had played a remarkable part as commander of the Third British Division in Belgium, but outside of England few people had ever heard of him until he took command of El Alamein.

essential industrial enterprises were to be closed. Employers were entitled to extend the work week up to 72 hours. Universities were ordered to prepare lists of students who should be assigned to work in Germany, but this plan came to nothing. However, students were required to sign a loyalty oath "to refrain from all actions against the German Reich, its armed forces, or the Dutch authorities." They were also informed that they would have to work in Germany for six months after completing their studies. The students were given one month to consider that strange pledge. The attitude of the still-operating universities differed. The denominational schools advised against signing. The Municipal University of Amsterdam left the decision to the individual. At Delft, the faculty told the students to sign, but later rather shamefacedly revoked the decision. The government-in-exile ordered students not to sign, and eventually only about 15 per cent signed the loyalty oath. All those who had refused were called up for labor draft in Germany, their families threatened with reprisals if they failed to report. About one-third of the nonsigners relented and were shipped to camps in Germany, from which many escaped. The majority went into hiding and the German police made no great effort to find them.

But the most incisive measures were still to come. On April 29, 1943, a communiqué signed by General Christiansen ordered all Dutch army personnel to be reinterned. Ingratitude for their lenient treatment in 1940 was given as a motivation, but in reality the measure had been conceived by Himmler as a new method to conscript cheap labor. It caused enormous excitement and led to the first open outbreak of resistance since February 1941.

The trouble started at the Stork Company plant in Hengelo, which functioned mainly for the Germans. The news spread at noon, when workers were at lunch. Most of them did not resume their work; others left the plant spontaneously. Former union officials encouraged striking, and management made no effort to curtail it. The movement quickly spread to other factories. During the afternoon, strikes occurred in widely separated parts of the country. The next morning, several hundred thousand workers all over Holland went on strike. The strike was not limited to industry. In the rural province of Friesland, dairy farmers refused to deliver milk to factories. Quite contrary to the outbreak in February 1941, the strike assumed nationwide character. However, in several ways history seemed to repeat itself. Again, as on the previous occasion, Seyss-Inquart happened to be absent and left Rauter in command. The latter acted with his usual decisiveness and brutality. He immediately declared a "state of siege" and sent a German police detachment to Hengelo. Riot-act posters, announcing capital punishment for strikers and an eight o'clock curfew, appeared everywhere. Workers were arrested and placed before German police courts, which almost invariably sentenced the defendants to immediate death by firing squad. On May 3, the first 26 executions were announced. In the Philips factory, a police court was established, seven persons executed, and the bodies exposed on the premises. Nevertheless, four days elapsed before the big plant resumed its work. In Friesland, where hatred of the Germans was particularly fierce, almost a whole week passed before the police had the situation under control. In the province of North Brabant, the strike grew almost into open revolt. Crowds demonstrated in the streets and tried to liberate political prisoners. A witness described it as follows:

> Dairy carts of farmers who didn't side with the strikers were overturned. Striking workers of the flaxseed factories marched through the streets. Suddenly, a shout: "The green police is coming!" The crowds dispersed. From my hiding place I could see the police trucks and heard shots. Five minutes later the trucks returned after three prominent citizens had been arrested as hostages. In front of the city hall two seriously injured men lay on the ground. The burgomaster, an N.S.B. member, was raging and threatened those who did not return to work with the concentration camp.°

The people stared at the sky. Was there no Allied air armada coming to their aid? But no help from the other side of the Channel arrived. Requests from the Dutch government-in-exile to the British were in vain. The Allies were not ready for full-scale

°B. Voeten: *Doortocht.*

invasion and did not fashion their strategy with regard to events in the occupied countries. From a general point of view, they were right. For the brave men who risked their lives opposing the Germans, it was a very bitter pill to swallow.

Between May 1 and May 8, about 80 persons were executed by the German police, and 60 more lost their lives by fusillades on strikers or demonstrators. Rumors greatly exaggerated the number of victims, and it was generally believed that more than 1,000 patriots had been killed. However, the Germans were careful not to indulge in mass slaughter. They had been surprised by the fierceness of the Dutch reaction. Some strikers were released when their comrades returned to work.

The lack of advance preparation made the May strike a confused affair. There was practically no political leadership. The railroad personnel, except for a few small local groups, stayed on the job. On the other hand, many white collar workers of the post and telegraph service and at the department of trade at The Hague went on strike. In the town of Arnhem, even the stores closed up.

On May 15, the state of siege was finally rescinded, but one week before its discontinuation, a new regulation ordered all men between eighteen and thirty-five years of age to register for work in Germany. Three age groups were promptly called up and transported to Germany. At first, certain categories like miners and agricultural workers were exempted; but many exemptions were later canceled, and the bearers had little chance to escape; their data were, of course, well known. The Dutch authorities who had to cooperate in the conscription acted as usual halfheartedly. The acting Secretary-General of Social Affairs, A.T. Verwey, was no Nazi, but did not refuse to collaborate. He even designated members of his own department for deportation, whereby persons of good society or higher education were given a far better chance to remain in Holland. Just as the Jewish Council ended up delivering its own staff to the Nazis, so were reputable civil servants caught in a vise and forced to deport their countrymen. Of course, the Dutch labor force was not destined for extermination, but frequently had to work under highly unfavorable conditions. At least 5,000 of them perished by air attacks or starvation.* Like his colleague, Frederiks, Verwey was often violently attacked by the underground press. Here again, a basically decent civil servant had become the tool of the occupying power.†

Actually, resistance against reinternment of military men and labor draftees became so widespread that the authorities were often almost helpless. Of the approximately 300,000 army veterans in Holland, the Germans never succeeded in interning more than a fraction. Many were working in the civil service or in vital industries, and their internment would have led to a complete breakdown of the economy. Many received exemptions, and a very great number simply failed to report.

The Germans had greater success with their labor conscriptions and succeeded in transporting 148,000 workers to the Reich during 1943. However, deportation of entire age groups proved very cumbersome, and the system was changed to a selection of sorts based on the type of work an individual performed in Holland. If it was considered irrelevant to the war effort, deportation followed. Obviously, a cooperative employer or a well-meaning civil servant at the registration office could change the status of a conscript. By opposition, sabotage, and delay, that whole system nearly broke down in 1944.

The May strike and the reaction of the population toward the labor draft destroyed any German hope for winning over or at least neutralizing a sizable segment of the Dutch people. Seyss-Inquart, who seems to have disapproved of the reinternment of soldiers, was well aware of this. Knowledgeable Germans like Admiral Canaris had always warned that the mistreatment of the French, the Belgians, and the Dutch would lead to very serious consequences. He was not listened to, and the open contempt he showed for Hitler and his creatures led to his downfall.‡

*According to some sources, that figure was much higher.

†Verwey thwarted the Germans on some minor issues.

‡A colonel of the Abwehr has preserved the following incident: Driving with Canaris along a herd of sheep, the latter suddenly got up and saluted. To the astonished question of his companion, he replied: "Perhaps one of my superiors is among them."

The deportation of workers, students, and military personnel to Germany gave a strong impulse to underground activities. Up until then, only Jews and individuals pursued by the S.D. had gone underground. But now thousands of young men were faced with transportation to the Reich and promptly went into hiding. The result was twofold: an enormous demand for false documents and ration books, which forced the resistance into desperate actions. At the same time, the ranks of the "illegality" were greatly strengthened. In 1942, the resistance was still numerically weak. In 1943, it became a mass movement.

CHAPTER TWELVE

On February 5, 1943, the doorbell rang at General Seyffardt's home. When the sponsor of the Netherlands Legion opened the door, he received one bullet in the liver and one in the kidney. He was rushed to a hospital and died on the following day.

A very similar attack was made a few days later on the newly appointed Secretary-General H. Reydon. His wife was shot to death, and he himself received a bullet through his spine. He died several months afterward.

A few weeks later, several men dressed in Dutch police uniforms requested admittance at the Amsterdam office of public registration. Upon entering, they overpowered the personnel and set fire to the building. The perpetrators were later apprehended and executed. Among them was a well-known Dutch writer, Johan Brouwer.

In Hengelo, armed men attacked the state employment office, drenched all files with gasoline, and set them afire. In Apeldoorn, the city hall burned down. Dr. F. Posthuma, a former minister of agriculture turned Nazi, was shot by a man on a bicycle while he sat at his window. In Leeuwarden, all registration cards referring to young men under the age of 25 were confiscated by Dutch policemen who later turned out to be resistance fighters. In Huizen, a great number of ration cards were stolen from the distribution office itself. The Germans sent the civil servants who were employed there to the concentration camp in Vught because they had not opposed the intruders.

Such incidents became daily occurrences. The Germans answered with arrests and executions, thereby only stimulating further resistance. The patriotic action groups concentrated on Dutch police officers and informers who worked for the occupying power. In Utrecht and Nijmegen, the chiefs of police were assassinated. In the eastern provinces, several farmers who were known for their N.S.B. sympathies were killed and their houses burned. Altogether, 40 Dutch Nazis were liquidated during the first eight months of 1943. Opposition was developing into underground warfare.

There were other strange events. Fritz Schmidt, one of Seyss-Inquart's deputies and Mussert's guardian angel, fell or was pushed from a riding train. The Dutch resistance was not involved in this and the facts of the accident were never fully disclosed. It was known that Schmidt and Rauter were on very bad terms, and rumor had it that the puissant police chief welcomed and, perhaps, planned his enemy's demise. From that time on, the Dutch Nazi leader's influence was on the wane. The May strike had convinced the Germans that Holland would never turn into a National Socialist country by its own accord. The radical wing of the party, which clamored for outright absorption into the Reich, got the upper hand. Soon Mussert quarreled with the commander of the Dutch S.S., J.H. Feldmeyer.* The conflict was finally patched up on German insistence. The N.S.B. press and radio still tried to convince the Netherlanders that Germany would eventually win, but the course of events clearly pointed to the contrary. During the summer, the Reich suffered three severe setbacks. The German army, slowly driven back in Russia, was now completely on the defensive. Sicily fell to the Allies, and the regime of Mussolini collapsed. And — most important! — Admiral Doenitz' U-boats were destroyed in such numbers that they ceased to be a decisive factor. Men and materiel from the U.S. began arriving in enormous quantities in England and North Africa.

Another fact that German propaganda could not hide was the ever-growing air offensive. The R.A.F. had been joined by the Eighth U.S. Air Force, and a hail of bombs began hitting German cities by day and by night. From the spring of 1943 on, the

*Feldmeyer perished in 1945 during an air raid.

inhabitants of Holland could observe the American planes flying overhead in greater and greater numbers, air battles were often watched from the ground. When darkness fell, the British started flying across the coast under the constant thunder of the German antiaircraft guns. People living close to the German border could often observe large fires; stories — sometimes exaggerated — about the destruction were circulated. The successful raids on the Mohne and Eder dams in the Ruhr made a deep impression in Holland. The enormous attacks on Hamburg, which destroyed

German antiaircraft battery on the Dutch coast
Library of Congress

about 60 per cent of that great city and killed about 100,000 persons, were greeted with a mixture of horror and satisfaction. Rotterdam was avenged. Had the Allies been able to continue such air strikes in quick succession against other large cities, German transport and production may have broken down. However, they dissipated their forces, and their losses were too high to continue blows of such severity to the enemy. Later on, the front in Italy and France somewhat relieved the weight of the attacks on German cities. Many smaller attacks were also flown against strategic objects in the Netherlands. Single raids on moving trains became more frequent.

The Allies began to shower leaflets on the occupied countries in which workers were warned against working in armament factories. Unfortunately, most men had no choice in their work as they had to feed their families. The Germans, who had so far belittled the Allies, now changed their tactics and warned of the horrors of a future invasion. Lurid posters showing scenes of destruction appeared. On one poster, a child was bending over a dying mother. The text read: "Mommie, is this the second front Daddie was always talking about?" At the same time, young men were still exhorted to join the German army and navy: "Serve your country and take service in the German navy!" Such slogans sounded false and became mainly an object of mockery.

The Germans made a somewhat deeper impression with their anti-Soviet propaganda. The disclosures about the mass graves of Polish officers at Katyn caused a certain uneasiness. However, the admiration for the military feats of the Red Army counterbalanced the effect, especially as the Germans were committing so many atrocities right under the eyes of the Dutch population. That the "second front" was still not established sometimes worried people, as it was feared that Russia would eventually dominate all of Europe. When the Allies landed in France, that feeling of uncertainty gradually disappeared.

The rising resistance and sabotage, coupled with the growing threat of invasion, drove the German authorities to two important decisions in 1943. Rauter had previously recommended confiscation of all radio sets. Shortly after the May strike, he ordered owners to hand in their sets, but the decree was never fully obeyed. Many persons delivered old, broken sets and kept the good ones. Sometimes razzias from house to house were held, but it is estimated that about 20 per cent of the existing wireless sets remained hidden. Confiscation indirectly stimulated the printing of illegal news sheets and secret construction of tiny radio sets that were easy to conceal. The "green police" was badly overworked and could not possibly search every house in Holland. When the Italian surrender was announced by the B.B.C. on the evening of September 8, 1943, the news spread with amazing speed, and many people were openly jubilant. The number of clandestine news bulletins and other publications rose to 150 after the radio confiscation. Radio hookups, which functioned only via radio Hilversum, the German-controlled Dutch transmitter, were not confiscated. By and large, Rauter's decree had no great effect on the attitude of the population. Since many persons had only indirect access to the news, rumors frequently arose and greatly exaggerated reports circulated, generally unfavorable to the Germans.

The German police were aware that many people were disappearing into underground existence. It also became quite apparent that a growing number of persons carried falsified identity cards. In the beginning, patriotic men would simply give their documents to people in hiding. The photo had then to be replaced and necessary changes made on the document. The original owner went to city hall and claimed he had lost his papers. This procedure worked only as long as the number of "divers" was small. The German police made lists of allegedly lost identity papers, and its agents were equipped with a book that contained numbers and names of all suspicious identification cards. Moreover, the S.D. sometimes used quartz lamps to meticulously examine the documents. A comparison of fingerprints would also disclose false identity, as it was impossible to change those on the card.

Therefore, when the number of persons in hiding rose, other methods for large-scale forgeries became necessary. From 1943 on, the underground frequently carried out raids on offices in which blank identity cards were kept. Many were also stolen by patriotic civil servants and forwarded to local resistance groups. The cards were then filled in with data that would fit the owner and contained its original photo and fingerprints. The printing of false identification cards was also attempted, but it turned out to be very difficult to counterfeit them to perfection. The bearer of a forged identity card could hope to pass superficial inspection, but rarely a close inspection at a police station.

By the middle of 1943, the use of false documents had become so widespread that Rauter decided on an elaborate scheme "to drive the army of divers to desperation." A new regulation decreed that ration books would only be issued to persons who presented their identity card at the distributing office. Before issuing the ration book, the identity card was to be stamped, and on the book itself a seal was to be placed. The latter would have a validity of six months only. It had then to be replaced by a new one. This complicated procedure would subject the entire adult population to periodic inspection and registration. As Rauter had very little confidence in the reliability of the Dutch by then, he had the stamps and ration books printed in Vienna.

If this measure had worked, all persons with nonvalid papers would have faced starvation. Obviously, people with false identity cards could not risk close inspection by trained personnel. However, the plan backfired completely. In the first place, many civil servants employed at rationing bureaus sabotaged the plan. A series of raids on such offices and on the agencies that kept population records followed. In one case, the official of a small town in Brabant handed over all new ration cards to the resistance with his regrets that he had only four thousand. In their attacks on government offices, the underground proved very imaginative. For example, at Oegstgeest, a suburb of Leyden, resistance men appeared in uniforms of the "green police" and confiscated all cards. Another rather amusing aspect of several raids of this kind was the brandishing of toy guns. The resistance was still desperately short of arms. Because of the England-spiel, all weapons dropped during 1943 had fallen into the hands of the Germans. What little armament existed, consisted mostly of booty from attacks on police stations. From the May strike on, single policemen, even entire units, more and more often suddenly disappeared. Their uniforms and weapons were, of course, a welcome help to the underground. Rauter angrily threatened the arrest of the families of police deserters. It was all to no avail. On several occasions, the Dutch police even joined the attacks on city agencies and station houses. The guards then disappeared with the intruders, taking their rifles and revolvers with them.

After months of growing chaos, Rauter had to admit that his scheme had failed. Apparently, he finally realized this himself, or perhaps he was worried that further rigid continuation of his ration-book control would create even greater trouble. The whole procedure was quietly dropped, and people applying for new ration books were not closely examined.

The mounting unrest also caused Rauter to forbid travel to the five eastern provinces. Furthermore, any offense with regard to identification or rationing cards was threatened with trial before a German police court, a euphemism for the death penalty. However, the most amazing and never-published reaction of the German authorities was the so-called "Operation Silver Fir." This code word was used for sanctioning the assassination of Dutch patriots in reprisal for the killing of members of the N.S.B. In September 1943, Rauter authorized the murder of persons whose only crime was that they were known to be loyal Dutchmen. It was decided that the death of one Nazi should be avenged by killing three prominent citizens. This is one of the rare occasions in history in which governmental agencies ordered outright murder of perfectly innocent people and gave full protection to the assassins. Whenever a Nazi was killed, the S.D. would choose three persons living in the same town or region and send out special commandos in civilian attire to carry out the murders. The killers were then spirited away by the German police to avoid discovery by the Dutch authorities. The murders were carried out mainly during darkness. The newspapers reported these crimes without having any knowledge of their being committed by order of the highest German police authority in the Netherlands. Forty-five persons were assassinated in this manner. The most renowned victim was the author A.M. de Jong, a Catholic novelist from North Brabant. None of the murdered men had been accused of any actual offense against the occupying power. The whole matter would sound almost incredible had Rauter not freely testified to having ordered this action at his trial in 1948.* Along with this astonishing practice of lynch justice, the German police frequently shot prisoners as a reprisal and later claimed that the men had tried to escape.

Certain prisoners were made to disappear under the "Night, and Fog Decree" signed by Field Marshal Keitel. This regulation prescribed that persons having acted against Germany should only be court-martialed if their death sentence was virtually certain. If their guilt was in doubt, they should be shipped to a German concentration camp in complete secrecy, and it was silently assumed that they would never return. They would vanish without a trace; no information was to be given to their next of kin, and even their burying places were held secret. The decree was especially aimed at the conquered territories in the west.

By the summer of 1943, the occupation regime had degenerated into a naked reign of terror. It is sad to report that of the many Germans in leading positions during all five years of occupation, not one raised a single word of protest against the continued violations of human rights and international law. Christiansen's chief of staff, Lieutenant-General Helmuth von Wuehlisch, seems to have had some qualms and was, therefore, characterized by Rauter as "a dandy without inner hardness and resistance, weak and soft, one of those who want to keep a clean vest." Christiansen himself, according to a former superior† "a very good-natured character," kept aloof and tried to see and hear no evil.

The increasing bitterness of the underground struggle produced very mixed reactions. The Dutch government-in-exile at first disapproved of political assassinations. They were mainly

*A number of participants in those murders were apprehended after the war and sentenced to long prison terms.

†General-Colonel Kurt Student.

the work of a new illegal organization, the "Council of Resistance in the Kingdom of the Netherlands." It had come into existence shortly before the May strike. Its main goal was sabotage, espionage, and aid to persons in hiding. The organization functioned through very small groups to avoid heavy losses in case of arrests. Politically, it was definitely to the Left. Its relationship with the very conservative O.D.* was none too good. Because of the presence of many Communists within the organization, the London government was slow in recognizing its merits, but gradually cooperation greatly improved.

The Council's attitude toward the Germans and the N.S.B. was dictated by the demands of total war and, more radical than that, of the ministers in London, who were not actually experiencing the stress and strain of occupation. A gentleman's war against an invader who maintained concentration camps, executed hostages, and deported women and children for extermination was not possible. Elimination of dangerous Nazis, especially of traitors and informers, gradually became accepted policy. The Germans claimed later that S.O.E. had ordered the assassination of 14 N.S.B. members and even provided revolvers equipped with silencers. This order was allegedly received over one of the contaminated channels and was never carried out. There is no proof that any Dutch government agency in London ever gave such a directive. Whatever the truth, no one can doubt that the majority of patriots in Holland approved of the liquidation of traitors. The illegal press, whose staff was constantly hunted by the S.D., did not exactly rejoice at the killing of Dutch Nazis, but considered those deeds inevitable. Attacks on members of the German armed forces were not encouraged, for they achieved little and always led to savage reprisals. Unfortunately, pent-up hatred and the bitter necessities of the underground struggle were hard to control.

Because of the Englandspiel, espionage and sabotage had made little progress during 1943. However, a new way for transmitting information was found via Switzerland. The contact man in that country was a Protestant clergyman, Dr. W.A. Visser

*See page 74.

't Hooft, who was the secretary-general of the World Council of Churches in Geneva. He paid a visit to London in 1942 and communicated with the Dutch government. As he was still in touch with friends in the Netherlands, he seemed the right man for establishing a link with his occupied homeland. Naturally, all letters to foreign countries were censored by the Germans. Besides, the sender had to deliver them in person at the post office. Therefore, only the most trivial information could be sent through the mails. Valuable news could only be transmitted by couriers. Such a person was Miss H. Kohlbrugge, a young member of the underground group Vrij Nederland. Furthermore, Dutch businessmen, whom the Germans considered to be reliable, were occasionally permitted to travel to Switzerland. Gradually, a regular information service was established. Reports were sewn into books and microfilm rolls were inserted into shaving soap sticks; in that way, a permanent, illegal traffic grew with contacts in Brussels and Paris. The "Swiss Road" became an important source of information for London. Of course, it suffered from slow communication and could not be very effective in a military sense. The organization of a competent intelligence service still lay in the future.

Great hopes for a speedy Allied victory had been raised by the surrender of Italy, but the succeeding events proved very disappointing. Progress toward Rome was painfully slow, and the winter passed while the "millimeter war" provided little satisfaction. The news from Russia was better. By the end of 1943, a great part of the Ukraine had been liberated. The war in the west remained a war in the air, with Berlin getting most of the R.A.F.'s attention. The last event of that hard year was the sinking of the *Scharnhorst* near the North Cape, which left the German navy with only two more battleships, both of them damaged. The German surface fleet had by this time ceased to be a threat to the Allies and the U-boats — according to Hitler "my first line of defense in the west" — were suffering the same fate. For every ship they had sunk, the Allies were building four. They were getting ready for their great assault on Fortress Europe.

CHAPTER THIRTEEN

A silly little song had become extremely popular in Holland. It was called "Old Tough One," and neither the text nor the tune was very remarkable. But somehow it caught on, and almost everybody was singing or whistling it. Perhaps it was the philosophy it expressed. You had indeed to be an "old tough one"* to survive. Very little fuel was available that winter, and many people had to use peat that smelled badly and gave almost no warmth. The food rations were progressing from bad to worse, and clothing was unobtainable. Bread, though sufficient in quantity, was of miserable quality. Soap contained mainly clay, and jam — so beloved in the Netherlands — was a reddish jelly that consisted mostly of water.

The dreary winter turned into a nervous spring. Everyone was edgy and restless. Almost 300,000 Dutchmen — workers, soldiers, and students — were working in Germany or slaving in concentration camps. Many girls and women had lost their partners. Some — not too many — consoled themselves with German soldiers and were regarded with contempt by their countrymen. The constantly growing army of "divers" was also an element of unrest. Many of these young men in hiding were completely cut off from their normal occupation and found themselves in very strange surroundings. To live day in and day out with strangers — often quite uncongenial — caused problems. Life in the country, where the young men could work on the farm, proved easier than in the city where time weighed heavily on

*In Dutch *ouwe taaie*. The text of the ditty had nothing to do with the war, nor did it make much sense.

active people who had to hole up in an apartment or perhaps a single room.

Late in 1942, an organization whose main task was helping people in hiding had been formed by a housewife and a Calvinist minister. It grew very fast, and by the beginning of 1944, it had expanded over the entire country. It called itself L.O. (Landelijke Organisatie) and eventually became the largest underground organization in the Netherlands. The early members and most of its later leaders were as unlikely a group of rebels as ever existed. They were deeply religious people, devout Calvinists, and many of their contacts were made through the reformed churches. The L.O. was particularly strong in the countryside, where it was still easier to hide.

Originally, the efforts of the L.O. were largely humanitarian. In the early days of its existence, most of its wards were Jews, especially Jewish children who were placed with foster parents in the provinces. After the May strike, the need for shelter, food, and identification cards grew tremendously, for thousands and thousands of young Dutchmen were driven to the underground. The L.O. developed a complete technique for such activities. A great effort was made to forestall difficulties by placing "divers" into homes similar to their own. Consultation took place among the leading members of the organization, and young men were trained and advised how to overcome the everyday problems of underground life.

With the struggle growing more bitter, the L.O. was forced to a more aggresive policy. Raids to seize ration books and identification cards became necessary, and in the fall of 1943, a more militant subdivision, the L.K.P., was formed. The name — Landelijke Knokploegen* — derived from those early action groups who had fought the N.S.B. in Amsterdam.† At first it had only a few hundred members.

The L.K.P. had its roots in the Calvinist Churches like the L.O., but as they were small fighting teams they were actually partisans. They liberated political prisoners, attacked small Ger-

*Regional Action Groups.

†See page 64.

man detachments, and committed acts of sabotage. Their most glorious enterprise was an attack on the prison at Arnhem, whereby more than 50 political detainees were freed.

Where did the L.O. and other underground organizations receive the financial aid to carry on their widespread operations? Much was collected from members who often generously gave part of their salaries to the organization. Other funds were provided by the churches, which stoutly maintained the old Calvinist spirit of sacrifice and mutual help born in the religious wars of the sixteenth century. However strange as it sounds, the resistance also had a banker of its own, the National Aid Fund (N.S.F.). This peculiar banking operation had originated as an assistance fund for the families of Dutch seamen serving with the Allies. When other persecuted persons required financial help, the fund expanded, and under the leadership of an Amsterdam banker, Walraven van Hall, it became a large organization. Contact with the former Director of the Netherlands Bank, J.L. A. Trip, was established. The latter promised that the government would reimburse, after the war, those who gave loans to N.S.F. On this basis, considerable contributions were made to the Fund, and by the beginning of January 1944, the Dutch government in London authorized the disbursement of 30 million guilders. Much of this money went to various resistance organizations. All banking operations were carried out in the meticulous Dutch tradition, though naturally in code. Although bankers do not fit the picture of the valiant resistance fighter with rifle and hand grenade, their part in the liberation struggle of the Netherlands should not be underestimated. Two of the founders of N.S.F. were later executed by the Nazis.

If the Dutch were nervous in the spring of 1944, the Germans were even more so. Along the western coast of Europe they had to defend a shore line of 1700 miles. Another poorly defended coastline stretched 300 miles along the Mediterranean. The enemy could strike anywhere from northern Norway to the Spanish border. To protect this immense area, Hitler had ordered the construction of the Atlantic Wall. It was strongest in the 300-mile zone between Flushing and Cherbourg, as it was correctly assumed that this was the area that the Allies could adequately cover with their fighter aircraft from British bases. However, the work had not been done very systematically. Because of the great damage from air raids in the Ruhr, much manpower had been diverted to that area. Between Le Havre and Antwerp fortifications were very strong. Field Marshal Gerd von Rundstedt, the Commander in Chief on the Western front, was completely convinced that the Allied onslaught would be made in the Pas de Calais. The old, dignified Field Marshal, "the last of the Prussians," had his own, very definite ideas about the German defense system. He would hold the Calais area and a few vital French ports and for the rest rely on a mobile reserve of infantry and armor. Von Rundstedt had little confidence in the planning of his subordinate, Field Marshal Erwin Rommel, whom he secretly despised as an upstart. Nevertheless, the latter made a few innovations. Underwater obstacles were constructed along the coast, and rail obstructions — in Holland called Rommel asperges — were rammed into the ground to prevent airborne landings.

By the spring of 1944, von Rundstedt had a total of 60 divisions under his command. Four infantry divisions and a weakened Panzer division were stationed in the Netherlands; the remaining forces were dispersed over France and Belgium. An uneasy, listless air of uncertainty enveloped the three countries. Where would the great blow fall?

The Dutch Nazis were even more uncomfortable than their German patrons. Mussert had again paid a visit to Hitler at the end of 1943, and again he had returned home with nothing but vague promises. His party members, frightened by resistance attacks, cried out for better protection, and in cooperation with Seyss-Inquart, Mussert established a new organization, the Netherlands Home Guard (Landwacht). Of all his creations, this one was certainly the most contemptible. His reservoir of N.S.B. manpower was exhausted, as many younger men were now fighting the Russians in German S.S. uniforms. Another armed unit (Landstorm), originally intended to defend the Netherlands against invasion, was later used by the Germans in Belgium. What remained was a rabble of ruffians and desperadoes without discipline and proper training. This strange home guard was officially under the command of C. van Geelkerken, but in reality it was controlled by Rauter, who equipped it with shotguns and used it as a sort of auxiliary police. That peculiar armament immediately earned it the nickname of Janhagel.[*] Mussert, whose influence was now at an ebb, soon lost all control over this newest formation. He later even protested the way Rauter used those bully boys, but the S.S. chief — as usual — ignored him.

Despite the home guard, the resistance became more aggressive than ever. In April 1944, a group of men seized the plant of a provincial newspaper at Schoonhoven and at gunpoint forced the personnel to print illegal copy, which was immediately distributed.

This idea caught on. For a short time, the Germans had produced an illustrated magazine called *The Shout (Gil)*, which satirized the Allies and the resistance. An Amsterdam group managed to produce a copy that at first sight looked like the German-controlled paper, but contained attacks on the regime and the N.S.B. It was sold out within one hour.

Another outright parody of a Nazi paper appeared on June 5, 1944, as an imitation of the *Haarlemse Courant*, a local daily. It contained a mock article ostensibly written by Goebbels and a paraphrase on one of Rauter's frequent proclamations, in which a curfew on dogs and ducks was imposed; furthermore, a sarcastic comparison was printed between the Nazi promise and the realities of the day. By sheer coincidence, this trick was played on the authorities just one day before the Allies landed in France. The consternation among the Nazis was considerable because they jumped to the completely unwarranted conclusion that the resistance had timed their publication for D-day. Actually, the Dutch underground had no information on the date of the Allied landings, and even the French resistance received their orders only eight hours before Ridgeway's parachute troops landed at St. Mère Eglise.

The activity of the Allied air force increased as the days grew longer. An extensive bombing attack on the submarine base of

[*] "Jan Bird Shot." But the word means also rabble.

Ijmuiden took place in full daylight; thousands of people watched the event. The whole Dutch coast shook under heavy explosions and the superiority of the Allies in the air was further demonstrated by the complete lack of molestation of their bombers, by German fighters. The R.A.F. also undertook a raid on the building in The Hague in which all public records were kept. A number of office workers drowned in the air raid shelter, which filled with water. This raid was undertaken on request of the Dutch resistance.

In May 1944, the hunt was on for everything moving on rails. Travel became very dangerous, and the Netherlands railway had to restrict its traffic. Some lone fighter-bombers chased trucks or even streetcars.

The Germans worked feverishly at their Atlantic Wall. For the population, the worst consequence was a growing number of forced evacuations. At first, most inhabitants of the island of Walcheren in the province of Zeeland were ordered to evacuate. Then, the far more densely inhabited coast zone around Rotterdam, and The Hague became a fortress area. Thousands of persons had to move, and many of the buildings in the defense zone were wrecked. This caused great unrest, as rumors were afloat that a 30-mile belt of fortifications would be constructed in the coastal area. Fortunately, this turned out to be exaggerated, but the destruction and misery caused by the evacuations were bad enough. Furthermore, the inhabitants were often compelled to work on the fortifications under supervision of German soldiers. Some areas near Rotterdam were inundated. In May 1944, a large number of Rotterdam citizens were forced to work at Hook van Holland. However, the deportation of Dutch workers to Germany was temporarily delayed by obstruction and protraction, and only 20,000 could be transported during the first half of 1944.

The plunder of the Netherlands went on with undiminished speed. That the country was saddled with all occupation costs can be considered normal, as conquerors have practiced this policy since the dawn of history. But with the deterioration of Germany's war position went a steady spoliation of the occupied territories that was sheer robbery. Evacuation was sometimes followed by confiscation of furniture. There was even a special agency that concentrated on art treasures, which sold at a handsome profit to Nazi "art collectors" in Germany. Men like Goering, von Schirach, and Kaltenbrunner filled their palatial homes with the stolen paintings of Dutch masters. The agency was run by one Dr. C. Muehlmann, another Austrian Nazi, who fared very well as an art expert under Seyss-Inquart.

The defeats the German army suffered in 1943 stiffened the will to resist in many persons and whole groups. The attitude of the medical profession deserves some comment because it shows that courage and solidarity could still achieve a great deal. In the autumn of 1941, the Germans, over the protest of more than 4,000 doctors, set up a National Socialist physicians organization. An N.S.B. member, Dr. C.C.A. Croin, was appointed chairman. The Loyalist physicians replied by organizing a secret organization called Medical Contact. They simply refused to join Dr. Croin's Nazi association, though membership was made compulsory. The frustrated chairman thereupon fined 80 doctors, with the result that he received 6,000 letters of resignation from the medical profession. They even put tape over the title "physician" on their office signs. The authorities, somewhat dismayed, ordered the doctors to continue their practice, but did not force the issue for the moment. When new pressure was brought to bear, the doctors sent a letter of protest to Seyss-Inquart of which a few sentences must be cited. "If it should come to the point, where unacceptable demands would be imposed on us as physicians, then we will have to throw our freedom and our life into the balance in spite of your threats. We expect that you will spare us this conflict and will allow us to continue our work in liberty and peace, according to our consciences."

Seyss-Inquart's reaction was predictable. He had 360 doctors arrested and shipped to the concentration camp at Amersfoort where they were treated in the most humiliating manner. Many physicians then went into hiding, and it almost looked as if medical service in the Netherlands would come to a standstill. However, both parties hesitated to let matters go too far. Finally, a face-saving device was found. The medical profession offered its apologies to the high commissioner, who had declared that the physicians' letter was a personal insult. The arrested doctors were released, and no further pressure was exerted on the profession.

The doctors had also pointed out that the health conditions in Holland were badly deteriorating. The authorities denied it, but the rise of mortality due to tuberculosis could be proved from official figures. By the spring of 1944, many people were badly undernourished and had very little physical resistance. The real catastrophe came half a year later.

Tuesday, June 6, 1944, seemed a day like any other. The first morning news at 7 o'clock reported nothing of particular interest, but one hour later, the German radio gave the first report of Allied landings in Normandy. At 9:30 A.M., the B.B.C. announced the invasion. Prime Minister Gerbrandy later addressed the Dutch population. The German troops in Holland were immediately alerted, but most of them remained in their barracks. It was a strange, quiet day; no air raid warnings sounded. During the night leaflets containing Eisenhower's appeal to the people of Western Europe and Gerbrandy's speech were dropped all over Holland. Mussert, for his part, sent a telegram to Hitler swearing eternal loyalty.

The Germans were by no means certain that the Normandy landings represented the main offensive against Fortress Europe. Von Rundstedt believed consistently that the main blow across the Straits of Dover was still to come. As late as June 19, a second large-scale landing was still expected. All political prisoners were hastily evacuated from Scheveningen to the camp at Vught. On June 10, the country was suddenly wild with rumors of Allied landings at Flushing, at den Helder, at Delfzijl. The truth was that a minor encounter had occurred at sea near Ijmuiden, and German soldiers had been hastily ordered to their stations.

For almost two months, the battle of Normandy raged with unremitting fury. The unrest in Holland grew, the German terror increased, the Allied air raids became more frequent, and the potato ration was lowered. Hardly a day passed without an attack by the resistance on distribution bureaus, and in some parts of the country the conditions approximated civil war. Incidents with he hated Landwacht were particularly frequent.

In Rotterdam, a certain van Dalen, who had denounced many citizens to the German police, was assassinated in his apartment. The Germans replied by executing several persons who were under arrest for underground work. The funeral of van Dalen was attended by a group of home guards, and persons who did not show their respect to the dead informer were dragged off to prison. The system of executing prisoners as a reprisal became an almost common event. Frequently, the victims were individuals who had committed minor offenses against the occupying authorities, though in Rauter's proclamations they were invariably referred to as "terrorists." Only a blind fanatic like Rauter could expect to pacify an occupied country in such a manner. Hatred and resistance mounted with every execution. The underground movement lost many of its best men in that period. One of them was the well-known sculptor Gerrit J. van der Veen,* who had commanded an unsuccessful raid and was severely wounded in action. He was arrested some time afterward in an almost paralyzed state and sentenced to death. He was carried to the execution on a stretcher, but, at his request, the other doomed men lifted him into a standing position; he fell, facing the firing squad.

While the battle of attrition went on in northern France, the German front in Russia started crumbling. By the end of July, the Red army was already in eastern Poland and Estonia and seriously threatened Rumania and the Ploesti oil fields. Farther south in the Balkans, a dozen German divisions were engaged by Tito's partisans. In Italy, the Allies had reached the river Arno, and the Germans retreated to the Gothic Line. To those military men in the Reich who were not completely blinded by propaganda, it was by then clear that Germany had lost the war. The attempt on Hitler's life on July 20, was mainly a result of that conviction, though a few of the very inept conspirators had nobler motives. The high command in the Netherlands was not involved in the conspiracy, but the general consequences of the ill-fated plot were extremely serious. The Wehrmacht lost all

---

*In his honor, the Euterpestraat in Amsterdam, where the offices of the S.D. were located, is now called Gerrit van der Veenstraat.

influence, and Himmler and his S.S. were solidly in the saddle. Hitler himself insisted on making even minor military decisions, and the trembling generals carried out his most absurd commands like obedient servants. There is nothing more characteristic than the reply of S.S. General Dietrich when urged to object to a particularly senseless order by the Fuehrer. "If I want to get shot," he answered, "that's the way to do it!"

In August, disaster came abruptly to the German armies in France. The Seventh Army got trapped in the Falaise pocket and lost two-thirds of its men and most of its heavy equipment. The fall of Paris only confirmed the disintegration of the German forces. What was left of them retreated behind the Seine. Of the 2,300 tanks with which the Germans had started the battle of Normandy, only about 100 were left.

Moreover, on August 20, the Russian steamroller thundered into Rumania. The 300-mile-long front was covered by 27 German and 20 Rumanian divisions; the latter were in no mood to fight. Three days later King Michael of Rumania ordered "immediate cessation of hostilities." Five days later, Finland asked for an armistice, and Bulgaria, which had never done any real fighting during the war, declared its neutrality. Soon afterward the Red Army entered Bulgaria in triumph. Within less than two weeks, the Reich had lost three of its satellites.

In the meantime, the Allies had invaded southern France and marched up the Rhone valley. In Poland, Warsaw was in full revolt. In the Baltic States, no less than 30 German divisions were tied up because Hitler had refused to shorten his front out of fear that the Soviets would invade the Baltic and cut off the vital iron-ore transport. Under those circumstances, not a single man could be spared in the east. To make matters worse, the damage due to the bombing of synthetic oil refineries and the loss of the Rumanian oil began to tell on the Luftwaffe. On August 30, the total stock of aviation fuel had fallen to a five-week supply. The effect of the V-1 flying bomb, which Hitler regarded as a decisive weapon, proved to be negligible. It killed many civilians, but did not seriously impair the movement of Allied troops from Britain to France.

A change had taken place in the German command on the

western front. Von Rundstedt had been deposed by Hitler at the beginning of July and replaced by Guenther von Kluge, who had earlier taken the command of the seriously injured Rommel. The latter and von Kluge himself had been on the fringe of the plot against the Fuehrer. Hitler learned of von Kluge's involvement when the catastrophe in France was in full progress and replaced him by Field Marshal Walter Model,* an excellent choice for handling a desperate situation. He had fought with great distinction on the eastern front, proved himself an able tactician, and was popular with his troops. His loyalty to Hitler was beyond question.

On August 29, the Allied left wing began to move. Montgomery's spearhead was commanded by Lieutenant General B.G. Horrocks, an extremely aggressive leader, who had distinguished himself in Tunis. His first action was a lightning blow at Amiens. The good citizens of that town could not believe their eyes when they woke and saw British troops in the streets. On the morning of September 3, Horrocks raced into Belgium, driving the fleeing Germans before him. The Belgian resistance rose everywhere, and the British tank columns sped along the roads at 30 miles an hour. By late afternoon, they were in Brussels, greeted by enthusiastic crowds. On the next day, an armored British division occupied Antwerp, its great docks undamaged.

The German collapse in Belgium presented the Allies with a unique opportunity. Several weeks before, Montgomery had advocated "one powerful and full-blooded" thrust into Germany. The vital Ruhr valley was now vulnerable. If the Allies could succeed in gaining, or at least immobilizing, this great industrial area, the war would be over in 1944.

However, Eisenhower had other ideas. The supreme commander believed in an advance on a broad front. In good time, both the Ruhr and the Saar would be captured, the ports of Antwerp, Le Havre and Dieppe opened to Allied traffic, and finally the Siegfried Line would be overrun and the Rhine crossed. The very speed of the Allied advance had created vast transport problems. The main supply base was still the artificial "Mullberry" harbor

*Von Kluge committed suicide on August 18. He feared being tried for his participation in the plot of July 20.

at Arromanches. The channel ports were either still in German hands or badly damaged. Antwerp could not be used without complete control of the Scheldt estuary. Roads and railways in northern France and Belgium had been heavily bombed and were in need of repair. The disruption of the railroad system had greatly contributed to the German defeat, but under the changed circumstances, it slowed the Allied advance. There can be no doubt that personal rivalries also played a certain part in the decision to follow Eisenhower's plan of broad advance. The British were far more bent on victory in 1944, partly for political and economic reasons. On the other hand, Eisenhower did not wish to stop Patton's Third Army, which was moving in the Moselle area. In the end, a compromise was reached. An effort would be made to circumvent the Siegfried Line in the north by crossing the Lower Rhine.

Historians will debate for the next hundred years whether Eisenhower's decision to abandon the idea of a "pencil-like thrust" into the Ruhr was right or wrong. But there can be no doubt that it had the most tragic consequences for the Netherlands.

On September 4 — the day Antwerp fell — von Rundstedt was reinstated as commander in chief by Hitler. The aged field marshal fell heir to a situation of extreme gravity. The Fifteenth German Army was isolated in Flanders and could only be saved by transporting it to the Scheldt estuary. The beaten Seventh Army was retreating toward the Maas and the Ardennes. Between these two armies, a 50-mile-wide gap had to be closed at all costs. In Holland, two infantry divisions, the garrison troops, and one brigade of the Netherlands S.S. were available. Another division of convalescents was hastily brought from Germany. As these troops would never have been capable of holding an Allied offensive, a new army composed of parachutists and air force ground personnel was formed in the greatest hurry and put under the command of General Kurt Student, who led the assault on Rotterdam in 1940. This First Parachute Army was deployed on the Albert Canal, which runs from Antwerp to Maastricht. Behind this lay the Maas-Scheldt Canal as a second water barrier. The terrain was highly suitable to defense.

The next move was up to the Allies. In a somewhat heated conference between Eisenhower and Montgomery, the latter's

Eisenhower and Montgomery

U.S. Army Photograph

plan for an airborne landing in Holland was approved. Montgomery repeated all his arguments for his pencil-like thrust to the Ruhr, but had to be content with a limited project that was designed to secure the crossings of the rivers Maas, Waal, and Neder Rijn (the Lower Rhine). This plan, "Operation Market Garden," was based on landing three parachute divisions at the crucial bridges and invading Holland at the same time from Belgium. While the airborne troops would capture the bridges over the three large rivers and five minor waterways, General Horrocks' armor and infantry would cut a diagonal corridor through the Netherlands. If a bridgehead over the Neder Rijn was won, the Allies would advance to the river Ijssel, then penetrate into the Ruhr.

It was a bold plan that involved heavy risks. However, it was only a limited action, not a concentrated assault. And like all operations based on parachute landings, it strongly depended on one unreliable factor: the weather.

CHAPTER FOURTEEN

Tuesday, September 5, 1944. During the night, the news of the
fall of Antwerp became widespread. People of The Hague, who
left their homes in the morning, observed three things. In the
first place, the streetcars were not running. Secondly, German
troops seemed to have vanished from the face of the earth. In
addition, all walls were plastered with new posters announcing
martial law. The decree, signed by Seyss-Inquart, made the
death penalty mandatory for any action against the occupying
power.

Also, people who happened to pass the railroad station noticed
that a large number of men, women, and children were obviously in great haste to leave town. The members of the N.S.B.
and their families were suddenly in a rush to make a trip to the
east of Holland or even farther. In Amsterdam, the large Central Station was mobbed with travelers. The square in front of
the station was filled with onlookers who regarded this
sudden exodus very derisively. The men of the "new order" who
had talked so much about comradeship, heroism, and resistance
to the end were running off in plain daylight. For more than
four years, they had berated the Queen and her government for
leaving the country. Now that the war was finally approaching,
they wanted to quit.

This sudden mass evacuation was completely unorganized.
A large number of the National Socialist refugees had to be
housed temporarily in the almost-empty Jewish transit camp at
Westerbork, much to the wry satisfaction of the remaining Jewish internees, who watched the inglorious arrival of their tor-
mentors. Others fled straight to Germany. Mussert maintained

enough courage and dignity not to join in the panicky flight of his supporters. But quite a number of prominent Dutch Nazis in high positions turned on their heels. Several were later expelled from the party, but the damage was done. The Germans were so disgusted with the behavior of their satellites that for several days sharp criticism of the N.S.B. in some Dutch newspapers was not held up by censorship.

On the morning of September 5, the B.B.C. reported that Allied troops had reached the town of Breda, which lies south of the Moerdijk bridges. This report turned out to be incorrect, but it created a flood of rumors. Around noontime, excited citizens told each other that British columns had already liberated Dordrecht and were moving toward Rotterdam and The Hague. The disruption of almost all telephone service provided fuel to the rumors. The strange, unreal atmosphere of that day is best described by a Rotterdam citizen who happened to be at The Hague:

> I was at The Hague for a meeting. When everybody asserted that Rotterdam was occupied by the Allies, that no trains were riding and The Hague itself surrounded, I hurried to the station hoping to get the last train. There everything was quite calm, the train from Amsterdam arrived in time, and I returned with less trouble than previously. In Rotterdam, nothing had happened, no military action. The mood was tense; sometimes it gave the impression of a Queen's birthday crowd. Flags appeared and many children, but also adults, were singing *Oranje boven*. German troops were seen hastily retreating toward Utrecht.*

While The Hague celebrated the "liberation" of Rotterdam, farther north at Amsterdam the Allies were said to have taken The Hague and Haarlem. At the main roads, crowds appeared carrying flags and flowers. At the Berlage bridge, where the Germans had once entered Amsterdam, people waited for the British spearheads. Enterprising merchants were already selling orange buttons and pins. In Leyden, workmen left their jobs to greet the liberators. It was a brief moment of enthusiasm and

*F.A. de Graaf: *Op Leven on Dood* (W.L. and J. Brusse N.V., Rotterdam, 1946).

self-deception. Soon the green police appeared and drove the people from the streets.

September 5, 1944, has entered Dutch history as "Mad Tuesday" *(Dolle Dinsdag)*. When it ended, people were disappointed but still hopeful. For days, the B.B.C. hardly mentioned Holland; the German police, heavily armed, drove through the cities, but after all, the Allies were only a few miles off the border. In the south, across the rivers, large German formations coming from Belgium were in full retreat. An Allied offensive could be expected every moment.

Three days after "Mad Tuesday," the population of The Hague was disturbed by a tremendous noise. It sounded as if a gigantic train was thundering through the skies. The day was cloudy and

The Arnhem airdrop

U.S. Army Photograph

windy, and it was impossible to observe what was transpiring. But the next morning, when the sky cleared, brought the explanation. A new rocket, the "V-2," was being fired at England from bases near Wassenaar, a suburb of The Hague, which was shortly afterward evacuated. The rocket, looking like a torpedo with a white cloud of steam behind it, shot up almost vertically and was visible over a great distance. It gradually gained speed, and on its arrival in the target area, it could not be heard because it traveled faster than sound. The news of the new weapon was followed by the final decision of the Allied High Command to attack as soon as possible. On September 10, the preparation for "Operation Market Garden" began. On the next evening, American troops crossed the German frontier near Aachen. On September 13, Maastricht, the first Dutch city to be liberated, was occupied without much resistance. Listeners to Radio Orange could follow the event.

September 17 was a Sunday. The weather was fine, but cloudy. General Kurt Student was at his desk at headquarters in Vught when he was disturbed by a roaring in the air of mounting intensity. The general went to the balcony. What he saw can be best described in his own words: "Wherever I looked I saw aircraft; troop carriers and large aircraft towing gliders. An immense stream passed over the house. I was greatly impressed, but during those minutes, I did not think of the danger of the situation."

It was then about 1 P.M. Student later admitted he was completely surprised by the Allied operation. He was not the only one. Field Marshal Walter Model had his headquarters at Oosterbeek, an Arnhem suburb. A few days earlier, Rauter had suggested to him the possibility of air landings. Model had shrugged this off, with the remark that a cautious general like Montgomery would not plunge into mad adventures. Seeing British parachutists coming down ail around him, Model raced into Arnhem. The local garrison commander had just been killed, and the field marshal himself immediately took charge of the bewildered troops. His first action was to call in reinforcements from the Ninth S.S. Panzer division (S.S. Hohenstaufen), parts of which had been in the Veluve area, north of

German P.O.W.'s under escort during "Operation Market Garden"
U.S. Army Photograph

Arnhem. Dutch resistance had informed London two weeks earlier that these forces were stationed between Zutphen and Arnhem, but the message seems to have been ignored. A second S.S. Panzer division (S.S. Frundsberg) under General Bittrich, just recently reinforced and resting in the Achterhoek, was also alerted. A few hours later, orders for the whole airborne operations found in an American glider were in German hands. This, and the quick availability of the German armored forces, strongly influenced the outcome of the battle at Arnhem.

The Allied plans called for a number of airborne landings spread out like a carpet. A glance at the map is necessary to fully understand the strategic situation. Two American airborne divisions were dropped at the lower end of the corridor, one near

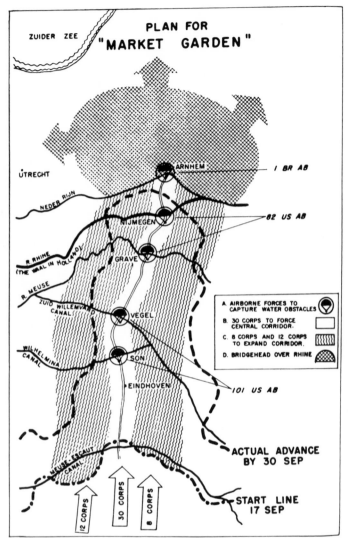

Plan for "Operation Market Garden," September 1944. From *The Memoirs of Field-Marshal the Viscount Montgomery of Alamein, K.G.* Published by the World Publishing Company. Copyright 1958 by Bernard Law, Viscount Montgomery of Alamein.

The first U.S. Paratroopers greeted by Dutch children

U.S. Army Photograph

Grave at the river Maas and one near Veghel, where four bridges
were taken intact. The fifth, near Son, was blown right in their
faces, but the Wilhelmina Canal was nevertheless straddled. At
Grave, General Gavin's parachutists very quickly captured the
large bridge from both sides, then moved immediately over the
Maas-Waal Canal toward Nijmegen. By nightfall they were
established at the Groesbeek ridge and one battalion penetrated
into the city, with its large bridges over the Waal. But here they
found growing resistance and were temporarily stopped.

While the air landings were in full swing, General Horrocks'
armored troops were deployed on the white concrete road to
Eindhoven. When he received word that the landings were
proceeding according to plan, his artillery put a rolling barrage
five miles deep into Holland, while Typhoon fighters sent a hail

General Gavin, Commander of the 82nd U.S. Airborne Division, at Nijmegen

Office of War Information, National Archives

of rockets into the German positions. By dusk, the Irish Guards were in Valkenswaard and on the next day they joined forces with the Americans in Eindhoven, where they were hailed with enormous enthusiasm. However, German resistance had been heavy, and the offensive was already behind schedule. The next step led over the broad Wilhelmina Canal, where a big Bailey bridge had to be constructed within 12 hours.

On September 18, heavy fog lay over the airfields in England, and about 1,200 gliders and their fighter screen left with delay. They were landed partly near Nijmegen, partly at Arnhem. In Nijmegen, the landing was executed under heavy German fire and Gavin's troops had to fight desperately to hold the enemy off. Meanwhile, the Germans formed a perimeter around the large road bridge. Field Marshal Model had ordered its defense, as he felt that destruction might hamper future German troop movements. Only on the evening of September 20 did the bridge fall into Allied hands after American parachutists crossed the fast-running river in assault boats. A last-minute attempt by the Germans to blow the road bridge failed. A bridgehead was established on the northern side of the Waal, but supply through the narrow corridor was slow and badly hampered by wreckage in Eindhoven's streets, caused by German air attack.

American airborne troops examine glider that crashed during battle of Arnhem.

U.S. Army Photograph

Dutch civilians explain the local situation to soldiers of the U.S. 101st Airborne Division.

U.S. Army Photograph

Thus, on September 21, the Allied controlled a long, narrow salient from the Dutch-Belgian border to Nijmegen. From Eindhoven to Grave, a distance of 30 miles, it was little wider than the road itself and under frequent shelling. Nevertheless, a new attack toward Arnhem was made on that day, but it was halted in the maze of dikes and channels, south of the village of Elst.

The airborne forces at Arnhem were meanwhile facing a desperate struggle. General Urquhart's First British Airborne Division's main objective was to take the bridges over the Neder-Rijn. The division consisted of crack troops of the highest caliber. However, they had been landed too far from the vital road bridge, and the railroad bridge was immediately blown up by the Germans. Furthermore, the gliders loaded with armored jeeps had been lost enroute. Nevertheless, the large road bridge was reached during the evening of September 17 by one British battalion. The German guards at the northern end had fled, and the only person present in the area was one lonely Dutch policeman. While the British held the northern approach, a party of S.S. troops sealed off the southern end. The 500 British parachutists were soon isolated by other German troops that had been hastily thrown into battle. Urquhart's main force was dispersed west of Arnhem, fighting a confused battle and waiting for reinforcements from the air. These arrived on the next day, five hours behind schedule because of bad weather. By then the Germans were attacking with tanks while the British had only infantry weapons. The British did gain a foothold within the city, and the Dutch resistance seized the local telephone exchange, but communication remained poor, and the wireless link with the R.A.F. was not working. By Tuesday evening — 48 hours after the bridge had been blocked — the situation was rapidly becoming desperate. The number of soldiers in the embattled bridgehead was dwindling and the main force held an oval-shaped perimeter around the Hotel Hartenstein at Oosterbeek. The plan was to reinforce the defenders by a Polish airborne brigade, but bad weather prevented its landing until September 21. By then, the British near the bridge were out of ammunition and could hold out no longer. The Germans now controlled the road bridge, and the Frundsberg Division was thrown against the advancing Allies at Elst.

The Poles were finally dropped at Driel on the southern bank of the Neder Rijn, opposite the British perimeter. They were too late to play a decisive part. In the meantime, the Germans commanded the surrounding heights, the ferry over the river had been sunk, and the compressed perimeter lay under heavy attack by infantry and armor. Ammunition and food parachuted to the besieged had fallen almost entirely into enemy hands. On the evening of that day, Urquhart reported: "Resources stretched to utmost. Relief within 24 hours vital." Indeed, his stocks of food and water were almost exhausted, and ammunition was running low.

On the next day, a British relief force advanced from the Nijmegen bridgehead. One column managed to reach the Poles on the southern river bend, but could not get across to the British. Moreover, the Allied corridor was disrupted by German tanks at Veghel. It was only cleared after heavy fighting. On the night of September 23, some supplies and 250 Polish soldiers crossed the river. Another attempt was made during the next night, but was repulsed, with heavy losses.

On September 25, the ninth day of the battle, the shrunken perimeter, now manned by only 2,500 British and Polish soldiers, seemed lost. The Germans could only be held back by artillery fire across the river. It was now decided to retreat during the night. At 9 P.M., a murderous bombardment was directed against the German positions, and under its protection the exhausted survivors were brought across in boats. The night was rainy, windy, and dark, and the Germans did not realize at first that the Allied troops were being withdrawn. By daybreak, about 2,300 men had been ferried across; the rest had to be abandoned. About 500 men were hidden by the resistance; some later rejoined their units. About 6,000 men — many wounded — fell into captivity, and 1,500 were laid to rest in the cemetery of Oosterbeek.

The battle of Arnhem destroyed any chance of a speedy Allied victory. Though a 60-mile salient had been carved into German-occupied Holland, the strategic object, the bridgehead over the Lower Rhine, had not been secured. The great river remained an effective barrier for six more months; neither the move to the Zuider Zee nor any attack against the Ruhr developed. The two main reasons for the failure lay in faulty execution of the landing, which took place too far from its immediate objective, and the weather, which prevented adequate reinforcement and supply. Both Montgomery and Student considered the weather a decisive factor. Many other incidental mischances, like the unexpected presence of S.S. armored units, repeated signal failures, and the slow advance towards Nijmegen, also played a part in the drama. The final word about it was spoken by Winston Churchill:

Heavy risks were taken in the battle of Arnhem, but they were justified by the great prize so nearly in our grasp. Had we been more fortunate in the weather, which turned against us at the critical moments and restricted our mastery in the air, it is probable that we should have succeeded. No risks daunted the brave men, including the Dutch Resistance, who fought for Arnhem.

After the war, an ugly story about betrayal of the Arnhem airborne landings circulated in Holland and England. It was claimed that the defeat was due to treason committed by a defector from the Dutch resistance, one Christiaan Lindemans. What is the truth of that tale?

Lindemans was one of those individuals whom the war carried along as a stream carries flotsam and refuse. A man of gigantic stature and strength, very vain and a great lady's man, he had originally worked at a garage in Rotterdam. After its destruction in 1940, he became a truck driver for the Wehrmacht and also a member of the underground. He took part in helping people escape via Belgium and France and became known in the resistance as "King Kong." However, his vainglorious behavior inspired little confidence, and he was therefore not greatly trusted. In March 1944, Lindemans' brother was arrested by the S.D. This, and his grudge against other resistance workers, made him change sides. He made contact with a Dutch V-man, who arranged a meeting between Lindemans and Lieutenant-Colonel Giskes of the Abwehr.* The latter had Lindemans' brother released, and "King Kong" started working for the German counterintelligence at good pay. Quite by accident, he was shot at, injured, and captured during a German razzia. Giskes had him "liberated" and Lindemans could then pose as a hero of the underground. He was instrumental in betraying two agents who had escaped from Haaren† and a number of other patriots. When the Allies occupied Belgium, Lindemans joined a unit at Neerpelt that was secretly sent to Eindhoven. On September 15 — two days before the start of "Operation Market Garden" — he passed through the Allied lines, was captured by the Germans, and

*See page 103.

†See page 108.

on his own insistence brought to Abwehr headquarters at Drie-
bergen near Utrecht. Here he told Giskes' subordinate, Kiesewetter, that an attack against Eindhoven was being prepared
and that paratroops would participate in this action. He did not
mention Arnhem, for he had no knowledge of the dimensions
of the subsequent Allied offensive. Kiesewetter seems to have
put little credence in Lindemans' story and sent him back to
Eindhoven. There is no indication that the Germans took any
action on Lindemans' report.

"King Kong" returned to Eindhoven, which was occupied two
days later by the Allies. Swaggering in the uniform of a Canadian Lieutenant Colonel, he raised the suspicion of a Dutch intelligence officer; but nothing was done about him for the time
being. Soon afterward, the man who had introduced Lindemans
to Giskes was arrested and confessed the whole story. This led
to Lindemans' capture. He was first shipped to England for interrogation, then extradited to the Dutch authorities who intended to try him for treason. The trial never took place. Lindemans fell ill at Scheveningen and was transferred to the prison
hospital. He still had a way with women and tried to escape
with the aid of a nurse, enamored of him. This attempt failed,
and the pair decided to end their lives by taking an overdose
of sleeping pills. This suicide pact brought death to "King Kong"
though not to the girl. Her life was saved by pumping out her
stomach.

The strange end of Christiaan Lindemans created some excitement and gave rise to the rumor that he had been the "traitor
of Arnhem." Some authors still maintained long after the war
that by betraying the full Allied plan this man had singlehand-
edly greatly prolonged the war.

CHAPTER FIFTEEN

The village of Putten lies on the road from Amersfoort to Zwolle in one of the prettiest parts of Holland, the Veluwe. Near that village, on the night of September 30, 1944 — a few days after the battle of Arnhem — a German car with four passengers was fired upon by a resistance group. One German officer was killed, a second one wounded and abducted by the resistance fighters. Two other Germans escaped. The injured officer was later released by his captors.

When General Christiansen was informed of this incident, he flew into a rage and shouted: "The place has to be burnt down and the whole bunch put up against the wall!" The result was that his chief of staff, General von Wuehlisch, sent the following order to the regimental commander in that region: "Shoot the guilty persons. Burn the whole village. Evacuate women and children. Arrest all men between 18 and 50 and deliver them to the S.S. for deportation." The commanding officer, Colonel F.W. H. Fullriede, was a soldier of good reputation and had no desire to play the executioner. He did not execute anybody, as the culprits were unknown. He had 87 houses burned, but spared the greater part of the village. Women and children were only briefly interned, then released. However, the arrest of the male inhabitants was carried out, and the S.S. transported them first to Amersfoort, then to a German concentration camp at Neuengamme. Of the 590 men deported, only 50 survived. The manner in which those unfortunate farmers came to their death has never been clearly established.

After the war, when the full impact of that terrible command was fully realized, all officers involved were arrested by the

General Christian
Christiansen
World War II
Collection of
Seized Enemy
Records, National
Archives

Allies. Von Wuehlisch took his own life in prison; Christiansen and Fullriede were tried by a Dutch court. The latter, who had carried out his task only halfheartedly, got off lightly. However, Christiansen was found guilty on three counts* and sentenced to 12 years in prison.

The tragedy of Putten illustrates the situation in Holland during the fall of 1944. The high officers, who ordered a whole village burned and its male population deported, were not professional mass killers. Christiansen was well liked by his subordinates and is described as a decent and good-natured person

*The Putten affair and the shooting of hostages on two occasions.

"incapable of inhuman actions." Von Wuehlisch had repeatedly opposed terror measures and was, therefore, hated and slandered by Rauter. How was it possible that such men signed their names to orders that the unwilling executioner, Fullriede, considered "inhuman?"

One reason was certainly the extreme nervousness of the German leadership. On the day of the first airborne landings, hundreds of thousands of leaflets had been dropped over Holland calling on the population to aid in the liberation. The proclamation began with the words: "The long-awaited moment has arrived." At the same time, the Netherlands' government-in-exile broadcast an order to all railroad personnel to lay down its work. On the next morning, almost all railway traffic came to a stop.

During the first four years of the occupation, the Dutch railroads acted on two principles: complete independence and regular traffic. The organization remained completely in Dutch hands, but the commands of the occupying power were carried out without fail. The railroads, highly centralized with more than 30,000 permanent employees, worked for the Germans. They, in turn, abstained from political interference, for their main interest was to keep the flow of transport intact. The railroad management refused to have anything to do with Dutch Nazi organizations, but for the rest its attitude was more pragmatic than ethical. The railroads efficiently transported Dutch workers, Jewish deportees, German troops, and immense quantities of loot to the Reich. Only two weeks before the Arnhem battle 5,000 political prisoners from Vught were shipped to Germany.

The concept of a massive railroad strike had been developed quietly in 1943. Management and personnel worked together on that project, and it was decided that an order for work stoppage from London would be promptly obeyed. In May 1944, all employees received one month's advance salary in case of emergency. The Germans ordered this money to be returned, and it was then kept in the safes of the station masters who were completely loyal to the railroad management in Utrecht.

Early in September, the British informed the Dutch government in London that a railroad strike coinciding with an airborne offensive would be desirable. After some confusion, the order was issued at 6 P.M. on September 17 while fighting was already in full progress at the river crossings.

On Monday, September 18, while American and German troops were fighting it out at Nijmegen, most railroadmen left the stations. Many assumed that the war would soon be over anyway. In two northern provinces, Groningen and Drente, the strike did not fully succeed, but only in a few border regions did the trains keep running. Of course, the Germans brought in their own railway personnel. Eventually, 5,000 of them worked in Holland, and about 500 became casualties.

When it became apparent that no fast decision had been reached at Arnhem, the strike nevertheless continued. Morally, it was a splendid act of defiance. The Germans could not break the strike, but replied with a food embargo that greatly contributed to the famine in the western part of the country. Many railroadmen went underground, and the German police was by then too overextended to chase them all, although there were a few arrests and executions.

In the words of a postwar inquiry, the strike was "a spectacular act of resistance of the Dutch people, an act whose psychological significance cannot be overestimated." This is certainly true. Those men who for years had obediently served the German war effort, much to the anger of the resistance movement, had finally delivered a solid blow in favor of the Allied cause and gained the respect of their countrymen.

Strategically, the railroad strike was of lesser importance because the Allied retreat at Arnhem changed the situation. During the first days after the airborne landings, lack of transport handicapped the German effort, but when the situation became more stable, it ceased to be decisive. Nevertheless, the London government urged that the strike be continued, and so it was, to the bitter end.

In some ways, the strike asked great sacrifices not only from the participants but also from the whole Dutch nation. On the day it began, hopes for a speedy German defeat were very high. Few people expected that the war in the Netherlands would go on for another eight months. When the Allied offensive came página

to a stop, it became necessary to aid the strikers financially. This was finally achieved after prolonged deliberations with the help of the N.S.F., which we have already mentioned as the banker of the resistance.* In the end, most employees received their full wages during the duration of the strike.

The food for the great cities in the western part of the country came mainly from the northeast. Furthermore, coal was a necessity, not only as a source for heat but also for electricity. The small amount of coal that came into the hands of the Dutch authorities had to be reserved for the public kitchens that were soon to feed the majority of the citizens in urban areas. The strike limited the transport from Germany to a few trains per week.

As reprisal for the strike, Seyss-Inquart prohibited all food transports from east to west for six weeks. This hunger blockade against defenseless citizens was finally lifted on November 8 at the insistence of two influential Dutch officials, H.M. Hirschfeld and S.L. Louwes. But by then it made little difference. The Germans had begun the final plunder of the Netherlands, and trains, rails, machinery, and all kind of equipment were disappearing rapidly toward the eastern border.

The last eight months of war in the Netherlands could have formed the original for Goya's famous etchings "Los Desastres de la Guerra."† But before describing that winter of horror, we have to return for a moment to Arnhem.

When the fighting at Arnhem and Oosterbeek ceased, the beautiful city and its suburbs were in ruins. On the sixth day of the battle, the Germans ordered the citizens to evacuate the whole area, and about 90,000 persons were driven westward and forced to leave practically all their possessions behind. When the battle ended, Arnhem was systematically stripped, and all movable goods were transported to Germany. Even Rauter was disgusted by this open act of robbery and forbade his subordinates to enrich themselves from the booty.

Rauter's position had undergone a change during these weeks. From July until the end of October, every remnant of process

*See page 152.

†The Disasters of War.

of law disappeared due to an order from Berlin: Persons apprehended in the act of sabotage were to be shot on the spot. If they were caught later on, they were simply executed by the German police without any form of trial. This gave a free hand to any local police commander. Rauter temporarily took command of an army group and did not devote much time to security affairs. Shakespeare's words, "I fear there will a worse come in his place" sound inappropriate when we consider Rauter's reputation and character. However, they came true as his deputy, Eberhard Schoengarth, was even more cruel and ruthless.

Seyss-Inquart once remarked that Rauter was "a big child with a child's cruelty." Other testimony and Rauter's own attitude at his trial rather show him as a dedicated hangman who had lost every conception of right and wrong and considered his occupation not only useful but highly praiseworthy. It is true, however, that he was an orderly person and punished corruption or thievery in his own ranks.

Schoengarth had been S.D. commander in Poland and was ordered to The Hague in May 1944, as his predecessor Naumann had shown himself a complete failure. Schoengarth, characterized by his subordinates as a very poor chief and possibly an alcoholic, left all responsibility to the local German police commanders. They received orders to act "with hardness, discipline, and moderation," but there was hardly any control, and the consequence was an orgy of butchery and arson. Schoengarth also introduced a new refinement: executions on public squares with a captive audience.

Of course, the resistance had become far more dangerous to the occupying power, now that the war was raging on Dutch territory. After the tragedy of the Englandspiel, both the Dutch and the British had learned their lesson. In London, S.O.E. had been reorganized, and a new Dutch intelligence service B.I.* founded. This office selected and instructed agents, and even before the Arnhem offensive, 33 had already been dropped in Holland. Radio communication was finally functioning, and small resistance groups began to specialize in certain tasks. Some

*Bureau Inlichtingen (Information Office).

transmitted political news; others sent out meteorological data for the Allied air forces, one even concentrated on the German V-weapons. Many agents were still caught by the Germans, but others continued their work. One particularly successful agent, P.L. d'Aulnis de Bourouill, was active for two full years until the liberation and set up three meteorological stations. This man also operated a transmitter with a 130-foot antenna, no small achievement as the German radio-spotting cars were always on the alert. As a nice aside, it must be mentioned that d'Aulnis established his transmitter in the house of his future father-in-law. That 34 of 43 B.I. agents were killed or imprisoned attest to the danger of this kind of work.

Droppings of arms and equipment were stepped up considerably in the autumn of 1944. Many of them were still lost because the planes often had great difficulties in finding the reception zone due to the misty haze that frequently lay over the Netherlands. The weak light signals were often impossible to detect. Of the arriving supplies, about one-third were discovered by the enemy, but slowly the underground became better armed, and acts of sabotage against the German communications multiplied. From the first day of the Allied offensive, the men of the underground gave their full assistance to the advancing troops. Many of these brave young men lost their lives, like Jan van Hoof, a student from Nijmegen, who sabotaged an explosive charge on the vital bridge over the Waal. He was shot a few hours later by the Germans.

We have given credit to the great efficiency of the Abwehr in the earlier years of the war, but in 1944, it was on the decline. Otherwise, the almost incredible blunder the Germans committed at Geertruidenberg would not have come to pass.

This small town in the province of North Brabant is the seat of a large power plant with its own telephone net. All normal telephone links were strictly controlled by the Germans, but this industrial communication had been completely overlooked. An underground organization, "Group Albrecht," took possession of this telephone service, and after the occupation of Eindhoven by the Allies, innumerable conversations were conducted with an intelligence post in that city. Geertruidenberg is strategically located just south of the big rivers and formed an excellent post of observation. For almost six weeks, until the small town's liberation by Allied troops, military information was constantly telephoned to Eindhoven. Similar telephone communications were also established with Nijmegen. But the Germans finally got wise to this rather simple manner of transmitting intelligence.

What was the activity of the government-in-exile, now that their country had become a theater of operations? Until the invasion, only the small Dutch navy and air force had actually been fighting the Germans. The light cruiser *Jacob van Heemskerk* took part in the Mediterranean war, and the destroyer *Isaac Sweers* was lost by submarine action. A number of smaller ships — some built in England — saw action in the North Sea. Of the large merchant fleet — about 800 ships — 50 per cent was sunk, with 3,000 casualties. The Princess Irene Brigade, Holland's contribution to the Allied armies, passed the Dutch-Belgian border on September 20 and took up the watch at the important bridge at Grave.

The hour had struck for a better coordination of the underground. Even in 1944, the resistance was very far from being a unified organization. Two years previously, a committee of five politicians sent a secret request to London, asking to be recognized as a sort of provisional government that would oversee the resistance. London refused. Four months later, this committee fell into the hands of the S.D.*

As the resistance consisted of many small groups, some political, others purely military or humanitarian, a true unification was almost impossible. Queen Wilhelmina had a strong preference for the men of the resistance as future leaders of a renewed, democratic Holland. Most resistance groups were jealous of their independence and individual merits. Those who were politically inspired, like the Communists, insisted on maintaining their separate identity. Other groups with strong religious motivation, also desired a degree of independence. Besides, contacts were dangerous for security reasons. In general, all these organizations had a limited sort of liaison, but there was

*See page 107.

no full cooperation. From 1943 on, a mixed group that called itself "The Nucleus" (de Kern) held regular meetings in Amsterdam. Technical and political questions were discussed, but its main effort was directed to a more efficient organization of the wartime struggle against the occupying power. However, since it did not function as a high command, the resistance remained a movement of many facets and convictions. By the autumn of 1944, it had almost become a "state in the state," with a press of its own, finances, food transport, and a modestly armed fighting force. Contacts ran in all directions, even to the German underground. At one time, van Heuven Goedhart, a prominent resistance leader, later minister of justice, held a conference with a German colonel by the name of Staehle, who took part in the conspiracy of July 20, 1944, against Hitler. On this occasion, the Dutch resistance learned about the fate of the Jewish deportees in Poland. Staehle was executed after the collapse of the plot against the Fuehrer. Van Heuven Goedhart managed to reach England and joined the government-in-exile.

Finally, a so-called contact commission was founded in which leading personalities from various groupings were active. The whole movement was divided into three great sections, more or less according to their political positions. That commission held its first meeting on July 12, 1944. The Germans were well informed about the whole setup. A memorandum of the S.D. that has been preserved shows a very complete and almost entirely correct review of all underground organizations. It is amazing that all these groups, with their numerous publications, still managed to survive.

The London government also appointed five prominent citizens, who would be considered as its representatives, as trustees. The appointment of these gentlemen took place in a rather unorthodox manner. The message was delivered through a paratrooper who carried it in the form of a microfilm in his cufflink. The five men were identified by code names; for example, Professor Cleveringa — known for his courageous attitude at the University of Leyden* — was called "Cleopatra." Eventually, this commit-

*See page 59.

186

tee was augmented by two more members. The task of these
men was to prepare the road for the future government of the
Netherlands. In the traditional Dutch manner, they planned
to have an orderly transition. In this, they were successful. When
liberation finally came, no major excesses occurred, and the
often-uttered threats of the "hatchet day" did not materialize.
Among the trustees was one future Prime Minister of the Netherlands, Willem Drees. He had already spent one year at Buchenwald and had also been arrested as a hostage.

We shall not discuss all the activities of the commissioners and
committees. Drees himself has described their actions and his
many adventures during the last months of the occupation.*
Those men had to work under strange and difficult conditions,
always under the threatening cloud of arrest and execution.
On "Mad Tuesday," the representatives had a proclamation to
the Dutch people ready and printed, but due to the change of
events, it was never distributed. The railroad strike made underground contact more difficult. Drees traveled repeatedly in
the company of a Dutch policeman who carried forged papers
that "proved" that he and his fellow traveler were working
for the Germans. The vehicle was an ordinary car that was
designated as a police automobile.

In September 1944, the London government established the
Netherlands Forces of the Interior (Nederlandse Binnenlandse
Strijdkrachten), most often simply called B.S. As mentioned
in an earlier chapter† armed fighting teams had so far acted
quite independently. The three main groups (O.D., R.V.V.,
and L.K.P.) were now integrated under the formal command
of Prince Bernhard. Later on, Colonel H. Koot was appointed
to direct the B.S. in the occupied territory. The internal organization was based on the so-called "delta," a triumvirate of the
chiefs of the three militant groups.

Notwithstanding all these improvements, the B.S. never became a real army. It still lacked heavy arms, and there was little
opportunity for thorough instruction. Organization remained

*W. Drees: *Van Mei tot Mei*

†See page 152.

somewhat shaky, due, probably, to a shortage of experienced field commanders. Collaboration with the Allies increased, and some units played an effective part during the last great offensive in the eastern Netherlands.

In the liberated areas, the B.S. acted as an auxiliary force to the Allied armies. One of its main tasks consisted in arresting members of the N.S.B. and other unreliable elements. This was necessary because the regular Dutch police was strongly infiltrated by pro-German elements. In some places, the hated policemen hardly dared to show their faces in the streets. However, the B.S. had never been trained as a police force, and the pent-up hatred for traitors and collaborators often prevented impartial investigations. In Maastricht, not less than 1,400 persons were immediately imprisoned and treated very badly. Many of them were undoubtedly guilty, but errors or personal animosities often led to unjust arrests. The general atmosphere of excitement and revenge was hardly conducive to fair and meticulous procedure. Very soon, there were conflicts between the civil authorities and the B.S., who were not overanxious to spare their former persecutors. That attitude is understandable after the horrors that were discovered in the liberated area. When the concentration camp at Vught was occupied, it turned out that the Germans had executed about 500 prisoners before closing the camp. The greater number of inmates had been shipped to Germany. Then the camp got new inhabitants: Dutch Nazis.

In the black summer of 1942, the actual resistance was a cadre of a few thousand dedicated patriots. By the fall of 1944, it had beome a mass movement. Two years of German terror and German defeats had brought a great change. Many people who had been too cautious or too indifferent in the past were eager to join. Collaborators who had gotten rich on Wehrmacht orders made generous gifts to the underground. Women who had been only too intimate with enemy soldiers were suddenly very anxious to offer hospitality to "divers." In the liberated parts of the country, many persons who had never been in the resistance and were mainly motivated by a desire to jump on the band wagon joined the B.S. Similar events have taken place in all formerly occupied countries and, last but not least, in Germany, where the ex-Nazi judge who sends the Nazi defendant to jail became a standing joke.

The prolonged war in the Netherlands placed the government in London before extremely complicated problems. Even in May 1944, a so-called legal agreement had been concluded with the Allies for the formation of a Dutch military government when Holland became Allied territory. At this time, nobody foresaw that the small country would be a theater of military operations for a duration of eight months. It was generally believed that the military government would merely be a brief interregnum. Major General H.J. Kruls was appointed chief of staff and transferred to Brussels shortly before the start of the Arnhem offensive. About 700 persons had been trained for future offices in Holland, but the first newcomers had neither transport vehicles nor typewriters. Kruls was a good organizer and a very independent character. He had no desire to let the London government interfere too much in a territory that was now a fighting ground. It took until December 1944 before the first Dutch ministers from London could enter Holland. The military government controlled all finances, and the poor ministers had to apply for money at the general's office. The conflicts between the military and the civilian governments soon led to a crisis that shall be described in a later chapter.

At the beginning of October, 1944, the Netherlands were in a situation that has few examples in history. By far the greatest part was still under German occupation and quickly reaching a state of economic collapse. The small Allied salient had two governments, one in Brussels and one in London, the latter for a time almost powerless. And the big battle was still to come!

CHAPTER SIXTEEN

The Allied position after the battle of Arnhem was far from favorable. What became known as the "Nijmegen corridor" was a 50-mile salient stretching from the Belgian border to the village of Elst, south of Arnhem. The first task was to enforce the narrow corridor, which was extremely vulnerable. Gradually, it was expanded until it was 20 miles wide. The important bridge at Nijmegen was damaged, though not destroyed, by German air raids and demolition charges.

Further to the south, the Germans were still in full control of the Peel, a bleak moorland area difficult to penetrate in the rainy season. North of the corridor the Germans still held most of the province of North Brabant, their main strength centered around the town of s'Hertogenbosch. On October 22, British, Canadian, and Polish troops began attacking this area with a pincerlike movement. S'Hertogenbosch was taken after three days of bitter fighting. Breda and Tilburg were also captured, and on November 4, the Allies reached Geertruidenberg at the river Maas.

A fearful drama took place at the small town of Heusden. About 190 citizens had taken shelter from the artillery bombardment in the ancient city hall. It was blown up without warning by a German demolition squad, and 134 persons hiding in the basement were killed. The exact circumstances of this senseless slaughter have never been fully explained. It is not clear why the building was blown up nor who was responsible for ordering the demolition.

On November 7, the Germans retreated over the Moerdijk bridges that their paratroopers had captured undamaged on the

189

morning of May 10, 1940.* This time the mighty span over the
Hollands Diep did not survive. The bridges at Heusden and
Keizersveer were also destroyed. The northern front then
stretched along the river Maas. It remained there until the end
of the war.

At the same time, a second Allied offensive was undertaken to
open the great port of Antwerp. The city, with its mighty docks,
had fallen undamaged into Allied hands. It was the biggest
harbor in Western Europe next to Rotterdam. At this time, the
Allies were dependent on Cherbourg and Arromanches, both
now far behind the front. LeHavre, Dieppe, Boulogne, and Calais
had been captured, but in a state of complete destruction.
Several other French ports were still in German hands.

Therefore, Antwerp assumed a vital importance. But the port
was unusable, as the Germans controlled the mouth of the
Scheldt. In order to open the harbor, it was necessary to clear
the shores of the estuary. On the left bank of the mighty river in
Zeeuwsch Vlanderen, stood the 64th German division under the
competent General Eberding. This front became known as the
"Breskens Pocket." The main position on the north shore was
the island of Walcheren, one of the strongholds of Hitler's Atlantic Wall. Its defender was Major General Doser, commanding
the 70th Division. Walcheren was the key of the German defense, which also included the South Beveland peninsula, connected with the mainland by a narrow isthmus.

Both parties were fully aware of the importance of the Scheldt
estuary. "At this hour the Scheldt fortifications play a decisive
part in our people's future," reads a German order of the day.
On October 9, General Eisenhower gave priority to the opening
of the approaches to Antwerp and wrote to Montgomery: "Unless we have Antwerp producing by the middle of November,
entire operation will come to a standstill. I must emphasize that,
of all our operations on the entire front from Switzerland to the
Channel, I consider Antwerp of first importance."

The task of capturing the approaches was given to General
Crerar's First Canadian Army. The whole operation was divided

*See page 34.

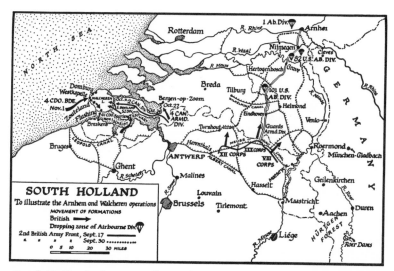

South Holland, showing Allied offensives in fall 1944. From *Triumph and Tragedy* by Winston S. Churchill. Published by Houghton Mifflin Company. Copyright 1953 by Houghton Mifflin Company.

into four separate actions directed against Zeeuwsch Vlaanderen, the Kreekrakdam on the shore of Brabant, Zuid Beveland, and Walcheren. It was undoubtedly one of the most difficult and complicated operations of the whole war. The offensive began on October 6 with a thrust against the Breskens pocket and a second move against the Kreekrakdam near Woensdrecht. The western shore of Brabant is fairly high and dominates the dike. After 10 days of fighting, the Canadians captured Woensdrecht, but only on October 24 did they succeed in crossing the isthmus. The South Beveland peninsula was then sealed off.

In the meantime, the Third Canadian Division launched a frontal attack against the Breskens position, which was later assisted by an amphibious landing in the right flank of the enemy. It was a bitter and frustrating battle in flooded areas, the men often waist-deep in water. The weather was bad, and during the first two weeks the air force was severely handicapped. Breskens fell on October 2, but the Germans still held the old Fort Frederick Hendrick, which was three times stormed by the Canadians and three times recaptured by the Germans. The fourth attack left it in Allied hands. Finally, the remnant of the German division that had fought so well was pressed onto Belgian territory and surrendered on November 3 near Zeebrugge, where the British had won another victory in 1918. Among the last men to surrender was Major General Eberding.

Meanwhile, the operations against Zuid Beveland and Walcheren had been started. The former was taken by land and by sea. Canadian troops advanced on the isthmus while the 52nd Scots Division was ferried across the Scheldt. The Germans then retreated behind the narrow Sloedam, which forms the only connection of Walcheren with the larger Zuid Beveland peninsula.

The Dutch population, which had to live for weeks under constant artillery and air bombardment, suffered heavy casualties. People lived in cellars and basements without electricity, often without water. In Zuid Beveland, the main water system was destroyed, and water had to be rationed, one quart per person a day! In one village, the Germans ordered evacuation, because allegedly somebody had signaled to the British. The column of evacuees was promptly attacked by the R.A.F., which mistook them for Germans on the march.

Of the German defense system, only Walcheren now remained. That island is invariably described as being formed like a saucer, and there is, indeed, no better description. The saucer's rim consists of sand dunes that secure it against flooding from the sea. On the western edge, there are no dunes, but the man-made West Kappelse Zeedijk, 30 feet high and 100 yards wide, protects the land.

The island had been made into one big fortress. Strong artificial defenses had been built, and about thirty batteries of artillery distributed over the whole area. Those of large caliber stood in concrete emplacements. Rail obstructions made airborne landings an unprofitable venture, not to mention land mines and antitank obstacles. The large guns could fire over a distance of 30 miles and gave considerable aid to the defenders of the Breskens pocket across the estuary. An attack by land alone across the Sloedam was almost suicidal. It is a narrow causeway without the slightest natural protection. The western end was heavily defended by artillery.

Walcheren's Achilles heel was the fact that the greatest part of the island is largely below sea level. If the rim were broken, the sea would stream into the saucer. On this geographical matter rested the Allied plan of attack. The Dutch government was not informed of the operation, but leaflets forewarned the population to leave the island. Unfortunately, this was impossible, as the Sloedam, the only tenuous connection with the mainland, was constantly under fire.

On October 3, the great dike at Westkapelle was bombed by the R.A.F. A gap of about 400 yards was smashed into its wall, and the sea poured into the breach. Two later raids created more breaks that were constantly widened by the tides. Walcheren was drowning, and many of the German bunkers filled up with water. The few towns that were above sea level were crowded with refugees. In Middelburg, the population doubled within a few days.

We have the description of an eyewitness of what happened on that day at Westkapelle. Forty-seven persons had fled to a windmill during the bombardment. The mill received a hit and collapsed while the water came pouring in from the breach in the dike. The 47 were pressed together under heavy beams, and the water was rising. Help arrived and tried to dig them out. Three were eventually saved; the others drowned miserably in the ruins of the mill.

Although Walcheren was partially inundated, the Germans were still far from beaten. Many of their heavy batteries were operating. They were placed on the saucer's rim and maintained a heavy fire against the attackers. The British decided to capture the island by specially trained commandos. After a vigorous artillery barrage, the first group landed at Flushing (Vlissingen) and took the town after two days of heavy fighting. But the main thrust was made at the gap of Westkapelle. This amphibious operation has almost become a classic example of landings under heavy enemy fire. The assault force embarked at the Belgian port of Oostende, and on the morning of November 1 — coinciding with the attack on Flushing — the lighthouse of West-kapelle came into view. The force sailed for the gap in the dike and scrambled ashore on both sides while the old battleship *Warspite*, a veteran of Narvik and Salerno, opened fire from her 15-inch guns. Two British monitors and a squadron of armed landing crafts joined in the bombardment. A planned bombing from the air had been canceled because of bad weather, but the landing troops were sustained by Typhoon rocket-firing aircraft. One commando group advanced toward Domburg; the second one ran into he fire of a powerful German battery that was embedded in a concrete emplacement. But now the Canadian artillery from across the Scheldt came to their aid, and during the night the battery was overpowered.

On the eastern tip of the island, the Canadians tried for three days to storm the Sloedam, but were thrown back again and again. On advice of the local B.S. commander, they made a new and successful attempt by land and by sea on the night of November 3. The German garrison was then under attack from all sides. While the Allied forces joined hands around the rim, the German main group retreated to Middelburg, which was packed with civilian refugees. The Allies were informed by a Dutch doctor who daringly canoed to Zoutelande that the Germans had no anti tank guns. Thereupon, an advance force of 100 men moved on to Middelburg in amphibious vehicles. General Doser decided to surrender the crowded city without any further fighting that would have meant a horrible slaughter of civilians. On the next day, November 8, the remaining Germans, pressed into the dunes, also laid down their arms.

The Scheldt estuary was in Allied hands, and minesweepers set to work to open the waterway. On November 28, the first Allied convoy entered Antwerp. Within a short time, 40,000 tons of materiel arrived per day, plus oil and gasoline. German V-1 missiles were then launched against the big harbor, but had very little strategic effect. Hitler fully realized that the opening of the great harbor was a mortal blow; the recapture of Antwerp became his final objective when the decision for his counter-offensive in the Ardennes was taken.

In the southern Netherlands, the Germans still possessed a

U.S. Paratroopers marching through destroyed Nijmegen

U.S. Army Photograph

powerful bridgehead on the western shore of the river Maas, south of the Nijmegen corridor. The British had advanced toward the river while the Arnhem battle was still in progress, but had been stopped by German Panzers at Overloon. Shortly afterward, an attempt was made to reduce this bridgehead by the 7th American Armored Division, which Eisenhower had transferred for that purpose to Montgomery's command. This attack failed, with heavy casualties. On October 12, a second attack on that front was launched by the British after a terrific artillery barrage. The Germans — mostly paratroopers and S.S. — resisted with utmost vigor. Overloon — the "second Caen"* — finally fell after

°Caen in Normandy. It was the scene of heavy fighting in July 1944.

a murderous infantry battle. It raged with particular fury around the little village of Venray, which houses a large insane asylum. The British troops, who finally entered the institution, found several hundred female patients in the cellars. Again the Allied offensive came to a standstill. It was renewed on November 14, and this time the Germans were driven over the Maas, except for a small but strongly fortified bridgehead at Blerik. Most of the German artillery was positioned on the other side of the river at Venlo. This bridgehead was finally eliminated on December 3 after an artful deception that warrants description. A number of loudspeakers, connected with record players, were placed in an area difficult to observe. They recorded the noise of riding tanks. The German artillery opened fire, thereby disclosing the positions of their camouflaged batteries.

On the morning of December 3, those batteries were drenched with a rain of shells. Then British flail tanks, followed by infantry broke through the German mine fields. In the afternoon, the Blerik bridgehead had ceased to exist.

The land west and south of the river Maas was then free. But no actions of greater importance took place in the Netherlands until the middle of January. The German offensive in the Ardennes* caught the Allies off balance and delayed all further activity on the front in Limburg. Although the German onslaught was eventually frustrated, it took about four weeks until the Allies were capable of renewing their attacks in the southern part of Holland. Even then only minor progress was made, and the liberation of the province of Limburg was only completed on March 1, 1945. For three months, this part of the country had been the stage of almost continuous fighting, and the damage suffered was immense. In Venlo and Roermond. the population — or what was left of it — lived for weeks in their basements while artillery fire and air raids ravaged their cities. There was neither gas nor electricity — nor proper water supply — and houses were often looted by German troops. In January,

*Better known as the "Battle of the Bulge" or the "von Rundstedt offensive." The latter is a misnomer. It was Hitler's personal plan. Von Rundstedt was skeptical about the outcome.

Dutch refugees riding on horsecart, after being ordered from their home town

U.S. Army Photograph

198

about 60,000 persons were evacuated to the northeast in unheated trains under the hardships of a very cold winter. However, the misery in the west, with its large cities, was even greater.

From October on, the situation in the densely populated provinces of North and South Holland* became tragic. The internal unrest can best be illustrated by the following, condensed excerpts of police reports at Rotterdam during a period of two weeks.

1. Two police deserters to be traced.
2. The corpse of an N.S.B. official has been found in a moat at Overschie.
3. A mail truck has been stolen at The Hague.
4. One of the chief officers of the labor service has been ambushed.
5. Six more policemen have disappeared and must be traced.
6. Two Dutch officials have been assassinated in reprisal of the murder of the N.S.B. member, mentioned under 2.
7. Two arrested men have been liberated by three armed persons during transport to a camp.
8. A man has been arrested in his home, after his own wife has betrayed him to the police.
9. Seven saboteurs from the town of Zwolle to be traced.
10. A citizen has been shot by a German soldier in the Maas tunnel.
11. A citizen has been killed by shots fired from a German military car.
12. The body of a N.S.B. police chief has been discovered in a ditch.
13. A citizen has been killed by two German soldiers. They claim he was under arrest and attempted to escape.
14. The house of an N.S.B. member has been burglarized.

These are the reports from just one area. The prisons were filled with men who were designated as "death candidates," an expression coined by Rauter. They were, so to speak, the reservoir for future executions. When an act of sabotage occurred, a number of

*This territory includes the cities of Amsterdam, Rotterdam, The Hague, Haarlem, and Leyden.

persons were chosen from their midst and executed, generally in public.

At the end of September, the systematic destruction of Dutch harbors was begun. Every day the citizens of Rotterdam and Amsterdam could hear the heavy explosions, that were destroying their once-flourishing ports. Cranes and dock installations were dynamited. The workers who were forced to take part in that scorched earth policy wept when they saw the pride of their cities fall into ruins.

On October 23, a German S.D. officer was shot and killed on the Apollolaan in the southern part of Amsterdam. Early on the next morning, 29 "death candidates" were dragged to the spot where the shooting had occurred and executed. In addition, two private houses at the corner of the street were burnt down. The inhabitants, who had not the slightest connection with the whole affair and were still in bed, had to leave their homes within seven minutes. Of course, they lost all their property. The practice of burning the homes of completely innocent persons was common among the local police commanders who were in no way restrained by their maniacal chief, General Schoengarth. However, shortly afterward, Rauter resumed his office as the highest police authority in the Netherlands and made a belated attempt to remedy the situation. The regime of Schoengarth had almost led to anarchy, for every little German police lieutenant took the law in his own hands.

During September and October, the Germans persistently conscripted civilians in the war zone for work at the front. Often, these pressed laborers had to dig while being exposed to Allied artillery fire. This type of conscription was undertaken, on the insistence of the Wehrmacht, for the building of defensive lines along the rivers Maas and Ijssel. In the German frontier area, the railroad system was more and more disrupted by air raids. Workers were urgently needed. In Hengelo and Enschede factories were surrounded, and thousands of workers dragged off. In other towns, for example in Venlo and Kampen, men were ordered to report for labor service under threats that hostages would be executed if the decree were not obeyed. In Kampen, the men stayed home, and three were actually shot as a warning to the population. A similar event took place in Apeldoorn, where the local commander even threatened to bomb the town. Ten men were executed, their bodies exposed on the streets. Schoengarth's "Polish methods" became daily routine.

We can dismiss Schoengarth as a ferocious bully boy, but the Wehrmacht had a certain motivation. During the disastrous campaign in France, the German army had been harassed continuously by the Maquisards. They also knew that in the liberated south the B.S. was already being formed into shock troops. There were 60,000 men of military age in the still-occupied Netherlands. The authorities seriously considered capturing them all and transporting them to Germany as forced laborers. This proved impossible, as such a measure would have required far more troops than were available. Furthermore, Rauter and Schoengarth were anything but enthusiastic about such gigantic razzias. They argued, quite logically, that such measures would drive the whole male population into the arms of the resistance.

On October 30, a secret conference took place in Hilversum at General Christiansen's headquarters. It was decided to arrest and deport all men between the age of seventeen to forty from Rotterdam, Amsterdam, and The Hague. The main responsibility for that order — of course, in complete contradiction to the Hague Convention signed by Germany — fell on General von Wuehlisch° that otherwise correct officer who seemed to have lost his head after the airborne landings. He had already proposed shooting all men who took part in the railroad strike. Rotterdam was chosen as the first object for a full-scale razzia.

On November 10, at 4 A.M., the unsuspecting population was awakened by the noise of German sound trucks repeating the command: "All men between seventeen and forty years of age are to assemble immediately in front of their houses. All other persons have to stay within." At the same time, leaflets with the same message were distributed. Persons who tried to re-

°After the war von Wuehlisch was first held as a witness, but gradually his participation in various illegal actions came to light. Faced with trial as a war criminal, von Wuehlisch committed suicide in 1946.

sist, escape, or hide were threatened with immediate death and their houses, with destruction. The conscripted men were promised good food, cigarettes, and pay and were admonished to carry warm clothes, strong shoes, and other necessities.

Most men were completely surprised by the German action and did not even try to escape, especially as the German troops frequently fired to intimidate the population. There was practically no resistance. About 50,000 young men were rounded up and marched to the east or transported under atrocious conditions on river barges. We shall let a Dutch woman tell the story:

> I have seen them march. We lived on the road to Gouda and after the "combing out" of that part of Rotterdam we noticed that the barricade at the bridge was removed. Everywhere you could see women carrying clothes or blankets. It was a cold, windy day with much rain. . . . Then the shout went up: "They are coming from the Hoflaan!" Indeed, if you looked into that direction, you saw the road crowded with a compact multitude of men. They moved slowly toward us, stopped, then started moving again. There was a deadly silence, you did not hear a word. Soldiers with their rifles in readiness accompanied the men on the pavement.*

Whenever such transports passed, they were followed by crowds of women who tried to say one last word of farewell to the prisoners. Sometimes young girls broke ranks, slung their arms around their boys, and marched with them until the German escort intervened. Shouts of "keep your chins up, boys!" and "Orange above all!" accompanied the marching columns. In many cases women attempted to supply their men with food and clothing. The German guards felt most uncomfortable among those weeping, shouting crowds and occasionally fired shots into the air to discourage demonstrations. Those tragic scenes went on for many hours as transport after transport was conducted along the roads lined with angry and desperate spectators. Only very few prisoners managed to escape during the march.

The whole procedure had a ghastly similarity to the Jewish deportation of two years ago. Here, too, the greatest part of the

*L. de Jong: *De Bezetting*, Vol. 5 (Querido, Amsterdam, 1965).

victims were too intimidated to resist. Many consoled themselves with the thought that the war would soon be over. Not everybody believed it, though! A bitter joke of those days tells of two Dutch boys standing in front of a firing squad. A German officer suddenly stops the execution. "Orders changed; we are going to hang them." One of the condemned men turns to his comrade: "They are losing the war. They lack ammunition!"

The razzia of Rotterdam caused tremendous excitement throughout the country. Most people believed — quite correctly — that others would follow. Many started looking for hiding places, preferably in their own house because it was obvious that the manhunt would start during a curfew. On November 21, it was the turn of The Hague. However, this time their success was a modest one; only 13,000 prospective slaves were captured. Many persons hid under floors or behind walls, even in closets. Some of the German soldiers showed no great eagerness for this degrading chase for civilians. Still, there was a great deal of shooting in the air, and many persons got frightened and surrendered. The usual abominable scenes occurred: parents forcing their sons to surrender for fear of reprisals; women whose husbands had been caught betraying other men out of envy or petty hatred. Others relied on German permits that were supposed to exempt the owner from labor service. Here, too, the parallel with the "privileged" Jews was obvious. The German authorities did not always respect such papers. However, the resistance was now better prepared for similar emergencies, and the falsification offices had a heyday. Sometimes men saved themselves by presenting false documents with a show of self-confidence. The Germans were too shorthanded to investigate every single case.

The author spent that day in a rather peculiar manner. At 7 a.m., German loudspeaker trucks started bleating out their message for all men below the age of 40 to surrender. The author's home at that time was a furnished room in a boarding house run by a somewhat eccentric spinster and mainly inhabited by older ladies and gentlemen. For days, a hiding place under the main floor had been prepared. Now the planks were removed, and the author crawled into the empty space between the sandy, humid ground and the wooden floor, carrying a blanket, candles, a little food, and a switchblade, the latter for ultimate emergencies. The hide-out was far from comfortable, approximately 25 inches high, so that the occupant could only assume a horizontal position. It was a cold, wet November day, and the dungeon was of course quite unheated. After about three hours, there was some commotion above, and the heavy steps of German boots were clearly audible. The house was searched, but as the other male lodgers were over forty years old, the enemy departed without carrying off any victims. The author's clothes had simply been placed in the closet of one of the older gentlemen who was approximatley of the same stature. However, the manhunt went on all day long and there was no certainty that the Germans would not return. So the author spent eight hours in that dark hole until the "all clear" was sounded by one of the ladies. Only then he ascended from the nether world, somewhat chilled from the cold, but none the worse for the experience.

The normal life at The Hague was disrupted for days. The public kitchens, which at that time fed many inhabitants, were closed. In the center of the city, hungry people attacked food stores and started to loot. The Dutch police were absent or helpless; and finally, the "green ones" appeared and opened fire on the looters. The once-civilized residence of royalty and diplomacy became the scene of riots that would have seemed fantastic years before.

In November 1944, The Hague gave the impression of a beleaguered city. German soldiers and green police patroled the streets. Younger men stayed in their houses, for nobody knew if the razzia would be repeated. The lack of food was already apparent; endless lines formed in front of grocery stores and public kitchens. From time to time, the thunder of the V-2 rocket rose over the city. At night, the giant flying torpedoes, with their fiery tails were a spectacular sight.

No great razzia occurred in Amsterdam. The Germans changed their tactics and returned to more bureaucratic methods. There were other exciting events. An accurate bombing raid destroyed the S.D. building in the Euterpestraat. The Dutch physicians once more raised their voices and accused Seyss-Inquart in an open letter of starving and enslaving a whole nation. They also warned that epidemics were now a serious danger. It was a cold, rainy, and very stormy fall, and sometimes the wind carried the sound of the artillery fire from Zeeland and Brabant to the large cities. There was no gas, no electricity, and no telephone. Coal was almost unavailable and reached fantastic prices on the black market. The people lived in fear of razzias, of air raids, of the icy grip of the winter that was now approaching, and, most of all — of hunger.

CHAPTER SEVENTEEN

The winter of 1944–45 is always referred to as the "hunger-winter." It was the most serious famine of World War II that occurred in Western Europe. The famine was concentrated in the cities, in an area of about three and one-half million people. The rural sections of the Netherlands were far less affected. There were shortages of all kinds, but the farmers did not suffer from starvation. Strangely enough, some regions in the immediate neighborhood of the front were far better off than the cities that were almost isolated from their bases of food supply.

In a sense, it was a man-made famine. After the start of the railroad strike, the German authorities simply refused to operate food transports to the west of Holland. When this reprisal was finally abandoned, the stocks that had existed in the larger cities were badly depleted. Furthermore, rail and port installations had been destroyed, and the razzias caused chaos and deterioration of services. Among the persons deported were also bakers, milkmen, and green grocers. Cars and trucks had been confiscated, and cyclists had to be in possession of a special permit. That these permits were forged in large numbers was finally noticed by the Germans, and bicycles were constantly confiscated in the streets — permit or no permit. River barges and other small craft were also mainly in the hands of the Wehrmacht. The result of this lack of transport was a steadily diminishing food ration. By November, it was down to 3 pounds of bread, 4 pounds of potatoes, and a little cheese of poor quality per week. There was no meat, no fat, no eggs, no milk, no sugar, and only few vegetables.

The Dutch government-in-exile foresaw the disaster when it

became clear that the war would continue through the winter. Prime Minister Gerbrandy asked the Allies to permit food transports to Holland, but his request was rejected. It was feared that the food would end up in the field kitchens of the Wehrmacht. He then turned to neutral Sweden and asked that food be delivered in Swedish ships. After two months of endless wrangling, the belligerents agreed to admit Swedish freighters at Delfzijl. The food would then be distributed under neutral control. However, for the moment, the agreement brought no relief; the Baltic was frozen and transport impossible. It took until the end of January for the first Swedish freighter to reach Delfzijl and then another month before the food was actually distributed. By then, people were dying from starvation.

On December 16, Gerbrandy made a desperate attempt to speed up the liberation of Holland by an appeal to Eisenhower. He wrote: "The Dutch Government cannot accept the fact that merely corpses will be liberated." On that same day, the Germans started their offensive in Belgium, and the Supreme Allied Commander clearly had worries of his own. Later, in February, Gerbrandy repeated his request and was kindly told by General Bedell Smith: "To comply with that most natural and justified request of the Dutch government is impossible. We have no troops for it, and the war may last until autumn 1945." Winston Churchill was much disturbed about the famine in Holland and suggested to General Ismay, chief of staff to the British minister of defense, that something should be done about it. But an attack on the western part of Holland had never been planned since the failure of the Arnhem offensive. Strategically, it was more promising to bypass the Netherlands and make the Ruhr and the north German plains the main objective. The loss of the Ruhr valley would then automatically lead to a collapse of the Reich, and Holland, Denmark, and Norway would fall without further fighting. It was also felt that a frontal attack across the big rivers toward the Dutch coast would be very costly and cause even greater hardships for the civilian population. The Germans were expected to inundate much of the area in case of an Allied offensive. This had already been done near Elst, south of Arnhem, where the water of the lower Rhine poured

through an open dike. This made a further advance toward Arnhem practically impossible. Another obstacle was the powerful
German position on the river Roer, stretching from Roermond
to Dueren on the German side of the border. This strong
bridgehead was a constant threat in the direction of Maastricht
and the important Allied base at Liège. During the German
offensive in the Ardennes, that bridgehead formed a constant
danger. Only at the end of December, with the force of their
great offensive spent, did the Germans slow activity in the sector. By then, it was too late for another German attack, but the
Allies had taken alarm and decided to destroy the bridgehead
before starting a major offensive on the Rhine. Bad weather made
this thrust impractical until the middle of January when the
ground was temporarily frozen. On January 31, the enemy was
finally pushed behind the river, and another small piece of
Holland was liberated.

In any event, the Supreme Allied Command was determined
to undertake no greater offensive in a northern direction before
the main natural obstacle, the Rhine River was crossed. The
Allied plan foresaw an assault across the great river in the
northern part of the Rhineland. Only then would the British
and Canadian armies turn north and advance into the Netherlands from German territory. Eventually, all German troops in
Holland would be isolated and forced to surrender.

This was certainly excellent strategy, but it meant a long delay. In the meantime, the still-occupied part of the country
was in the grip of a terrible winter. The decision to strike north
only after gaining access to the Rhineland was undoubtedly
correct. Strategy is rarely determined by humanitarian considerations.

Even in October it was obvious that new ways had to be
found to feed the urban population. For this reason, public
kitchens were organized. The citizens had to submit ration
stamps and received about one pint of warm food, mostly a potato and vegetable stew, with occasional small particles of meat.
Sometimes a hot cereal was substituted. For this meager portion,
people lined up on the cold streets, often in streaming rain, for
hours. The distribution of the food portions was handled by

208

city personnel, mostly bus and streetcar conductors who were otherwise unemployed. In Amsterdam alone 160,000 persons were fed every day by these public kitchens at 22 different places of distribution.

There is nothing as demoralizing as hunger, but it is also a force that gives birth to unexpected ideas. Suddenly, reports appeared in the daily newspapers about the great virtue of the sugar beet. It is true that for centuries it has been a source for sugar and syrup and can also be used for feeding certain mammals, for example, hogs. In any case, many citizens produced a sort of pulp from beets that was considered edible. One of the many disadvantages of this delicacy was an unpleasant feeling it caused in the throat. It gave the sensation of having swallowed thistles.

Another novel foodstuff was tulip bulbs roasted on the stove like chestnuts. They did not taste so bad, but easily led to indigestion. All kinds of strange concoctions, mostly of the gelatinous type, were also sold by former cafés and ice-cream parlors.

Needless to say, the black market flourished. Money gradually became valueless, but barter — the most ancient form of trade — made a remarkable comeback. Barbers offered their services for potatoes. Furniture, fur coats, and even jewels were bartered for food. Tobacco had also disappeared except for some home-grown varieties of a taste and scent that was absolutely obnoxious. Some people even tried to smoke tea surrogate — mostly dried strawberry leaves — in their pipes.

Thousands of other small necessities of life became unavailable. Textile and leather had completely ceased to exist, and many women wore shoes with wooden soles. Laundries had to close because of the coal shortage. Glass was so scarce that even empty bottles and jam pots became valuable. The newspapers became thinner and thinner, to nobody's regret, because of the paper shortage. The underground still managed to publish a number of bulletins and news reports; one illegal paper, *Trouw* (Faithful), printed 350,000 copies per day. They were helped by the American air force, which dropped its news reports almost every night. As there was no electricity in most homes, radios were often running on home-made dynamos.

The lack of electricity and coal forced most factories to close down or restrict production. More and more people became unemployed, but the constant hunt for food kept them busy. Most cities were without light, and the time-honored oil lamp made its reappearance. However, oil was scarce, too, and almost any available inflammable liquid — often stolen from chemical factories — became precious. In many homes, families sat virtually in the dark, with tiny wax candles their only source of light. People also learned to live without vacuum cleaners, pressing irons, and doorbells. Life seemed like a return to the middle ages.

But far more disastrous was the lack of fuel. Except for those who had a hidden reserve of coal or coke, the cold was almost unbearable. The west of Holland is not rich in wood, and proper firewood was only available on the black market or by barter. Some people, in utter desperation, gave their last warm socks and gloves for a few fagots. Soon, men, women, and children went to the parks — those beautiful, well-kept Dutch parks — and cut down any tree in sight. Later, they often found out to their disappointment that the fresh sappy wood gave no heat. But there was still another untapped reservoir: the abandoned houses. In The Hague, these were mainly small homes in the coastal area that had been evacuated when the Germans started building their Atlantic Wall. Officially, this was a restricted area, but the soldiers on guard had no stomach for chasing the desperate crowds away. They broke into the empty houses and battered down doors, beams, and windowsills, even whole staircases. Serious accidents were common, as ceilings and stairs often collapsed under this ruthless and slovenly despoilment. In Amsterdam, the old Jewish quarter, now completely abandoned, was thoroughly wrecked. In all cities, wooden blocks between the tram rails were torn out of the ground. These solid pieces of lumber gave a few hours of heat. A number of new emergency stoves were constructed that were supposed to heat a room with very little fuel. They were also used for cooking, as nobody could afford maintaining two different fireplaces. In many ways, the cold was even worse than the hunger. The very poor even burnt their own furniture. The urban population had already been undernourished for years and had little resistance. Older men or women frequently collapsed in those endless lines in front of food stores or public kitchens. Mortality in January 1945 almost doubled that of 1944. It rose especially among small children and older persons.

The rising demoralization was clearly visible to every observer. Baker's carts had to be protected by policemen for fear of looting. Black marketeers sold food on Amsterdam's streets at incredible prices: one loaf of bread — 100 gilders,* one package of margarine — 50 guilders. Dutch girls sold themselves to German soldiers for a few cans of pea soup with sausages. Starving children begged for bread in the streets. Even the terrible Schoengarth was moved by their misery. There were still butchers who sold meat to their customers, but it was wiser not to inquire too closely where this meat came from. A great number of cats and dogs mysteriously disappeared from the streets. Meat of that sort was identified as "roof rabbit."

The once-clean Dutch cities deteriorated. Refuse lay in the ravaged parks. The sanitation department lacked transportation, and the streets became very messy. Vermin multiplied in the filthy houses; rats were in great abundance. They were large and quite fearless, as if they knew that they were secure in the dying cities. The long-neglected sewers could not absorb the water; it poured out of the conduits and formed large, evil-smelling pools in the streets.

Even coffins became scarce because there was hardly any lumber left. Corpses remained unburied for days. In Amsterdam, the Zuiderkerk was changed into a morgue. The dead were laid to rest in cartons or blankets. In the cemeteries, the hungry, weakened burial crews could hardly cope with the growing harvest of death. The somber scenes so often depicted by medieval painters and sculptors, the dance of death, turned into reality. Ghastly quarrels occurred among the gravediggers, who accused each other of laziness.

A Dutch writer describes Amsterdam in the hunger winter as follows:

*1 guilder = $0.27

Memento mori.° Wherever you look, those two words seem to become visible. They floated in the gutters filled with feces, which rose from the cesspools of nonfunctioning sewers. They lay on swampy gaps between train rails, whose former lumber blocks have ended up in stoves and furnaces. They hung in the black, gaping voids of houses, demolished from basement to roof, as if ravaged by termites. They lay in the smelly refuse in parks and groves. They stood above the entrance of an old church, where corpses, nibbled at by rats, were kept because there were no caskets and no transport to the cemetery. Gates, lightpoles, and neon signs were covered with rust. The soil itself seemed to change into swamp on which that city once had been built. Stone and lumber showed the sickly sores of contagion. And on the streets of the rotting town walked shapes of hungry, dying people; their places on the cold stone floor of the old church were waiting. Decrepit dogs scavenged among the heaps of waste; their spindly bodies showed protruding ribs like steel rings on a motor block. But greedy fingers had already plucked anything edible from the heaps. Children with swollen bellies walked barefoot on shrivelled legs and death stared out of their hollow eyes. The women had lost all their grace and attraction, they were tired, ugly, and dirty. The girls looked waning, the men weak and exhausted. This whole generation seemed never to have been young, to be born in a half dying state. They were only shadows of the living, creatures made of mist, mildew, and microbes.†

As winter progressed, the starving city dwellers swarmed into the countryside to forage for food. They trekked through rain and snow in the icy-cold wind toward the farms in the hope of bartering their property for food. Those who still had bicycles or carts were a little better off, though many had to ride without rubber tires. Others dragged baby carriages or sleighs, anything that could serve as a vehicle. Not a few collapsed and were carried home, dead from hunger and exhaustion. The best chance for food was in the northern provinces of Friesland and

°Remember death!

†M. Dekker: *Josef duikt* (A.W. Sijthoff's Uitgeversmaatschappij N.V., Leiden, 1946).

Groningen, but the long distances made those trips desperate ventures, especially in January when a long period of snow and ice set in. Roads and dikes were often inundated, and a howling storm from the northeast chilled the trekkers to the bone. The farmers had little interest in money, but were generally willing to barter. Many showed only moderate compassion for their starving countrymen and drove hard bargains. Their closets were filled with linen, blankets. china, and jewelry. One farmer asked for a golden ring for 20 pounds of potatoes. The most unlikely objects, from tablecloths to shaving brushes, were offered for wheat, peas, beans, and bacon. We shall again let an eye witness speak: "The endless road behind Hoorn* was filled with fearful, anxious, hungry Amsterdamers. They stumbled along, towing carts and carriages. Some dropped along the road, they couldn't go any further and had no strength left. Women who had accompanied their sons or husbands sat now on the carts. And they were whipped by the wind and drenched by the icy, streaming rain."

Some farmers were helpful, but others felt uncomfortable and refused to deal with all that sudden influx of starving humanity. There had never been a very close relationship between them and the urban population. Boards and signs that read "No bartering" appeared on some farmhouses. Inns and restaurants in the rural areas were mostly closed, and the unfortunate trekkers had to walk mile after mile without even a cup of hot "Ersatz Coffee."

On all the major roads stood the C.C.D.,† the controllers of food distribution. They were entitled to confiscate food transported by private persons. Many of those men were no better than the hated home guards and even more corrupt. People who had traveled for days under the most trying circumstances were frequently robbed of the food they had acquired at great sacrifice. The confiscated goods ended up in the home of the C.C.D. officials.

At the beginning of October, the official food ration in oc-

†Crisis Controle Dienst, an organization to control food transport.

*A town in the north of Holland on the Ijsselmeer.

cupied Holland amounted to 1,400 calories. Three months later, it had dropped to 500. This was considerably less than the rations in the German concentration camps. Many people suffered from hunger edema, which led to ghastly swelling of the legs. Tuberculosis was on the rise, and persons suffering from malnutrition became easy prey to pneumonia and other diseases; 15,000 Dutchmen died of hunger and cold in that last and most horrible winter of World War II.

That hungry, freezing, and tired little nation was exploited to the utmost. In The Hague, the inhabitants were even forced to supply clothing for the German army, whereby soldiers went from house to house. Some of them found the job disgusting and closed their eyes. The action was not repeated in other cities. That the once proud German Army had to engage in legalized plunder perhaps made the initiators of that order hesitate.

Far more serious was a constant drain on manpower. The Germans organized a new system of labor draft, a kind of legalized razzia. Just before Christmas, a decree was published ordering all Dutchmen between the age of 16 and 40 to register within a period of three days. This new measure differed radically from the previous efforts to mobilize manpower. The Germans knew that to rely on Dutch authorities would be futile. Therefore, they used largely their own personnel. The draftees were promised good food and decent treatment, but by December 1944, only an extremely foolish and naïve Dutchman would trust such promises. This new labor draft* was considered extremely dangerous by the resistance. The conditions in Holland were by then so bad that many men obeyed the decree out of sheer hunger and desperation. The government in London reacted sharply and warned employment agencies and employers alike against furnishing the Germans any information. There were still 650,000 men of the critical age group in Holland. If the Dutch just refused any collaboration, the Germans would find the task of registering and deporting all these men almost impossible. The

*The Germans called it the "Liese action." Liese was Dr. Goebbels' representative in the Netherlands. His task was to integrate the country into the total war effort.

men of the resistance — hungry, cold, tired, but determined — fought back with the utmost resilience. In Amsterdam, one registration office was burnt down, another was bombed. But far more decisive was that the great majority of Dutchmen simply refused to register. The bitter lesson had finally been learned. Seyss-Inquart tried to convince the Dutch by one of his hypocritical speeches that they had to cooperate. At the same time, terror was once more "the order of the day." No young man was really safe in those months, he could always be arrested at any time, at his home or in the streets. If he could not present an exemption, he was either deported to Germany or put to work on the fortifications in the eastern Netherlands.

Nevertheless, the whole action failed. About 50,000 men were registered, but only a few thousand were sent to Germany. A greater number was forced to work on the Ijssel line, which the Germans were building in the eastern provinces. It was in that area where an Allied offensive was expected. It eventually came, but from a completely unexpected direction.

CHAPTER EIGHTEEN

During the rainy, dismal fall of 1944, the three southern provinces of Holland — Zeeland, Brabant, and Limburg, — were liberated. They were still in the front line and far from secure. At
the end of December, while the "Battle of the Bulge" was still
raging in Belgium, the Germans crossed the Bergsche Maas and
formed a new bridgehead. It was eliminated by Canadian and
Polish troops after a whole month of fighting. A second, similar
action by the Germans took place on the Maas, north of Venlo,
and was only repulsed after a bitter battle in a heavy snowstorm.
As we have already mentioned,* the dangerous bridgehead that
threatened Maastricht had also been destroyed by the end of
January. Only in February did the Allies start a massive offensive
from the Nijmegen area.

Life in those freed provinces was still difficult, though there
was no famine. A coal shortage existed because the production
of the mines in Limburg was still very small. General Kruls' military government did its best, but it had never been prepared for
those problems that multiplied every day. Actually, the whole
area ranged under the Supreme Allied Command, whose approval was necessary even for minor measures. The Dutch
government in London was in no position to help effectively.
Five of its ministers had been transferred to the Netherlands,†
but their influence was almost nil. Besides, conflicts caused dis-
turbances within the government. Queen Wilhelmina had no
great desire to maintain a cabinet that had been formed under

*See page 207.

†See page 188.

U.S. truck on a war-torn street in Maastricht

U.S. Army Photograph

completely different conditions and did not meet the emergencies of the present situation.

The five ministers resided in a hotel in the small town of Oister-wijk, somewhat to the north of the Belgian frontier. The men of the resistance regarded them with indifference. On one occasion, Mr. van Heuven Goedhart, the Minister of Justice, entered an office in which a number of B.S. troops sat around a table with their feet on top of it. When he introduced himself as the head of the justice department, they remained in this position and paid very little attention to him. The attorney general in Brabant almost immediately got into a serious conflict with the former resistance movement and had to leave his office. The minister of interior affairs was fired because of a radio speech that seemed to condone collaboration. Later on, the whole cabinet resigned and Prime Minister Gerbrandy formed a new government that was more to the right. One of the new ministers had played an important part in the long-deceased Netherlands Union.* It also included several men from the now liberated provinces. This second cabinet of Gerbrandy functioned until after the complete liberation of the Netherlands.

As the Netherlands had no army to speak of, they were bound to remain a junior partner among the Allies. By the winter, there were only about 4,000 "shock troopers," drawn from the ranks of the B.S., plus the Princess Irene Brigade. The larger part of the B.S. served as auxiliary police, but was neither trained nor armed for combat duty.

A very limited contact with the occupied parts of the country began. North of the mouth of the Bergsche Maas lies the Biesbos, a water maze of small islets very difficult to control. The same underground team "Group Albrecht" that had maintained the telephone contact with the Allies at Geertruidenberg conducted regular crossings in that inaccessible area. Arms, transmitters, and medicines passed from the Allied zone into occupied Holland by way of small boats and canoes. The crossings were always undertaken at night, not less than 400 during the last months of the war. The Germans were aware of those clandestine movements, but they could not watch every small water way. In January 1945, all inhabitants were evacuated from that area, but still the crossings went on. One intrepid river pilot, A. van Driel, took part in 53 crossings until he was caught and executed just five days before the German surrender. A great number of military reports were sent across the Biesbos to the Allies and proved their value when the Canadians started attacking the Ijssel Line. Very precise plans with 21 drawings were made of the German fortifications at Zwolle, passed on to "Group Albrecht," and finally smuggled through the lines.

Activities of this kind made the Dutch underground most valuable to the Allies. To fully appreciate this risky work, it must be

*See page 51.

218

realized that the railroad strike complicated matters considerably. Without trains, trucks, and cars, the resistance had to rely on courier services, most of them composed of young women. One group, which called itself with wry irony "Rolls Royce," established a real itinerary between Amsterdam and The Hague. All the work was done by girls on bicycles. They were in less danger of being controlled by German guards, and ladies' bicycles were rarely confiscated.

During the icy-cold January, the German offensive in Belgium had been stopped, and by the end of the month, the enemy was back where it had started on December 16. Now it was the Allies' turn. The first move was made by the First Canadian Army, which had been quietly concentrated around Nijmegen. On February 8,

U.S. Airborne Infantry advancing in Gelderland

U.S. Army Photograph

a terrific barrage from more than 1,000 guns was directed against the Reichswald, a forest area that stretches east of the Dutch border. After one of the most bitter battles of World War II, the Allies penetrated the big forest and reached the German town of Goch, one of the cornerstones of the West Wall. But no actual breakthrough was achieved; 11 German divisions positioned in the narrow strip between Rhine and Roer resisted to the utmost.

Farther south, the Ninth U.S. Army under General Simpson had also started operations, but the Germans destroyed the largest of the Roer dams. The whole area was flooded, and the offensive had to be delayed until the river subsided. Then the American infantry began crossing in assault boats. While the great mass of Germans was still involved with the Canadians, the U.S. infantry overran the enemy positions. and Simpson's engineers laid bridge after bridge across the Roer. On February 25, American armored cars were rolling toward the Rhine. They had by then reached flat country, without natural obstacles, traversed by many excellent roads. Rundstedt saw the disaster coming and asked the Fuehrer to permit a general retreat behind the Rhine. For two days, Hitler did not even deign to reply; than he briefly answered that such a move was out of the question.

Meanwhile, the last towns and villages of Limburg were freed by Canadian and British troops. An enormous Bailey bridge — the biggest in Western Europe — was thrown across the Maas at Gennep. A small group of German paratroopers put up a desperate defense at the old castle of Bleijenbeek until the R.A.F. smashed it with 1,000-pound bombs. On March 4, British and American troops joined hands at Geldern, and the last Germans along the Maas were forced to surrender. The dreadfully battered towns of Roermond and Venlo, which had so long been in the battle zone, were finally free.

The Reich's position had become desperate. The eastern front was in a state of collapse. Russian troops stood at the Oder no more than one hour's motor drive from Berlin. A large German army had been completely surrounded in Latvia, and only pockets of resistance survived in East Prussia. Another mortal threat had developed on the south eastern flank. After a long and bitter siege, Budapest fell on February 13, and its defenders were com-

U.S. Infantry in position in Limburg

U.S. Army Photograph

pletely annihilated. In Italy, too, the German defense was dis-integrating. Hitler did not know it, but one of his most trusted S.S. Generals, Karl Wolff, had already secretly decided to make contact with the Allies concerning an Italian surrender. Germany itself was reeling under the repeated blows of the Allied air raids. Under such circumstances, no government of reason would have continued the war, but Hitler, far from even considering sur-render, clung to the puerile hope that the Allies would quarrel at the last moment. Therefore, he ordered the West Wall to be held at all costs. On many points, the German army still resisted with vigor, but weak spots began to appear rapidly. "The willingness to fight has given way to resignation and apathy," wrote the com-manding general of the Cologne area.

But in the occupied part of the Netherlands, all these develop-ments seemed remote. The daily struggle for sheer survival continued. In the first week of March 1945, two events took place that spelled death and disaster for many families.

For weeks the Allied air force had been attacking the rocket sites and storage places of the V-2 around The Hague. This diabolic missile was the curse of the city. Many rockets exploded in the launching area, and some crashed directly in the heart of town. On every occasion, there were victims among the civilian population; constant glass damage added to the misery of many families, as it became almost impossible to heat the windowless apartments. During the month of February, air raids were so frequent that most citizens paid little attention to them. Few persons bothered to seek the protection of air-raid shelters. In previous years, the Germans had driven the people from the streets, sometimes even with shots, but by now nobody seemed to care. Then, on March 3, a great disaster occurred.

Out of a gray sky bombs came raining down on the Bezuidenhout, a densely populated district of The Hague. Large fires broke out and thousands of panicky people fled into other parts of the city. More than 500 persons were killed. Innumerable families lost all their possessions, which under the present miserable circumstances often meant more hunger and more cold. The bombardment had been intended to destroy the rocket sites, but because of faulty navigation, residential areas were devastated. When Churchill heard of it, he angrily denounced "the extraordinarily bad aiming which has led to this slaughter of Dutchmen." The attack had no direct effect on the rocket sites. They stopped functioning a few weeks later when the Germans ran out of rockets.

The second drama occurred on the night of March 6 at a place called Woeste Hoeve, north of Arnhem. A small Dutch action group planned to get hold of an automobile. They stopped an open B.M.W. car on the road, and both parties fired at each other. Finally, the B.S. men, retreated, leaving the car on the road with no less than 243 bullet holes. They did not realize that they had fired on Rauter, the "High Lord Executioner," and his staff. In the morning, Rauter was found in his car seriously wounded, but still alive. He was destined to die by Dutch bullets four years later. For the time being, he was brought to a German hospital where he was later apprehended by British soldiers. Rauter's deputy, Schoengarth, then engaged in an orgy of revenge. Altogether, more than 400 persons were executed as reprisal; 117 of them were dragged to the place in which Rauter's staff car had been ambushed and shot right there. The firing squads were working overtime; executions took place in Amsterdam, Rotterdam, and Utrecht. In all cases, the bodies were exposed on the streets until the next day. In Amsterdam, 36 men were shot in front of a waste dump at the Weteringplantsoen. Some courageous person later spread a Netherland tricolor over the corpses. The spot is now marked by a monument.

Bombed by their own Allies, executed or deported by the Germans, and dying of hunger and cold — such was the fate of thousands of Dutchmen in that last phase of the war. The resistance lost in those months some of its dedicated members. Among them was Jan Thijssen, one of the most active leaders of the Resistance Council and Walraven van Hall, the organizer of the N.S.F.,* banker of the resistance.

Those losses were particularly hard because at that time the resistance had to care for about 300,000 persons who lived underground with forged documents. This is without doubt the most impressive achievement of the Dutchmen who fought Hitler. They never represented a great military force, but each man, woman, or child saved in this manner is a living monument to their unbreakable spirit. Many families who had not enough food for themselves still managed to help "divers" whom they had taken into their homes. Often, just the poorest citizens showed the greatest compassion. The public kitchens were a new complication. A family often had more mouths to feed than its official members, a fact that could easily become known to neighbors or distributing personnel. Not all such persons were always trustworthy. Among the "divers" were quite a number of Allied pilots or paratroopers who had been stranded in Holland after the Arnhem battle. Some well-documented stories of persons in hiding are fantastic. One farmer managed to hide a group of Jews so well that a five-hour search by the German police proved

*See page 152.

unsuccessful. The slave-hunters threatened to return and burn his place. Thereupon, the Jews offered to leave during the night. The farmer replied: "The Lord did not save us today from the enemy to deliver us tomorrow into his hands." The Jews remained on the farm and survived the war.

The reign of terror was still riding high in the streets, but the force behind it, the Third Reich, which according to its leaders would last a thousand years, was crumbling. The great mass of the German people and its soldiers were still trusting the promise of some "miracle weapons" that would suddenly turn the tide. In fact, these grandiose new arms existed only on paper. It is true that about 1,000 new jet fighters were produced, but because of lack of the specified fuel, only a handful got off the ground. Of Admiral Doenitz' novel electro-U-boats, only two were put to sea. The chances for constructing atomic missiles had been lost when American bombers and Norwegian resistance men put the plant at Vemork in Norway out of order. The heavy water, the atomic fuel produced at Vemork, was sent to the bottom of Lake Tinn with its transport by a sabotage group. The truth was that the Germans were so desperately short of arms that when the Third U.S. Army crossed the Rhine at Oppenheim, there were only five tank destroyers to oppose it.

The German soldier still fought on, but General Blaskowitz — of whom we will hear more later on — found it necessary to decree "that all soldiers who announce themselves as stragglers looking for their units will be summarily tried and shot."

The beginning of decomposition was also felt in the Netherlands. A conflict over the home guard broke out between Mussert and van Geelkerken, who was nominally the Dutch commander of this worthy legion of cutthroats. When Rauter tried to use the home guards for combat duty, Mussert protested and asked van Geelkerken to resign. He refused, and the Dutch Nazi leader dismissed him from the party. However, the Germans ignored Mussert and kept van Geelkerken in command. During the last weeks of the war, several hundred home guards mutinied against being used for front-line duty. They were briefly interned at the concentration camp Amersfoort and finally released, with the promise that they would only have to fight the "enemy within."

Hitler's strategy — to fight for every inch of ground — had led to a very peculiar situation. In the east as well as in the west, the Allies stood on German territory. With the Allies on the Rhine and the Russians at the Oder, there were still large German armies on foreign soil. Not less than 30 German divisions were cut off on the Kurland peninsula, where they could do practically nothing and had eventually to surrender to the Russians. Other large inactive forces were in Denmark and Norway, where no fighting was being done. In the Netherlands, the Germans still numbered 118,000 men. Not all of these troops were of the best quality, but they still formed a disciplined fighting force.

The Nazi empire was also being threatened from two more directions. In Italy, Hitler foolishly had ordered General Kesselring to defend the plain south of the river Po, an extremely ill-chosen position. The Allies had complete mastery of the air and could strike almost anywhere at will. Even more serious was the Russian thrust toward Austria. Hitler had thrown eleven armored divisions into Hungary to save Vienna at any price, but except for a slight delay, they achieved next to nothing.

During the first week of March, the Germans on the western front suffered one blow after another. On the right flank, the Americans reached the Rhine near Düsseldorf, and Cologne was captured on March 7 against a weakening resistance. On the same day, troops of the First U.S. Army, to their own surprise, found the railway bridge at Remagen still standing and captured it in a bold, swift action. Hitler, in a rage, deposed Rundstedt (such actions seem to have become a habit with him) and had four officers shot as scapegoats. Ironically, it had been Runstedt who had counseled an orderly retreat behind the big river and had been rebuffed by the Supreme War Lord. Consequently, a speedy disaster overtook all troops that had remained on the western bank. The time was then ripe for the decisive assault in the north, the long-delayed action against the Ruhr valley.

An enormous concentration of artillery and an advance guard of 80,000 men was to be hurled forward. The main blow was to fall on the early morning of March 23. News of the great offensive was given to Hitler while he was discussing a number of very futile questions with his staff. The records of the meeting show that Hitler at this decisive moment had nothing better to do than to debate the value of Indian and Russian "volunteers" — of course quite valueless — and the desirability of cutting down trees in the Berlin Tiergarten for building a landing strip. At about the same time, from a hilltop near Xanten, Winston Churchill was watching a stream of 2,000 aircraft carrying two airborne divisions across the Rhine. This time the error committed at Arnhem was not to be repeated. Within four hours, the paratroopers linked up with ground units.

In Holland, hungry but hopeful men listened anxiously to their hidden radios. On April 1, the momentum of the Allied offensive became clearer. The British marched into the so-called Achterhoek and took the industrial town of Enschede. Finally, the liberation was under way.

CHAPTER NINETEEN

For five years the Dutch had looked to the west for their liberation. Hardly anybody had expected that the country north of the great rivers would be freed by an offensive from the east. During the winter, an assault across the rivers had seemed likely, but this front had remained in the state of almost complete inactivity. Except for occasional evacuations, life in the many villages and small towns along the rivers Maas and Waal was compartively quiet.

In fact, the Netherlands were now only a secondary front. The full force of the Allied offensive struck right at the heart of Germany. Three days after the start of the attack, a dozen bridges had been thrown over the Rhine, and armored divisions streamed into the bridgehead. Meanwhile, the Americans had taken Darmstadt, Frankfurt, and Mannheim. In desperation, the Germans tried to destroy the fatal Remagen bridge by V-2 rockets launched from The Hague. Eight missiles were fired against the target, but all went astray.*

With both Rhine flanks shattered, Hitler ordered Field Marshall Model to defend the Ruhr as a fortress. This was hardly realistic as there was not even enough food for the large number of soldiers and civilians surrounded in that area.

While the second British Army moved into northern Germany in the direction of Bremen and Wilhelmshaven, two Canadian army corps turned North into the Netherlands. They overran German resistance at the Twenthe Canal and seized Almelo

*The bridge did actually collapse on March 17. By then, four U.S. divisions were over the Rhine.

U.S. supply depot at Maastricht

U.S. Army Photograph

on April 5. A second offensive developed in a more westerly direction, and on the same day, the river Ijssel was reached after a fierce battle. The next obstacle was the town of Zutphen, which was fanatically defended by German paratroopers. After three days of house to house fighting, the badly damaged town was in Allied hands. The fortifications along the Ijssel that had been built during the winter were then attacked from the rear. Deventer and Zwolle were taken and it became quite clear that a northern thrust to isolate the Netherlands from Germany was well on its way.

A change took place in the German command on April 6. General Student and his staff were ordered to Germany to organize defenses at the river Weser. Christiansen, who was no field commander, was replaced by General Johannes Blaskowitz, who had so far commanded Army Group H at Emmerich and Wesel. Blaskowitz drove hastily into Holland via the Afsluitdijk, and the west of the country was declared a fortress area.

Blaskowitz was a capable military man of the old school. He had protested against S.S. brutality in Poland and was no favorite of the Fuehrer. Notwithstanding his dislike for the Nazi regime, he remained loyal to Hitler. In the last four weeks of the war, as Commander of the 25th German Army, he showed himself an energetic and ruthless leader.

While the Canadians began to move in the direction of the North Sea, another attempt was made to capture Arnhem and outflank the Germans by an advance toward the Ijsselmeer. However, this time no effort was made to force the heavily defended Lower Rhine. The whole area was covered with artificial fog, and a feigned frontal attack was made against the old battlefield of Oosterbeek. But the real blow came from the opposite direction. On April 13, the 49th Canadian Division crossed the Canal of Pannerden and, thereafter, the river Ijssel. The attack on Arnhem was made from the east, and after heavy fighing in the center of the town, it was finally occupied on the next day. It was completely empty, a devastated ghost town.

Meanwhile, a large pontoon bridge was prepared at Nijmegen and dragged to the Ijssel. Farther up the river, new crossings were made, and the important road center of Apeldoorn attacked. The first assault was repulsed by S.S. troops, who executed a number of resistance men before evacuating the town on April 6. Fortunately, the B.S. succeeded in informing the Canadians of the German retreat before a heavy bombardment of the town was opened. The apparent threat to cut German communications forced part of their troops to a hasty retreat. They managed to flee in boats from the small harbors of Harderwijk and Elburg. The rest retreated along the big road to Amersfoort and through the Veluwe forest area. This latter column ran straight into the staff of a Canadian armored division. There followed a confused battle. Staff officers, cooks, chauffeurs, and other personnel held the Germans in a desperate struggle until the Irish Regiment of Canada came to their aid and finished the Germans

ted suicide. On the same day, the Red Army reached the great highway to Berlin. The end of the Third Reich was only weeks away.

But what to do about Holland? Those few weeks could mean the death of many thousands of undernourished men, women, and children. The denouement came from a completely unexpected side: from Arthur Seyss-Inquart.

The Reichskommissar had visited Berlin and returned with orders to inundate the Netherlands if necessary and practice a complete scorched-earth policy. However, the Vienna Quisling had other ideas. Loyal as he was to his masters, he fully realized that the war was lost. But did wars not frequently end with negotiations? Was diplomacy not a better weapon than destruction? For five years Seyss-Inquart had served the Fuehrer assiduously. He may very well have hoped that peace might bring for himself not the end of the road but promotion. His ideas were not quite unjustified because in Hitler's last will and testament Seyss-Inquart was appointed Minister of Foreign Affairs. He never actually got the job, and his ultimate fate would have been no different if he had received the coveted advancement. But this is mere hindsight, and Seyss-Inquart seems to have felt that the time had arrived to show himself a great diplomat. Even during the winter he had toyed with the idea of neutralizing the Netherlands. Now he decided to seek contact with the Allies.

The man to whom Seyss-Inquart disclosed his plans was, perhaps, the most remarkable personage in the Dutch administration: Dr. Hans Max Hirschfeld, secretary-general of the department of Agriculture and Fisheries and the Department of Commerce, Industry and Shipping. Hirschfeld, like his colleague K.J. Frederiks, had remained in office because he stubbornly believed that he could serve his country by doing so. This was bound to lead him to a certain degree of collaboration. He saw things mainly from the economic viewpoint. A cool-headed man of unquestionable ability, Hirschfeld was respected by his staff and the Germans alike. The latter wanted to use his talents and ignored the fact that the Secretary General was not a full Aryan. He was often and not without reason attacked by the underground press. After the war, he received an honorable discharge, later served in other government functions. He also appeared as a witness at Seyss-Inquart's trial at Nuremberg.

On April 2 — the Canadian offensive was just starting — Seyss-Inquart invited Hirschfeld for a talk. Very cautiously, he hinted at the possibility of a separate surrender. If the Netherlands could be isolated, he — Seyss-Inquart — might act independently. Hirschfeld passed the information on to Bosch van Rosenthal, Chairman of Trustees of the London Government.*

In greatest secrecy, further discussions took place with Seyss-Inquart and the German plenipotentiary for South Holland, Schwebel. Of course, the Dutch government in London was informed of these negotiations. The clandestine meeting between German authorities and Dutch trustees went on for 10 days. General Blaskowitz maintained that he would only take part in a general surrender of the Wehrmacht. On April 12, Seyss-Inquart repeated this view but declared his willingness to prevent further destruction and to open the port of Rotterdam for food transports, provided that the Allies would stop at the Grebbe Line. The representatives of the Dutch government considered this concession important enough to send two men from their ranks to the liberated territory for discussion with the Allies.

The two emissaries, J. van der Gaag and L. Neher, met at first with Seyss-Inquart. It was a strange meeting. Both men were very active in the resistance, and van der Gaag had secretly been in Allied territory during the month of January, a fact of which Seyss-Inquart was well aware. Accompanied by Schwebel, they left on the same day for Gorinchem, where the N.S.B. mayor took them for important Nazis. Van der Gaag proceeded to a German outpost at the Merwede and rowed across the river wearing an Allied uniform. Of course, the German soldiers thought him to be one of their intelligence agents. He contacted Prince Bernhard, who ordered a one-hour cease fire and made it possible for the second emissary to follow his colleague. The men were then flown to London. They presented the problem as follows:

*See page 185.

Either a large airborne action against all important dikes and locks in Holland or an armistice that would make it possible to feed the starving population. Gerbrandy put the question squarely to Churchill: Can the Netherlands be freed until the end of April? We shall quote Mr. Churchill's reply, which was given in a letter dated April 19, 1945:

My dear Prime Minister,

I should not think there was any chance of the clearance of Western Holland being accomplished in any relation to the date you mention, namely April 30. In any case it would be marked by fighting and inundation and the destruction of the life of Western Holland.

I am however sending your letter to General Eisenhower who, I understand, is not unfavorable to the course you originally proposed.

The question also arises in view of what you say about Seyss-Inquart's untrustworthiness whether we should not now make him aware that his 100,000 officers and men, including himself, unless he flees like a coward, are in our grip and can certainly be placed high on the list of identified war criminals.

In view of the somewhat undecided character of your letter, I am suggesting to Mr. Eden in Washington that he should endeavour to have the whole matter put into General Eisenhower's hands.

With deepest sympathy for you and your much-harrowed country,

Believe me
Winston Churchill

Six more days passed until Eisenhower wired Seyss-Inquart that negotiations on feeding Holland by airlift could begin. In England, large stores of foodstuffs for the intended airdrop were prepared.

In the meantime, the negotiations between Seyss-Inquart and the Dutch representatives had leaked to the underground and caused considerable criticism. This was understandable enough. For years, the Allies had declared that the only terms they would accept from the Nazis were unconditional surrender. Meetings and disscussions with the hated Reichskommissar were considered unprincipled and repulsive. Violent protests appeared in several underground newspapers. The anger of the "illegality" was increased because Blaskowitz ordered the inundation in the north while negotiations were already in progress.

Of course, the underground leaders and the Germans did not know that a large-scale offensive in the western Netherlands was not planned by the Allies. Americans and Russians had met on the Elbe river and cut the fast-shrinking Reich into two parts. This coincided with the fall of Bremen. In Italy, surrender negotiations were in full progress. Berlin was encircled by the Russians, and Hitler's rats were scurrying to leave the sinking wreck. S.S. Chief Himmler — Hitler's "treuer Heinrich"* — was making overtures to the Allies in the incredibly naïve hope that he of all people would be acceptable to them as a new head of state.

Under such circumstances, a major offensive in Holland that would cause enormous destruction and loss of life made very little sense. Churchill saw the situation quite clearly and had already indicated in a letter to Roosevelt, dated April 10, that Holland was a distressed area, to be saved by a determined relief action.

On the other side of the fence, Seyss-Inquart was now practically free from control by Berlin. He declared his willingness to permit relief from the air. Dropping zones were indicated, and a meeting for further negotiations was to be held at the village of Achterveld, just within the Allied frontline near Amersfoort. The war in the Netherlands had reached its last phase.

*Loyal Heinrich.

CHAPTER TWENTY

For all those who lived in the occupied Netherlands during World War II, Sunday, April 29, 1945, will always remain an unforgettable date. It was the first day of the great airdrop, the day when the Allied planes came to the aid of a starving nation. The author will describe the event as he experienced it himself at the village of Waardenburg on the river Waal, only three miles behind the German front line.

Only a few days earlier, that area had been shelled by the British artillery during the fighting at Hedel.* The riverbank bristled with German antiaircraft guns, and the village was occupied by a detachment of paratroopers. The day was sunny and clear. Around 10 o'clock in the morning, there was a steady drone of many approaching bombers. When we looked up to the sky, we observed squadron after squadron of Lancasters and Liberators. They flew so low that the pilots were clearly visible. It was a unique moment. For five years, Allied planes had been watched with both hope and fear. This time they carried no bombs. But perhaps the most remarkable fact was that the German guns, which used to greet even single fighter or observation planes with their shells, remained silent. The gunners stood at their usual positions, but their orders were not to fire. Most of them were pale and nervous, and one of them raised his fist to the sky and shouted: "Those damned things up there!"

The radio had announced that relief planes would be coming, but the message was met with doubt and disbelief. Who had ever heard of planes dropping food parcels in territory occupied by the enemy? The Germans would never permit it!

*See page 233.

But now it had come true. Hundreds of planes passed very low over our heads. The whole population stood on the streets waving and shouting. Many were crying. And one excited exclamation was heard again and again: "Now we shall soon be free!"

The relief negotiations were held at a school at Achterveld. Eisenhower was represented by General Bedell Smith, Montgomery by General De Guingaud. Also present were Prince Bernhard and a Russian officer. The German negotiators arrived by car, were stopped at some distance from the meeting place, and proceeded on foot under a white flag. Both parties had brought their experts for organizing the relief work. Seyss-Inquart was accompanied by the Dutch food commissioner Louwes. The two emissaries who had returned from London, Neher and van der Gaag, were also present.

A few days earlier, the B.S. had captured a Mercedes that belonged to Seyss-Inquart, and Prince Bernhard had used this car to drive to Achterveld. The German prince-turned-Netherlander and the Austrian ex-lawyer in his German uniform gazed at each other with hatred and comtempt. To Seyss-Inquart's anger, the prince remained seated when the Reichskommissar entered the room.

Discussion started, with the participants facing each other at a large table. Again, Seyss-Inquart rejected unconditional surrender, because such a step would hurt him in the final judgment of history. An argument began between him and Bedell Smith and the latter impatiently exclaimed: "Come on, speak up! You know you will be shot anyway!" Seyss-Inquart replied "That leaves me cold." Whereupon the American scoffed, "It certainly will!"

The final agreement regarding the delivery of food was signed on May 2 while the airlift was in full operation. Ten dropping zones were designated, and truck convoys were to be admitted into occupied territory at Rhenen. The port of Rotterdam was kept open for three freighters loaded with supplies, and small craft were to transport additional food via the rivers and the Zuider Zee. The unofficial truce, which had been in effect since the last engagement at Hedel, was to be continued during the whole relief action.

The situation in Holland was certainly a most peculiar one. The population of the big cities stood on their roofs and balconies and cheered the Allied planes. For weeks, people had lived on two slices of bread per day and a few frost-spoilt potatoes and vegetables. The Dutch radio in London warned the populace "to avoid premature demonstrations," a message that most listeners found very strange. Thousands had already greeted the British aviators with Dutch flags. But the green police kept riding with helmets and machine guns through the streets of The Hague and Amsterdam.

Mussert had been in northeastern Holland and just narrowly escaped over the Afsluitdijk. He then came back to The Hague. He still had his car and gasoline, but the mousetrap had closed behind him. His military passport had expired, and he did not dare to apply for a new one because he was now on very bad terms with Seyss-Inquart. Finally, he resigned himself to the inevitable and remained in his office. From his window, he could see the Gevangenpoort, the medieval prison gate with its tower.

On May 1, the world was informed that Hitler was dead. As some wit put it: "He announced that he had fallen, fighting to the last breath." The communiqué was false, for the Fuehrer had already died the day before by his own hand. Admiral Doenitz, rather to his own surprise, found himself President of the Reich, which by now had almost ceased to exist. He started his brief reign with a hollow speech in which he once more tried to create trouble among the conquerors. He implicated that if the Allies continued to fight, they would do so "solely for the spreading of Bolshevism in Europe." He also appealed to God, whom the Germans for the last two centuries have always considered a sort of trusty retainer who is told to intervene when things go wrong.

All German troops in Holland were sworn in to obey the new head of state. This ceremony was performed with a great show of military discipline.*

Blaskowitz urged his men to "close ranks" — whatever this

---

*Doenitz reign was of short duration. On May 23 he was arrested as a war criminal. He was informed of his fate by a Dutch captain who served with the British at Flensburg, Germany.

meant at this last hour. In the meantime, Field Marshal Kesselring's armies had surrendered in Italy, and German resistance in Berlin was collapsing. Montgomery, only weakly opposed by General Blumentritt's depleted army, was nearing the Baltic port of Luebeck. Immense crowds of German refugees were fleeing westward to escape the advancing Red Army.

Doenitz then decided to act. The admiral was politically naïve and still lived under the illusion, long-nurtured by Nazi propaganda, that one Allied power could be played against the other. The poor man was to suffer some disenchantment. Planning to surrender northern Germany to the British while still holding off the Russians, he sent Admiral von Friedeburg to Montgomery's headquarters on the Lueneburger heath, 30 miles southeast of Hamburg.

On the morning of May 3, Doenitz' emissaries presented themselves at Montgomery's trailer. The Field Marshal, at his arrogant best, eyed them cooly, asking: "Who are these men? What do they want?" He must have enjoyed that visit immensely.

Von Friedeburg, accompanied by three other officers, advanced and offered the surrender of three German armies that were opposing the Russians, but were now in full retreat. Montgomery declined and told him to surrender to the Soviet army. Friedeburg started arguing, but Montgomery again refused and said: "Will you surrender to me all German forces on my western and northern flanks, including all forces in Holland, Friesland with the Frisian islands and Helgoland, Schleswig-Holstein, and Denmark? If you will do this, I will accept it as a tactical battlefield surrender of the enemy force immediately opposing me and those in support in Denmark." Friedeburg, who had not expected this attitude, declared he had no authority for such surrender. Montgomery shrugged and showed him the battle situation on a map. It was unconditional surrender or continuation of the fighting. The admiral was told politely to have lunch and reflect on his problem. The German officers were conducted to a separate tent. Friedeburg sat down and cried.

Their spirits did not rise when, after the lunch break, Montgomery delivered an ultimatum: no discussion without unconditional surrender in the areas he had named. Details of occupation and care of civilians would be determined later. They finally agreed to send this message to Doenitz and Field Marshal Keitel. Montgomery let Friedeburg and a second officer go back to Flensburg by car and held a press conference on the afternoon of May 4. During this procedure, Friedeburg's return was announced. The Field Marshal was so sure of acceptance of his terms that he asked the correspondents to attend the proceedings that followed. After seeing Friedeburg alone, he and the other German delegates were taken to a tent. Montgomery read the Instrument of Surrender and repeated his ultimatum. The Germans signed without further argument. Hostilities were to cease on Saturday, May 5, 8 A.M. Montgomery proceeded to prepare messages to his armies, the navy, and the air force in personal, colorful style.

This was factually the end of the war in Western Europe, though the full surrender of the remaining German forces was only signed on May 7 at Rheims.

In Holland, the great news was announced on the evening of May 4. Though only few radios were still functioning because of lack of electricity, the news spread immediately from house to house. The people celebrated in the streets. In Rotterdam, wooden trafffiic signs of the Wehrmacht were torn down and burnt. But the Germans still acted as if nothing had changed. The green police repeatedly opened fire on demonstrators. As late as May 7, a real battle took place at the Dam in Amsterdam in which 22 civilians were killed and several hundred wounded.

On May 5 Seyss-Inquart announced that an armistice was in force, but threatened that the German authorities would suppress demonstrations by force of arms. This was his last proclamation in the Netherlands and, like so many earlier ones, a complete falsehood. Only a few hours later, General Blaskowitz signed a surrender document at Waageningen. The ceremony took place at a small hotel with General Faulkes, Commander of the first Canadian Army Corps acting for the Allies. The Germans were ordered to collect their own weapons and to remove land mines. The next days passed in great confusion. Incidents between German troops and civilians were frequent. The author and several other people very narrowly escaped execution after a minor scuffle between B.S. and paratroopers.

The Germans were desperate and trigger-happy, always ex-

Field Marshall Bernard Law Montgomery
Office of War Information, National Archives

pecting to be ambushed by the resistance. In the presence of the author, a sixteen-year-old boy was almost shot because a search party found a hand grenade in his closet. It turned out to be a harmless souvenir without charge of explosive. The sergeant leading the group was slightly drunk and completely shaken by recent events. Fortunately, one of his men kept his head and examined the worthless weapon before firing at the boy, who had been placed against the wall and kept shouting defiantly "shoot, shoot, you fools, shoot!" Finally, the sergeant released him, muttering angrily "those damned partisans!"

The British and Canadian forces were slow in coming; in some areas, a very uncertain situation prevailed for several days. Conditions sometimes bordered on the absurd. Small groups of sparsely armed B.S. took over gigantic ammunition dumps.

It is to the credit of the Dutch population that the often-predicted "hatchet day" never took place. The members of the N.S.B. were rounded up, but there were neither lynchings nor massacres. Mussert, Blokzijl, and most other party leaders were arrested without much ado; only Rost van Tonningen jumped to his death from a window. Van Genechten later hanged himself in prison. Imprisoned Nazis were treated with comtempt, but excesses were rare. A number of girls who had been intimate with German soldiers had their heads shaved. By and large, the population acted calmly; to some observers this attitude after so many years of terror and deprivation, seemed almost unnatural. A British brigadier-general, M.B. Jenkins, watched a group of German P.O.W.'s marching through the streets of Utrecht. He noted that they were completely ignored by the inhabitants. However, there was sometimes bitterness because the German P.O.W.'s got more rations and cigarettes than the liberated civilians.

The attitude of the German soldiers was mixed. Of course, many were simply glad that the war was finally over. But the more fanatical Nazis adamantly refused to admit that they had lost. Years of propaganda had completely destroyed their common sense. A noncommissioned officer told the author in all seriousness that the capitulation was just a temporary one. The troops would be sent back to Germany and rearmed, and would fight on against the Russians. Probably, some German officers spread such rumors intentionally to keep the diehards quiet. Some very strange things occurred in the P.O.W. camps. On one occasion, a German camp commander had two deserters executed — the Canadians accommodated him by supplying the rifles for the firing squad. Seyss-Inquart submitted quietly to arrest; he seemed confident that not too much would happen to him. In this expectation, he was wrong. He was tried as a war criminal in Nuremberg, convicted, and hanged. Schoengarth was caught by the Canadians at Scheveningen. The arresting officer was astonished that so savage a killer looked "like a very innocent young man." Rather ironically, Schoengarth was never called to account by a Dutch court. It turned out that he had murdered an Allied aviator at Enschede, and for this crime — a mere trifle compared with the mass slaughter he practiced during his reign of terror — he was sentenced to death by a British military tribunal and hanged. Schoengarth, like his predecessors Harster and Naumann, was little known to the public at large; his full responsibility was only realized much later. Some of the worst war criminals of the Third Reich were faceless, unapparent persons. Adolf Eichmann, the organizer of the "final solution," was a name totally unknown to Netherlanders during the war years.

Rauter had been apprehended by British troops in a German hospital in which he was still recuperating from his injuries. He was extradited to the Netherlands and transported to Scheveningen in an ambulance. Because of the long and complicated investigation, it was not until April 1948 that he stood trial at The Hague. Rauter defended himself with great vigor and a flood of oratory spiced with all the old, shopworn Nazi phrases. He was found guilty on seven counts of the indictment and sentenced to death. He appealed on various legal grounds. The higher court confirmed the sentence after permitting Rauter to make a long speech in his own defense. It was noted that he constantly quoted from the writings of Jewish law experts, mainly on questions of international law. One of the judges remarked sardonically that Rauter would gladly have destroyed the men whose legal opinions he now offered for his protection. A further request for revision was denied and another one for clemency rejected by the crown. On March 25, 1949, the man who had been the main instrument of Nazi terror in the Netherlands died in the same manner as so many of his victims: in front of a firing squad.

But this all happened later. Following liberation, the Dutch people — tired, hungry, and somewhat bewildered — resembled a patient who leaves the hospital after a long and painful illness. Men who had been in hiding for months, sometimes for years, were back in the streets and often found it hard to get used to their new life of freedom. Political prisoners were released, and thousands of conscripted workers began slowly to re-enter the country of their birth. Due to the almost complete destruction of the railroad net, it was a slow and cumbersome repatriation. Small groups of pale, sick, emaciated people started to return from the concentration camps. Most of them had horrible stories to tell. Some came home, only to find that their whole family had disappeared. A Dutch doctor described their condition — much later, in 1964! — as follows:

> Perhaps you have met somebody who has been in a concentration camp or has been hiding for years in an attic. Perhaps he is difficult and a little strange in his habits or has certain characteristics which belong to the concentration camp syndrome: He is irascible, sometimes given to dark moods, cannot carry on a normal conversation without suddenly forgetting his subject. Sometimes he wants to be alone, and then again he needs company. A narrow room, like for example a telephone booth, will oppress him and make him scared; he can't even sit in a movie house. After a drink, even a glass of beer, he becomes intoxicated. Also he may not be able to consume coffee. He is always tired, sometimes cries without reason, perspires even without previous exertion. This is by no means a complete list of all symptoms.°

The liberation brought many small consequences that are quite unthinkable in a normal society. A newspaper published a list of children with description and name — sometimes not their true name. Where are the parents? Returning workers or P.O.W's found their houses demolished, their jobs gone, and

°Dr. J. Kater: *Algemeen Handelsblad.*

their wives entertaining Canadian soldiers. No wonder many had great difficulties readjusting.

Undoubtedly, some people had painful and disappointing experiences, especially brave resistance workers who quickly found that connections could be more valuable than actual merit. Others who had trusted their property to friends or neighbors found it gone with the wind. The hardships of the hunger winter had greatly lowered ethics. People who normally would not take a newspaper without paying for it helped themselves liberally to the property of others. But there were also heartening incidents. The author shall never forget his wonderful landlady — mother of two small daughters — who not only returned everything that had been left in her attic, but also blushingly confessed:

"I took one jar of jam, the children were so hungry" *Grandeurs et misères d'une victoire!* There were moments of enthusiasm and deep gratitude when Allied troops finally marched through the streets of The Hague and Amsterdam. There was Queen Wilhelmina's speech on the first day of the liberation:

> Our language has no words for what goes on in our hearts in this hour of liberation of all the Netherlands. Finally, we are again master of our house and hearth! The enemy, from east to west, from south to north is defeated. The firing squad, the prison, the torture camp have disappeared. Gone is the unspeakable oppression by the persecutor, who for five years has tormented you. Gone is the horror of famine.

The ceremony at The Hague was particularly moving. The representatives of the London government and the newly reinstated mayor S.J.R. de Monchy° stood on the stoop of City Hall and Bosch van Rosenthal read a proclamation which started with the words, "The Netherlands have regained their freedom." Tragically, the speaker had just recently been informed that his brother had been killed. When the Princess Irene Brigade marched into The Hague, a Jewish girl, still wearing the yellow

°See page 50.

star, advanced and handed a bouquet of flowers to the burgo-master. He removed the star among the cheering of the crowd.

Other sights were far less glorious. Food and cigarettes, drop-ped from the skies appeared quickly on the black market at outrageous prices. The number of prostitutes seemed suddenly to have multiplied. Many Dutchmen saw their otherwise well-behaved sisters and daughters turning into very easy conquests for the smartly uniformed liberators. As in all countries that had been under occupation, the gratitude of the female population took forms that were not always appreciated by their families. The Canadians could be generous with cigarettes and chocolate bars that added to their persuasiveness, much to the aggravation of many Dutch boys who could offer no such enticements.

For many, the liberation, and the strange manner in which it eventually took place, was a sort of anticlimax. Of all Western democracies, the Netherlands had suffered the hardest fate. In Belgium, liberation had been achieved in a few days of relent-less advance France had at least the pride and satisfaction of knowing that its own sons had effectively taken part in the mili-tary struggle. Also, large regions had hardly been touched by the war. In Norway and Denmark, the Germans surrendered without prolonged fighting. In Holland, eight months of military operations on the ground, heavy air attacks, and the frightful famine had taken their toll. The terrible strain of the last months had broken the spirit of a great number of persons who had to live in a constant chase for the barest necessities of life.

A Dutch writer, perhaps too pessimistic, expressed his feel-ings on the liberation as follows: "The spirit is sick, ethics are rotten, the chaos is far from having changed to order. The recup-eration, the decomposition of poison which has eaten into our soils and made them spongelike, will take a long time."

The feeling of disenchantment, most common among former resistance men, was of course partly due to the fact that suddenly, as if by magic, the enemy, the great rallying point, was gone. Though war is terrible, it also provides a great deal of drama and adventure. For the Dutch, who had lived placidly for so long in their clean little country, it was a unique experience. The author happened to meet a former comrade from the resistance a few months after the liberation. This young man, a member of the police force, had been a very courageous underground fighter. Now he was back in the normal routine of duty in the sleepy little town of Delft. "What kind of life is this, giving out summons for minor infractions of the law? What boredom! Wasn't the war wonderful?" The author left the former hero, who disconsolately went on directing the small-town traffic on an almost empty street in a provincial town. Indeed, the great days were gone! Normalcy would return, there would be no knock at the door from the green police, no air armadas thundering through the clouds, and listening to the radio was again a harmless, mostly boring pastime. Politicians began already to squabble; businessmen were taking inventory and wondered when they would again do business with Germany. On the market square of Delft, the peddlers sold flowers, vegetables, and rabbits. At the nearby church, a memorial service for executed L.O. men was taking place. Canadian soldiers, hoping secretly to return soon to Calgary, walked by with their girls. Suddenly, the war seemed terribly far away — an unlikely, absurd, endless nightmare. Somewhere a street organ struck up the "Wilhelmus," the Dutch anthem, followed by the still popular "Old Tough One." But nobody paid much attention to it.

The Netherlands was at peace again.

EPILOGUE

The Netherlands survived World War II not without honor. Small as their contribution to the total Allied effort was, the brave struggle of the resistance, the sacrifice of the navy and merchant marine, the record of the Princess Irene Brigade, and many small individual actions deserve recognition. These and the generally decent attitude of the civil population overshadow the ugly treason of the N.S.B. Unfortunately, every country under German domination had its quislings and collaborators, just as ancient Greece had her Ephialtes and the United States her Benedict Arnold. Modern history, with its ideological party lines cutting through nations and loyalties, has many more examples.

Basically, the political, social, and religious entity of the Netherlands remained intact. The prewar condition of parliamentary democracy returned as soon as the worst consequences of the five-year ordeal were over. Even the loss of the colonial empire, the fact that, of course, was not realized in 1945, proved to be less damaging than originally expected. The struggle in Indonesia, which continued until 1950, added a further burden to the nation's recovery. However, it can be assumed in the light of events in Asia that the East Indies would have sooner or later become independent in any case. The Japanese occupation and the condition of Holland after the war hastened the course of events.

The history of the Netherlands during World War II is characteristic of the tragic situation of small nations overcome by the advent of forces they cannot control. Because of the long preceding period of peace and relative welfare, the nation seemed particularly ill prepared for a struggle against a regime that considered violence a way of life. Even with better military organization, that fight would not have been successful in 1940. The inner strength, the fanatical will to defend every inch of ground, was lacking. In 1672, William III of Orange had declared: "My country is in great danger, but there is a sure way never to see it lost and that is to die in the last ditch." The Dutch leaders in 1940 were not of that heroic fiber, and the average citizen was too soft and, perhaps, too reasonable for such an attitude. It took years of growing oppression to nurture a spirit of defiance and sacrifice. Once resistance had taken hold, it grew and persisted, though for a variety of motives and with complete lack of uniformity. The Dutch people retained their highly individualistic outlook even at the height of the terror. One has only to glance at the innumerable clandestine publications during those five years to realize that they represented every kind of political and religious thinking. A separate book could by written about the underground press in the Netherlands.

The supreme individualism of the Dutch proved to be an excellent defense against the onslaught of the monolithic Nazi ideology. A nation that for centuries had learned to think and act along individualistic, humanistic, and religious lines will not easily fall for such blandishments. Totalitarian propaganda fails where democratic ideas are deeply entrenched. Conservatives and liberals, Catholics and Calvinists, Communists and Monarchists, Socialists and Capitalists recognized the enemy for what he was. All parties found at least one national symbol in Queen Wilhelmina. Here again, traditional devotion to the dynasty was far stronger than the cloudy, irrational slogans of demagogues. Once the war was over, people gradually flocked back to their own political parties. The influence of the churches was rather strengthened than weakened by the German occupation.

Small nations have often been victims of aggressors. Unless a very different spirit develops among the human race, they will always remain dependent — at least to an extent — on the good will of more powerful neighbors. The story of the Netherlands during World War II — with all its terror, blood, tears, and frustration — proves that evil is after all not always victorious. It was

Winston Churchill who said that "the wicked are not always clever, nor are dictators always right." That truth is confirmed by the behavior of the Nazi regime toward the Netherlands. The decision to invade Holland was adopted for purely military considerations. It is perfectly conceivable that a non-Nazi Government, at war with the West, might have taken the same step. The financial and economic exploitation of the Netherlands could perhaps be explained, though never justified, by the hard realities of total war. But no apology is possible for enforcing the National Socialist ideology with utmost brutality on an occupied country that quite obviously wanted no part of it. This stupid and totally unrealistic policy eventually led to a reign of terror. No valid excuses exist for the forced labor conscriptions, the concentration camps, the deportation of Jews and political prisoners, the murder of hostages, the reprisal killings, and the mass executions. At least a few Germans were aware of the madness and futility of such methods. General von Wuehlisch wrote a bitter memorandum in 1946, in which he blamed "the frequently corrupt commissaries, their equally corrupt administrations, and the inhuman methods of the Gestapo" for all his troubles and contrasts them with the correct behavior of German authorities during World War I. Admiral Canaris, the highly respected chief of the Abwehr, repeatedly uttered his rage about Nazi methods in occupied territories, but such voices went unheard or were muted by gallows equipped with piano cords.*

The Nazi terror did not profit Germany as a belligerent. In the last analysis, its consequences for the Reich were disastrous, as it triggered partisan warfare and tied down large numbers of occupation troops in various parts of Europe. As to the deportation of Jews, a German officer remarked sarcastically that "tying up so many freight trains was the greatest blow the Jews dealt to Germany."

Holland emerged from the war occupied by a foreign army,

*A special refinement introduced by Hitler. The thin cord does not break the neck but strangles the victim slowly. Canaris was executed in this manner.

fed by foreign supplies, with many of her cities destroyed, and a completely disrupted economy. Today, it hardly shows any scars of the war. If it were not for the various monuments, a casual visitor might not even realize that this was one of the most devastated countries in 1945. Fortunately, the forces of recuperation overcame all defeats and frustrations. We may rightly wonder at the invincible strength of the human spirit.

In Shakespeare's *Henry the Fourth,* Glendower boasts: "I can call spirits from the vasty deep." Hotspur skeptically replies: "Why, so can I, or so can any man; but will they come when you do call for them?" The spirits Hitler had called did indeed appear, but they finally destroyed him and his reign of madness. The Netherlands — sober, unspectacular, democratic, and humane — did survive.

BIBLIOGRAPHY

ARENDT, H., *Eichmann in Jerusalem*. Viking, New York, 1963

BERG, S., VAN DEN, *Deportaties*. C.A.J.v. Dieshoeck, Bussum, 1945

BOLHUIS, J.J. VAN, et. al., *Onderdrukking en Verzet*, 4 vols. Loghum Slaterus, Arnhem, 1950-54

BRADLEY, O.N., *A Soldier's Story*. H. Holt, New York, 1951

BRYANT, A., *The Turn of the Tide*. Doubleday, Garden City, 1957

BRYANT, A., *Triumph in the West*. Doubleday, Garden City, 1959

CHURCHILL W.S., *The Second World War*, 6 vols. Houghton Mifflin, Boston, 1948-53

COUVEE, D.H., *De Meidagen van 1940*. Daamen, s'Gravenhage, 1960

DEKKER M., *Josef duikt*. A.W. Sijthoff's Uitgeversmaatschappij N.V., Leiden, 1946

DREES, W., *Van Mei tot Mei*. Van Gorcum, Assen, 1958

EISENHOWER, D.D., *Crusade in Europe*. Doubleday, Garden City 1948

FERGUSSON, B., *The Watery Maze*. Cotluis, London, 1961

FRANK, A., *Diary of a Young Girl*. Doubleday, Garden City, 1952

GISKES, H., *London Calling Northpole*. Kimber, London, 1953

GRAAFF, F.A. DE, *Op Leven en Dood*. W.L. and J. Brusse N.V., Rotterdam, 1946

HARTOG, J.L., *En Morgen de Hele Wereld*. . . . Van Holkema and Warendorf, Amsterdam, 1960

HELMAN, A. (pseud. Lichtveld, L.), *Een Doodgewone Held*. De Spiegel, Amsterdam, 1946

HIRSCHFELD, H.M., *Herinneringen uit de Bezettingstijd*. Elsevier, Amsterdam, 1960

JONG, L. DE, *De Bezetting*, 5 vols. Querido, Amsterdam, 1965

256

KLEFFENS, E.N., *Juggernaut over Holland*. Columbia University Press, New York, 1941

KONING, B., *De Bevrijding van Nederland*. Callenbach, Nijkerk, 1960

MARTENS, A., *The Silent War*. Hodder and Stoughton, London, 1961

MASON, H.L., *The Purge of the Dutch Quislings*. Nijhoff, The Hague, 1952

MOOK H.J. VAN, *The Stakes of Democracy in South East Asia*. Norton, New York, 1950

MONTGOMERY, B.L., OF ALAMEIN., *The Memoirs*. World, New York, 1958

POSTHUMUS MEYJES, H.C., *De Enquetecommissie is van Ordel*. Meulenhoff, Amsterdam, 1958

PRESSER, J., *Antwoord aan het Kwaad*. Meulenhoff, Amsterdam, 1961

PRESSER, J., *Ondergang*, 2 vols. M. Njihoff, s'Gravenhage, 1965

PRESSER, J., *Breaking Point*. World, Cleveland, 1958

RAATGEVER, J.R. JR., *Van Dollen Dinsdag tot de Bevrijding*. Uitgeverij de Telg, Amsterdam, 1945

REILE, O., *Geheime Westfront*. Welsermuehl, Muenchen, 1962

RIJKSINSTITUUT VOOR OORLOOGSDOCUMENTATIE., *Het Proces Mussert*. M. Nijhoff, Amsterdam, 1948

RIJKSINSTITUUT VOOR OORLOOGSDOCUMENTATIE., *Het Process Christiansen*. M. Nijhoff, Amsterdam, 1950

RIJKSINSTITUUT VOOR OORLOOGSDOCUMENTATIE., *Het Proces Rauter*. M. Nijhoff, Amsterdam, 1952

SCHREIEDER, J., *Das war das Englandspiel*. W. Stutz, Muenchen, 1958

SHIRER, W.L., *The Rise and Fall of the Third Reich*. Simon and Schuster, New York, 1960

SOMER, J.M., *Ze sprongen in de nacht*. Van Gorcum, Assen, 1950

TAYLOR, T., *The March of Conquest*. Simon and Schuster, New York, 1958

TEMPEL, A. VAN DEN, *Nederland in London*. Tjeenk Willink, Haarlem, 1965

TOLAND, J., *The Last 100 Days*. Random House, New York, 1956

URQUHART, R.E., *Arnhem*. Norton, New York, 1958

VLIS, J.A. VAN DEN, *Tragedie op Texel*. H.J.W. Becht, Amsterdam, 1956

VOETEN, B., *Doortocht*. Contact, Amsterdam, 1946

VRIES, S. DE, JR., *Verduisterte Jaren*. W.L. Salm, Amsterdam, 1946

WARMBRUNN, W., *The Dutch Under German Occupation*. Stanford University Press, Stanford, 1963

WEBER, E.P., *Oranje Hotel*. Nijgh and van Ditmar, Rotterdam, 1946

WERTH, A., *Russia at War 1941-1945*. Dutton, New York, 1964

WHEELER-BENNETT, J.W., *The Nemesis of Power*. St. Martin's Press, New York, 1954

WILHELMINA, QUEEN OF THE NETHERLANDS, *Eenzam maar niet alleen*. W. Ten Have, 1959

WILMOT, C., *The Struggle for Europe*, Harper, New York, 1952

INDEX